Passing Time

An Autobiography
Tim Curr

MMV111

Septimus Publishing
Applegarth
Teddington

Passing Time

An Autobiography

Tim Curr

MMV111

Septimus Publishing
Applegarth
Teddington

ISBN-13 : 978-0-9560277-0-2

INTRODUCTION

What is it that stirs one to set out such personal thoughts and details that an autobiography must necessarily entail?

There is in most of us an innate desire to preserve and hold moments and things precious as we live our lives.

The pace and level of change, which affects everyone of us like it or not, can leave us bewildered and alarmed. We cling to and derive comfort from old memories and remembered long-gone values.

These changes are characterised not just in the physical sense but in a great mosaic of other more intangible influences.

As the years have passed so I have felt better equipped to comment on such issues which on looking back, have guided me and moulded my own attitudes and sensibilities.

So with advancing age comes a finer judgement of the satisfaction and personal achievement attained over the passing years.

I have attempted here to chronicle not only my own experiences but to overlay them as a commentary to the period which they encompass.

Thus I hope that this account will be of wider interest than that confined to the handful of friends, family and ex-colleagues who have all accompanied me on the journey described here.

Nevertheless, the debt which I owe to so many of my dearest friends and family must be acknowledged. They have supported me, provided companionship and tolerated all my peculiarities and peccadillo's over so many years.

To them all, I dedicate this book.

"This is the land of lost content

I see it shining plain

The happy highways where I went

And cannot come again"

THE EARLY YEARS

My story starts far away and long ago, in the Lowlands of Scotland. In the year of 1794, on New Years Day, a James Curr wed Isobel Hill and his union begat a family of four offspring, all born at Hamilton, Lanarkshire.

Their second eldest, also James, was born in 1804 and grew up to become a master gunner with the Royal Artillery, initially at Dumbarton Castle and later Fort William before moving to Woolwich Arsenal in London.

He married a Susanna Fife and they produced a large family of seven children. The second eldest child born in 1837, they christened James Fife - my great-grandfather to be.

He married Elizabeth Ogier in 1861 on the Channel Island of Guernsey. The meeting of the couple must have been brought about by James embarking on a maritime career, for in 1871 he is recorded as being a Pilot's assistant. He died in 1874 aged just 38, but not before fathering five children. The eldest, Albert carried on the seafaring tradition but his brother Walter Fife, born in 1874 followed the profession of hotelier. Walter married a Alice Parsons and between them they raised a massive ten children, comprising four girls and six boys, Reginald Roland, my father being born in 1901.

In his younger days Dad must have been something of a "Jack the Lad". At various times he worked in the family hotel trade, ran a car-hire and garage business, played football for Guernsey and also of all things, became interested in tap-dancing!

I am told that he apparently featured on a set of "footballer" cigarettes cards which I would dearly love to see.

Around this same time there was a young girl growing up in the hamlet of Woodmancote, a few miles north of Cheltenham in rural Gloucestershire.

Winifred Bessie was the elder of two daughters who, with their six brothers, comprised the family of Jim and Annie Surman.

Jim was the son of Henry Surman, the landlord of the "Wagon And Horses" public house. This idyllic inn nestled amongst the fruit trees at the edge of an orchard high above Stockwell Lane in Woodmancote. Henry was something of an entrepreneur, owning other property at various times. I have copies of an old transaction document on which he is described as a "gent". Nevertheless, when Jim became romantically attached to Annie Wilcox from Rose Farm just down the lane, her family vehemently objected to the relationship.

They perhaps considered their daughter a cut above the local publican's son, as they themselves were prosperous farmers, (and I suspect may even have descended from early Lords of the Manor, the Cocks family, from whom a "William Cocks" may have been shortened verbally to Wilcox).

However, love found a way and one dark night Jim actually placed a ladder against Annie's bedroom window and carried her off to Birmingham in a traditional elopement. When the ensuing furore had eventually subsided they returned to their home village where they settled for the remainder of their lives.

Winnie would today be described as something of a "free spirit". Her playground was the woods and fields arrayed below that edge of Cotswold, Cleeve Hill, and its fellow outlier, Nottingham Hill.

She attended the small stone-built school in nearby Bishops Cleeve, opposite the Norman church of St Michael's and All Angels.

Her headmaster was a Mr Cox, who thought very highly of her, helping her pass the Oxford Matriculation examination. Winnie subsequently stayed on at the school as a student teacher, having amongst the class under her charge, several of her own younger siblings.

With the ending of the First World War the lure of the freedom to travel was too strong for Winnie, and together with two close girl friends this intrepid trio travelled to Guernsey to take up teaching posts.

The stage is now set for the meeting with Reginald Curr and the lighting of the fuse to set off a train of unstoppable events.

In 1923 Reg and Winnie came back to her home village to be wed. The ceremony was held over the hill, in the small town of Winchcombe, which then held a position of some importance in North Gloucestershire.

The happy pair travelled by horse and trap through the lanes around Gretton to the Registry Office in Winchcombe's High Street. Winnie's brother Len accompanied the trap on foot, holding his sister's hand for the full seven miles.

A modest reception was held in the White Hart Hotel, virtually next door to the Registry Office, and so Reg and Winnie began a lifelong partnership together.

Some time after their marriage they returned to Guernsey and settled down to raising a family, Roland the eldest being born in 1924 followed by Tony two years later and then Jean, Sheila, Patrick and David, all at about two year intervals.

Life on Guernsey, whilst not particularly easy with a large family to keep, was at least enjoyable. Family picnics were held on the sandy beaches, sitting under the sea wall, there was bathing in the temperate waters and shell hunting expeditions to the neighbouring island of Herm.

This idyllic lifestyle was rudely interrupted by Britain's declaration of war on Germany in 1939. The Channel Islands became the focus of both sides in the conflict as a strategic prize. Rumours abounded amongst the Island's population and scare mongering stories were put about, concerning the awful consequences of a German occupation, with predictions of mass deportation of the population to camps in Germany. In the event such a scenario proved unfounded, but not before Reg and Winnie with their six children to care for had left their home and made a rapid return to the safety of Winnie's home village in Gloucestershire.

They carried between them all they could manage in the way of possessions and arrived late one night at Jim and Annie's cottage in Woodmancote.

Winnie Surman, my future mother, on right of picture with her young class at Bishop's Cleeve School c.1916.

My father and mother around the time of their marriage in 1923.

The winter of early 1947, villagers clearing Station Road, Woodmancote.

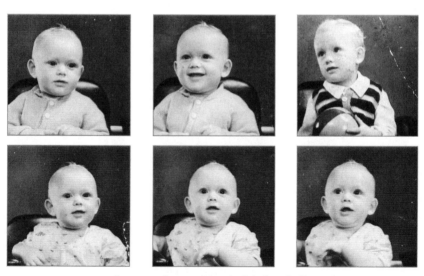

Some poses from my visit to the Polyphoto Studio.

8

What household goods and chattels that were of necessity left behind were never seen again.

In 1937 the Winchcombe Rural District Council had, in a programme of house building, erected a row of twelve semi-detached and terraced dwellings on Station Road, Woodmancote's main street. It was to one of these, number three Nutbridge Cottages, that my family settled.

On December the Twenty Seventh 1946 my mother at the age of forty seven, gave birth that evening in the tiny back bedroom to her seventh child. Timothy Noel had arrived.

From one's earliest years certain events and faces can be dimly remembered, as 'through a looking glass darkly'. I am convinced that I can recall sitting in my pram outside the back door of 'Number 3' and family friends and neighbours peering down on me, their visages large and distorted against a bright sky.

I can certainly remember being carted off into nearby Cheltenham, a rare trip in those days of early post-war austerity, and being photographed at the "Polyphoto" studio in Clarence Street. I still possess several of the minute pictures, cut from the large composite sheet which the studios supplied as proofs.

January 1947 is still remembered for the great snowfall. As a baby of just a couple of weeks old I knew nothing of the hardships which my parents endured. My bath water was of melted snow, thawed and heated in an old galvanised gas boiler which was mounted in one corner of the kitchen and its contents fed via a pipe through the wall into the adjacent downstairs bathroom.

Daily supplies had to be fetched by walking to Bishop's Cleeve across fields packed with hard driven snow, so deep in places that a sledge loaded with provisions would be drawn clean over the hedgerows.

And then came the sudden thaw and the River Severn being overwhelmed by the relentless rush of melt water pouring down from its upper reaches in the

Welsh mountains, burst it's banks, flooding Tewkesbury town and the surrounding vale of Gloucester.

Fortunately, Woodmancote being on the lower slopes of Cleeve Hill and some fifty or so feet higher than its neighbouring Bishop's Cleeve escaped the general flooding.

During the last years of the nineteen forties, life was still offering up its challenges to a family such as ours. There were eight of us living in what today would be described as virtual penure, a small three bedroomed council house, no piped hot water, no power points, certainly no central heating and just a tiny iron range incorporating a fireplace and side oven with a warming plate over it. The oven could actually manage to cook a simple casserole on a very hit and miss basis. My mother usually used it for drying kindling wood or airing her laundry. On one memorable occasion we were entertaining an American Major, from a nearby army base, to supper. He was fairly smitten with one of my sisters and out to impress. A smell of hot material wafted from the oven and he remarked in his trans-atlantic drawl "Say what delicious home cooking!" and with that my mother made a dash for the oven door and removed a flaming wad of her newly washed knickers and unceremoniously flung them out onto the front lawn. Life at Nutbridge Cottages was certainly never short of entertainment!

My eldest brothers had both embarked on careers with the Royal Navy during the war, Roland witnessing first hand the horrors of the atomic bombs dropped by the USA on the cities of Hiroshima and Nagasaki in Japan. He had got to know the artist Ronald Searle, who had been taken prisoner in the Far East, and spent time working on the infamous Burma railway. Roland said that to help endure the horrors Searle used to sketch the hellish scenes unfolding before him, often from the window of his prison cell.

Tony, my second eldest brother, seemed to have enjoyed a more charmed period of war service. He used to relate the story of how he was landed on Gibraltar and on consuming quantities of Canadian Club rye whisky he was late returning to port just in time to see the British Fleet including his own ship, disappearing over the horizon!

With so many of us living under one roof there was always a succession of callers to the house, girlfriends and boyfriends, especially the latter. Tradesmen made regular deliveries, in those days before the now ubiquitous family car and "destination shopping". The Co-Operative Store dropped off a large cardboard box of provisions at least once a week and a local grocers shop, Beckinsales from neighbouring Bishop's Cleeve, also came round, the little dark blue Ford 8 van being driven by the shop's proprietor, the genial Mr Blake. He and his son kept the business going until the early nineteen eighties when with overwhelming competition and the changing shopping habits of customers, eventually he decided to take a well-earned retirement.

We looked forward every week to the visit of the "Man from the Pru", a short bespectacled Mr Ivor Waite from over the hill at Winchcombe. He was a jovial fellow, and when he had checked and counted the insurance premium my Mother had handed him and initialled the amount onto the green card, he would settle down for a good gossip over a cup of tea. Heaven knows what time he eventually completed his round.

Many years later I received an unexpected windfall as one of those little policies in my name matured, and yielded several hundred pounds at a time when I was particularly short of money. I am sure the ghost of dear old Ivor was beaming down on me from above!

One particular visit which had hilarious consequences concerned that of one of my Mother's old friends from the days before her marriage.

Arnold Mustoe had been quite sweet on young Winnie Surman. I still have a book of Rupert Brooke poetry with the front piece inscribed "To little sister Win. With pleasantest recollections of Guernsey. From Big Brother Arnold. March 1921"

Arnold went on to forge an extremely successful career in civil engineering, mainly in India where he led the drive to build the dams and flood prevention schemes and other infrastructures essential to that vast developing sub-continent, and was rewarded for his efforts with a knighthood bestowed by the King. He came back to England and took the post of the Western Region Traffic Commissioner in what I imagine was preparation for retirement.

One morning a large sleek limousine drew up outside our humble home and who should step out on a surprise visit but Sir Arnold. My Mother had been baking jam tarts and I remember, as I sat on Sir Arnold's knee being fussed over, she offered him one straight from the oven. Of course it's contents were still scalding hot as Sir Arnold discovered to his extreme pain when he took his first and only bite. Both the tart and I were jettisoned, along with what decorum the occasion possessed, to the accompanying anguished howls of our gallant Knight!

At the age of four my little cosy world was turned upside down, for in the Autumn just before my fifth birthday, I was enrolled with Bishop's Cleeve School. It was the same school at which my Mother had taught as a young woman, but much expanded to cope with demands of a bourgeoning post war population explosion.

Locally this had been exacerbated by the removal from London of the instrument makers "Smiths" who had established themselves on a sprawling site, "the Newlands", just outside Bishop's Cleeve.

For me they were happy days, seemingly full of endless sunshine and laughter. I was taken initially to and from school by an Auntie, who worked there as a supervisor, sitting strapped in a metal seat attached behind the saddle of her ancient Raleigh bicycle.

Those old classrooms had a character all of their own. There was a certain unique smell, especially on returning from the Summer break, when the rooms had been closed up for several weeks, a smell of stale polish and ancient dust, overlaid with general mustiness. To experience such an odour today transports one back across the years and once again be sat as a nervous six year old, in an unyielding metal and hardwood tip-up desk, apprehensively starting in an older class.

Although the school possessed a canteen, for some reason the younger children took a packed lunch crammed into a brown paper bag - no plastic boxes in those days. The first words I ever learnt to write were those of my own name onto my lunch bag, which was then stacked with all the others onto a side table first thing in the morning.

The role call for the day was then made by calling out the register of pupils; you responded by shouting "present"! I recall my acute disappointment at there being no actual presents on offer!

As the nineteen fifties passed there were still certain shortages and deprivations that could be traced back to the war. Rationing of sorts was in force, although perhaps not taken quite so seriously as during the hostilities. I remember persuading Mrs Wood the village postmistress, who also ran a provisions counter in her lock-up shop, to sell me sweets without my ration book.

Gloucestershire is associated with the development of jet engines and aircraft going back to the nineteen thirties. Frank Whittle, the acknowledged inventor, although a Warwickshire man, had close links with our own County.

The experimental prototype jet plane was first demonstrated at Brockworth airdrome. There are conflicting eye-witness reports whether it actually made a genuine flight or merely "hopped" a few yards for the benefit of the watching V.I.P's. Nevertheless, Gloucester became the home of the Gloster Meteor, and I well remember planes, with their characteristic long fuselages hurtling through the skies above our village.

Cleeve Hill had been the site of at least one war-time air crash. One of my elder brothers visited the hill and ran home in triumph, bearing a trophy in the shape of a belt of live ammunition salvaged from the plane's gun turret.

My Father was horror-stricken, and promptly dug a deep hole at the bottom of our garden and buried the lethal article, where it probably remains to this day.

One evening we saw sweeping across the sky above the outline of Cleeve Hill a huge white apparition the size of a circus marquee. It was a barrage balloon which had broken loose from its mooring, possibly at the Gloster Aircraft Company's airfield, and tracked across the County with the prevailing wind. Our local Constable P.C.Saunders attempted to catch it but his only reward for his heroic efforts was a badly injured foot where the heavy cable had trailed across it.

War time detritus continued to surface a long time after peace was declared in 1945. I remember my father bringing an intact hand grenade home which he had unearthed in the course of his employment. It was kicking around in his shed for several years afterwards, but I do not know of its eventual fate.

Other relics which we prized as children were discarded gas masks which we scavenged from old dumps. The regular ones were a simple single cylinder type which was held tight over the mouth by rubber straps.

The more unusual, and therefore more prized by we children, were the "full face" masks which covered the eyes as well as the mouth, giving the wearer the appearance of some primeval reptile.

The working of these devices, where any poisonous gases would be "filtered" by a dispersion of carbon granules through which one drew breath, was totally flawed as a scientific principle. I am sure they were issued more as a morale-booster by conveying a false sense of security to the wearer. A modern-day comparison might be in giving parachutes to passengers of Concorde!

For many years the unofficial playgrounds for the village children were the fields which followed the footpaths ascending the slopes of Bushcombe Hill. The first of these fields and the only flat one, was eventually purchased and developed into a playing field with a village hall. When the Second World War

Grand opening by Woodmancote Parish Council of the village's new bus shelter c. 1950.

"Cobo," Nutbridge Cottages, Woodmancote.

13

Countess of Huntingdon Chapel, Woodmancote.

Villagers enjoying the Annual Outing to Weston-super-Mare.

had finally been laid to rest and all the troops welcomed home, somebody had whitewashed in enormous letters six feet high "V of J" - Victory of Japan, on the stone wall of an adjacent barn. These letters remained, proclaiming their celebratory message across the field for many years, until in fact the barn was eventually demolished in the 1970's.

When we were not enjoying adventures in these fields we would be out on Station Road, the village main street, which was then newly surfaced with asphalt, playing hopscotch on a crudely chalked grid, or even enjoying a gigantic form of tennis, lobbing the ball over the cats-cradle of electricity cables which crossed the road. On one of those occasions I was nearly struck by a car coming up the hill, it being such a rare and unlikely thing to occur, so unusual was car ownership in those days. Tradesmen, and of course the local doctor, used transport of the motorised variety, although the horse and cart persisted for quite some time after the war had ended. The rag and bone man drove one of the latter, his broken-winded old horse harnessed to a ramshackle cart loaded with the meanest, mangiest tat you could possibly imagine!

Another tangible sign of post-war social change were the bearded Indian Salesmen who came to the door. They were the first real foreigners I had ever seen, and as a seven year old child, I was fascinated by their ethnic dress and turbans.

They knelt on our front doorstep and opened up their large well-worn suitcases. I expected a display of exotic oriental goods, gold, jewels, fragrant spices, exquisite tea and other fine delicacies. Instead we were presented with an array of cheap lavatory brushes, dusters and polishes, perhaps in retrospect somewhat more useful!

Woodmancote enjoyed a local bus service to Cheltenham run by a company called Bowles from the hamlet of Ford near Winchcombe. They used to stop on the village green, a small triangle of grass formed by the junction of three lanes at the top end of the village. Later it was decided, by the parish council, to build a bus shelter just a few yards above our house.

At this time I was being taught to ride a bicycle by my brothers. They would get me underway by holding the back of my saddle and then let go of me unawares. On this particular occasion one of these derring-do lessons coincided with the wife of one of the local builders who were constructing the shelter, delivering the men's afternoon tea. Kitty Compton, our hapless victim, was tripping along in a pair of the extremely high-heeled shoes so fashionable at this time. Yours truly bore upon her from behind, completely out of control as she leapt for safety with the tea-tray, mugs, milk and sugar disappearing in an arc in the opposite direction. The dear lady took the incident with such good humour, but left me with a memory which I relish to this day.

A building which Woodmancote does not possess is a "proper" church, thus making what we referred to as a village actually a hamlet. There is a place of worship for the local inhabitants, a stone chapel, adjacent to the local inn, the Apple Tree in Stockwell Lane. It is one of a number founded by Selena, Countess of Huntingdon, in the South Midlands, and this particular edifice was formally opened in 1854.

It was in here that I sat as a very reluctant attendee of the Sunday School. I remember feeling cheated out of my precious weekend leisure time, when I would much rather have been out and about on my beloved hills. Instead I, and most of my fellow companions, were closeted together, huddled on the hard unyielding and extremely uncomfortable pine bench seats whilst being preached to by the well-intentioned Sunday School superintendent. Our weekly attendance was noted in the register and used as a device for subtle bribery, for you needed so many stars in the book to qualify for the Annual outing.

This inevitably consisted of a coach trip, usually to Weston-Super-Mare which was the only salt-water within a day's return travel from North Gloucestershire. I refrain from describing the resort as a sea-side for in reality, fringing the Bristol Channel, the waters are little more than the outfall from the River Severn. There is a huge tidal range of around forty feet, the second highest recorded anywhere in the world and consequently the scouring effect is tremendous, drawing up and depositing huge quantities of glutinous mud and forming dismal looking mudflats.

In Victorian times, when Weston was developing as a popular resort and railway destination, the quality of this mud was promoted as conferring health giving properties to anyone courageous or foolhardy enough to avail themselves of a generous plastering of the stuff.

Until recent times the Knightstone Baths offered a variety of submersions in their complex of treatment suites such as saline or mineral and, of course, the inevitable mud.

This high tide, coupled with a very gently sloping foreshore, meant that the "sea" was usually so far out that one needed a pair of binoculars to even see it. A marine lake had been constructed in one of the natural inlets on the town's esplanade, by means of a stone built bar with a walk-way along it's top. The water thus held provided a permanent facility for boating and swimming which was replenished twice a day by the incoming tides which swept over the bar.

On arriving at Weston our coach deposited us all on the seafront and departed to some mysterious far-off bus park. I remember feeling like some refugee landed in a foreign country.

We used to make our way onto the beach "en masse" where our teachers established "camp" for the day, usually erecting a flag on a wooden pole pushed into the sand. This reduced the chance of the younger children wandering off and ending up in the "lost children" office.

The day was spent in desultory games of beach cricket or rounders, the highlight being of course the picnic lunch, when seemingly endless quantities of food and drink were conjured out of voluminous bags and baskets.

We youngsters had all been presented with half a crown from the Sunday school coffers to spend. This thoughtful gesture meant that no child from the worse-off families, which meant most of us, would go without a little pocket money for the day. I remember on one occasion blowing my cherished two and sixpence on a Knickerbocker Glory from the nearby Forte Ice-cream Parlour, and promptly feeling extremely sick for the rest of the day.

It was a very tired party of children and parents who returned home that evening.

The coaches all left at six o'clock and we wended our way in those pre-motorway days back up the old A38 main road, passing under Brunel's great suspension bridge at Clifton and enjoying a "comfort stop" on the Downs, parking near the huge water tower. Then on northwards to Gloucester, over the swing bridge by the Docks and so to Cheltenham. Here we started dropping off weary passengers near their homes, finally arriving back at the bus shelter in Woodmancote with the remaining faithful few, tired but very happy.

Outings enjoyed somewhat nearer home were our family picnics. They achieved near-legendary status. My Mother would pack an enormous yellow enamel teapot and an old kettle, cut up a loaf into sandwiches and invite one or two other parents with children to join us. We would then all set-off "en troupe" up the familiar field paths with Mother at the head like some mythical Pied Piper, gathering other youngsters into our rank along the way. Our destination was usually the Washpool, at the very back of Cleeve Hill, where we would "pitch camp" by the source of the River Isbourne, a ready supply of drinking water. Cleeve Common is particularly bereft of trees but we managed to collect sufficient kindling wood in a nearby copse adjoining Postlip Hall. There is a small stone and tin shelter in this copse, just a weatherproof covering for a pump serving the nearby big house, but to our young eyes it became the cottage of "Snow White and her Seven Dwarfs".

We would spend the summer afternoon exploring the long-deserted quarries or visiting the Huntsman's Grave atop Postlip Warren, or, more likely playing in the infant Isbourne searching for fresh water shrimps or in the Washpool itself, which was then deep enough to swim in.

As the sun dipped behind the Malvern Hills to the west we would slowly all straggle our way homeward, bearing our various trophies or fossils, or maybe even live frogs or minnows, back over the hill and so down the lane and home.

The early years of the 1950's were ones of austerity. Our total family income was probably less than ten pounds a week when a black and white television cost one hundred pounds and a family car, perhaps a small Morris Minor or a Ford Eight, would be priced at several hundred pounds. Such a possession would be beyond our wildest expectations.

It was very much a period of "make do and mend". Clothes were handed down through the family, me being the youngest ending up with an array of second or even third hand items.

My Mother's friend, Nancy, from her Guernsey days, had "married well" and now lived at Sevenhampton Manor on the Cotswolds, and offered us pieces of their unwanted furniture fairly regularly. Today they would probably fetch a small fortune at an antiques auction. There was a large round pedestal rosewood table, a mahogany Pembroke gate-leg table, a huge Victorian bedside commode stool, a capacious brass-bound coal scuttle, a set of Regency dining chairs and a huge cumbersome rotary knife sharpener which you operated by laboriously loading its drum with upwards of a dozen knives and then optimistically whirling the handle attached on the side.

Food must have been a major item in any family's restricted budget, especially to one as large as ours. Living where we did, nestled on the lower slopes of the Cleeve and Bushcombe Hills, meant regular forays to gather Nature's Harvest of whatever was in season.

Blackberries, which hung like grapes from the copious brambles of the "Bushy Field" supplemented by a few windfall apples "scrogged" from the Apple Tree Inn's bountiful orchard, made a welcome pudding for a large family.

On a misty September morning we would don our Wellington boots, and in the half light wade through the dew laden fields to well-remembered glades where the finest mushrooms grew.

There was an element of good-natured competition with neighbours in these expeditions, as to who could get out first and take the pick of the crop.

We did enjoy a large garden at Nutbridge Cottage, although my Father was very much a reluctant gardener. We kept a few hens which resided in a wire-pen at the end of the back garden and these also had the run of the orchard which abutted our property.

My brother Tony, on one of his evenings out in Cheltenham, entered a draw and won of all things a live Cockerel. He claims he brought it home by leading it the full four miles using his necktie as a lead!

My long suffering Mother came into the kitchen to make the morning tea to be confronted by "Henry" as we christened him, perched on the back of a chair. Tony had unceremoniously let the poor confused bird loose there and disappeared off to his bed.

The green painted chicken hut became "Henry's House" and for many months we were aroused every morning by his alarm call. Eventually such a tasty potential dinner proved too great a lure for a hungry family and much to my bitter distress, poor Henry ended up on our plates.

The sole means of heating our home at this time was a small open fire in the living room which also warmed the black-leaded iron oven and hot plate which abutted it. It had a voracious appetite for coal, for most of the heat generated disappeared straight up the chimney. To supplement and eke out our precious

Family picnic at the Washpool, Cleeve Hill with my mother and me perched on her chair.

"Huntsman's Grave" Postlip Warren, Cleeve Hill.

My little Austin pedal car.

The only photograph taken of my mother with her seven children (plus young grandson Terry).

20

fuel supply, my Mother indulged in what she termed "wooding". This involved wheeling my pram, usually with me still in it, up the steep lanes to the woods which crowned the upper summits of Bushcombe. Here she gathered as many fallen branches and large faggots which could be loaded into the long-suffering pram and transported home, like spoils of war, with me perched precariously on top.

Another source of welcome timber was the telegraph poles which my father purchased as redundant stock from his employers, the GPO. These he and one of my elder brothers would saw up into convenient lengths using a long double-handled cross-cut saw on a crudely constructed wooden saw-bench. The bench was made from the telegraph pole "arms" to which the cable insulators would have been bolted. They were of a heavy mahogany-like timber and deemed too useful for burning and thus were embodied in a variety of constructions all around the garden.

The chimney at Nutbridge Cottages became the unintended centre of high drama in the village one Saturday afternoon. The coal which we had delivered was often of extremely poor quality, high in tar and consequently generated vast amounts of soot.

Old Mr Agg, the village sweep, was a frequent visitor to our home, and I used to delight in standing outside on the lawn looking up at the chimney pot, waiting for the black bristles of Mr Agg's brush to appear in a cloud of soot.

On this particular occasion my father had invested in a packet of the proprietry chemical powder called "Imp" which was claimed to obviate the need of tedious chimney sweeping. He rather impetuously emptied the entire packet onto the lit open-fire and with a violent "whoosh" flames consumed the entire flue and licked out into the living room itself. Within seconds the sooty contents of the chimney were alight, roaring like an express train, became loosened by the terrific heat and cascaded down onto the hearthrug and carpet, which immediately caught fire.

I arrived home from seeing my chums to be greeted by a fire-engine out in the road surrounded by half the village gawping around it.

On our lawn were the blackened smouldering remnants of the family carpet, with my father looking suitably sheepish as my dear mother was hopping up and down with exasperation at him and his foolish schemes.

The family home had recently been purchased from the then Cheltenham Rural District Council for the very reasonable price of eight hundred pounds. In fact the repayments were the same amount as the rent had been, for the mortgage had been advanced by the Council themselves.

My parents named their new possession "Cobo" after Cobo Bay in Guernsey. The Curr family had run the Rockmount Hotel there since the early years of the century, Walter Fife being the first landlord, and the bay enshrined many happy memories for my parents from their early married life together.

Of my parental partnership, my father played by far the more passive role. My mother, on the other hand was a great motivator. She was a natural adventurer, well read and cultured, a lady "to the Manor born". She had a lively, active mind and inspired all those around her. She used to become so agitated at her husband's apparent indifference and "laissee faire" attitude. He was a very difficult man to arouse into any sort of action.

I do not recollect him ever taking me out anywhere, playing games or showing any particular interest in my welfare or well-being.

With hindsight this seems a rather unfair judgement. For one thing he was in his fifties as I was growing up, and had already helped raise a family of my six older siblings.

For another, he had been wrenched from the idyllic island of his birth with the outbreak of war, leaving his home and business behind and arriving in what to him was a foreign country and being at first totally beholden to his parents-in-law's charity. He then had to virtually start establishing a home and career from nothing whilst feeling isolated from his own brothers and sisters who had remained on Guernsey. So all things considered he coped very well.

In the mid-nineteen fifties the war was still very fresh in many people's memories, especially to my parents whose lives had been so affected.

Therefore when the Suez crisis developed, and the prospect of hostilities seemed likely, the atmosphere at home was indeed very sombre.

By this time, of course, nuclear weapons were in the arsenals of the major protagonists and people genuinely believed that the end of the world was nigh.

To a degree, International and National politics never featured very highly on our agenda.

The only time the village was animated politically was at the General Election. Posters and slogans daubed on any convenient prominent surface would appear. Percy Moore whitewashed "Vote Tory" on his brown wooden garage doors and the words remained for several years thereafter.

W.S. ("Shakespeare") Morrison, our Member of Parliament came a-canvassing, his only ever visit to us as I recall. He paid a whistle-stop call at the bus-shelter, where a number of his devoted supporters gathered to hear him speak. On one occasion he did invite the members of the local Conservative Association up to London and I have a group photograph of them all posing outside the Houses of Parliament, looking extremely self-conscious and ill-at-ease in their Sunday Suits.

In this new Britain of the nineteen fifties there was an enthusiasm for redevelopment of the country's infrastructure and with it came a building boom in the housing industry.

Woodmancote was not immune, and one day the excavators moved into the orchard where once our hens scratched undisturbed. My poor mother was mortified, seeing her beloved village torn apart and she straightway formed an attitude of distrust bordering on contempt towards any local landowners.

Indeed, one or two farmers, having made their "packet" did move away, as if conscious of the village's hostility.

Technology had also taken a hold on society by now, mains electricity was commonplace in most homes which, along with piped running water was probably responsible more than any other factor in emancipating the average housewife from the humdrum drudgery of onerous daily chores.

Internationally, technology had captured the public's imagination with the launching in the Autumn of 1957 of the world's first satellite. I remember standing late at night in our garden, gazing steadfastly skywards and desperately hoping for a glimpse of the tiny specular reflection which was the Russian "Sputnik" as it crossed the great arc of the heavens on its celestial orbit.

My vigil was, alas, in vain, and I had to content myself with taking cuttings from the newspapers which reported this momentous event.

I took a fascinated interest in electrical gadgets, especially wireless sets and amplifiers. I used to regularly cycle into Cheltenham to visit a small shop called "Ray Electrical" tucked away down the Lower High Street and invest my pocket money in such hardware as copper "perlite" aerial wire, solder, variable condensers, resistors, thermionic valves and later, the most prized possession of all, the new transistors. The latter revolutionised the electronics industry into what it has become today. These early devices were so crude by comparison, and unbelievably expensive.

I remember with great apprehension purchasing a "Mullard OC71" transistor, about the size of a pea, with three fragile wires emerging from its body, for the high sum of seventeen shillings and sixpence. That was about seven weeks pocket money.

When soldering such a delicate item into a circuit great care had to be taken, avoiding too much heat from the hot soldering iron and at all costs keeping the correct polarity from the battery, otherwise disaster would strike and that seven week's worth of pocket money would be lost. Those years of experimenting have stood me in good stead ever since, for even now I will have a crack at repairing most items of kit that can be accessed, on the basis that there is so little to lose. Nowadays one can buy a new radio for just a few pounds and a video tape recorder for around fifty pounds. But money cannot buy that feeling of supreme satisfaction when turning the "on" switch and hearing the BBC radio programmes fill the room as a result of ones own ingenuity.

I built myself a reel-to-reel tape recorder, as a final project, before many people had experienced the fascination of hearing their own voice on tape.

It was assembled from basic components, a Collard Studio deck and a separate amplifier which I incorporated in a ply-wood cabinet. It had a three speed deck of $7^1/_2$", $3^3/_4$" and $1^3/_8$" per second and on the slowest setting, with a long-play reel of 2400 feet of $^1/_4$" tape, it would run for several hours unattended.

A second interest which ran concurrent to my electronics activities was photography.

I cannot remember the exact point in time when I decided to acquire a camera, but I was probably only about ten or eleven when my mother took me to Cheltenham and in what seemed a junk shop in the town's "second-hand quarter", bought a Kodak Hawkeye no 2 Model C box camera.

It cost just ten shillings. A box is really all it was, covered in black Rexine, with a simple fixed lens at one end and a small red window at the other, through which you observed the printed number on the film's backing paper when winding on after making an exposure.

Failure to wind the film caused double exposure to occur, often with hilarious results, such as a ghostly Aunt Effie peering out of the topmost branches of an apple tree.

Film cost and the cost of developing and printing at the local chemist shop was expensive, and with only eight frames per roll of film you made every shot count. Nevertheless, failures were plentiful in my early photographic career, usually as a result of being too ambitious. I took pictures under impossibly low light levels, often far too close to the subject, way outside the fixed lens focus, or else took "sporting" style pictures of speeding cars and trains which reproduced as mere smudges when the wallet of "snaps" was collected.

In an effort to keep the costs of this potentially expensive hobby down I started dealing with a firm called "Gratispool" based in Glasgow.

You posted off your exposed film and postal order as payment and a few days later back came a set of postcard-sized glossy photographs, your negatives and a replacement film.

The film base was of paper, which precluded anyone but "Gratispool" processing it, as presumably they were equipped with special epidiascope-type enlargers. Therefore in a clever marketing ploy, you were forced to remain loyal to them and as you received a "free" film every time it was a process which could endure "ad infinitum"!

I finally broke away and bought some darkroom equipment, yellow safelights, processing dishes and chemicals and some ex-government packets of Velox Contact paper cheaply. I constructed a crude stand with an electric bulb and an easel for holding the "sandwich" of negative and printing paper. The film itself I processed in the pitch darkness "see-sawing" the loose length of film, some three feet long, through the 3 dishes of chemicals: developer, acetic acid stop bath and the fixing bath, followed by a thorough wash in the kitchen sink.

Whilst all this was underway my long-suffering family were barred from the locked and blackened out kitchen, probably all wondering what on earth I was getting up to, closeted as I was in darkness for most of the evening.

Up until this time, my travel beyond the parish had been somewhat restricted by my lack of transport. My fellow playmates all had bicycles and on the occasions of trips to neighbouring villages and further afield I borrowed my older sister's Raleigh. It was a pretty basic machine with a fixed gear, rod operated brakes and unyielding saddle, all mounted on a sturdy steel frame. And worst of all, horror of horrors to a lad of ten or so, it had no cross-bar, which immediately identified it as being a ladies model.

Nevertheless, I made some fairly lengthy and arduous day trips on it, on one occasion touring the North Cotswold villages, panting and straining up the relentless gradients in the wake of my companions on their lightweight tourers.

This state of affairs all changed when one Christmas morning there was a gleaming electric-blue Armstrong Consort racing machine leaning against the settee by the Christmas tree. And at long last I had a bicycle with gears, a train of six operated on the "derailleur" principle.

My parents must have made quite an effort financially and I was overcome with disbelief and wonderment.

That bicycle became my closest friend and companion, and I never left the confines of our house and garden without it. The farthest we ever travelled together was a run to Hereford where I and two chums spent a short time around the Cathedral green before returning home via the steep climb across the Malvern Hills, where we made a visit to one of our trio's elderly aunts. It was probably a round trip of some eighty miles, good going for a twelve year old.

My relatively carefree days at Bishop's Cleeve Primary School were due to end in the summer of 1958. In those days, one's future schooling from then on under a County Council regime was determined by means of the 11+ examination. Depending on the degree of the pupil's mark, he or she would attend Cheltenham Grammar School, usually the preferred option, or failing that, the Technical High School. Until the Comprehensive School was built in Bishop's Cleeve then the final choice was merely to stay on at the same school until the age of fifteen.

I took the examination, including an intelligence test, and must have been classed as "borderline", for I was invited to an interview with the Headmaster of Cheltenham Grammar School, a Dr Arthur Bell. My mother dutifully accompanied me into Cheltenham on our local bus. "Interview" was too grandiose a term. It was really Dr Bell checking that I was reasonably respectable with a neat haircut and clean shoes. We couldn't have been in his study for more than five minutes. I evidently passed muster, for that following September saw a very timid boy, shiny satchel over shoulder and pristine black blazer with its "lion rampant" motif on the breast pocket, stepping into the Cheltenham bus. I was so nervous. It was my first journey on a bus unaccompanied for one thing and as the conductress drew nearer to where I was sat, clutching my eight old pence return fare in a clammy fist, my heart was beating faster and faster. I did breathlessly manage to gasp "return, please" and my ordeal was over. I never looked back!

Cheltenham Grammar School for Boys had occupied the same site on the High Street since its foundation in the fifteenth century by a certain Richard Pate.

During the late nineteenth century it was rebuilt and extended following a damaging fire. Its later stone façade presented a sort of mock Gothic appearance complete with castellated tower, an impression somewhat lessened by the adjacent Victorian Brewery which every morning enveloped the school's yard in swirling clouds of pungent hop flavoured steam.

One entered the premises via a small stone archway to the left of the frontage and then into the building itself by a rear door. Entry by means of the imposing central front door and flight of steps was strictly prohibited to us boys.

The interior was bleak "in extremis" with bare pine boarded and high ceilinged classrooms, still with their enormous stone fireplaces whose function had long been replaced by massive cast-iron radiators and pipework. The various lecture theatres were fitted with tiered wooden seating facing down onto the master's rostrum and blackboard.

The biology and chemistry laboratories were pervaded by the stinging aroma of raw chemicals especially from the formaldehyde baths of the former in which the macabre corpses of rats and dogfish would stare out with their lifeless eyes through the glass sides.

From my very first day at the Grammar School there followed the most miserable five years of my life.

I started, of course, as a very small fish in a huge pond. Everything seemed so officious and unfriendly. The masters (virtually all the teachers were men, I can recollect only one woman and she was the wife of the German master) addressed us by our Surnames, and we were expected to call our fellow pupils by theirs.

Correct uniform was to be worn at all times, naturally, and caps and mortar boards on the journeys to and from school. If we met a master outside then we were expected to acknowledge him by raising our headwear.

We were issued with a timetable of lessons on our first day and were responsible for being in the relevant room at the time indicated.

Games were compulsory, one whole afternoon per week, on a cycle of rugby, athletics and cricket. The school sports field was several miles away on the outskirts of Cheltenham. It presumably was once in open countryside but over the years the area had been developed into one of high density housing, local authority flats and terraced homes.

In my early years I used to lunch in the school canteen then catch one of the maroon coloured double-decker buses of the Cheltenham and District Traction Co. up to the sports ground. One problem of that arrangement was the return trip home that afternoon, which entailed a bus back to Cheltenham town centre and then the uncertainty of finding our own local one back to Woodmancote, such was the infrequent timetable.

Later on I devised a plan of actually taking a bus home after the morning lessons and cycling the seven miles or so to the sports field then straight back home again after the stint of rugger or whatever.

Rugby especially I loathed. Our tutor was a short belligerent little man with an army-style haircut who delighted at bawling at us until his cheeks became puce, and blowing an "Acme Thunderer" whistle until I would willingly have rammed it down his throat. He merely succeeded in putting me off competitive contact sports for life.

After our exertions we were made to endure communal showers, being herded through first a warm spray and then on through a freezing cold one. I have never taken a shower again to this day.

General discipline at the school was very rigid. There was a system of

Cheltenham Grammar School's Victorian frontage was a familiar feature on the town's High Street.

The school yard shared a common boundary with the Cheltenham Brewery.
Our canteen lies in the centre of the picture.

The 8.25 a.m. Kearsey's bus picking up outside Northam Stores, Woodmancote, 7th July, 1964.

Cheltenham Grammar School's Annual Sports Day held on the Hester's Way playing field c. 1960.

detention which took place on a Saturday morning. The school prefects were empowered to impose this stricture on our weekend freedom, which they did not hesitate to implement even to the extent if they merely didn't like your face.

We were expected to participate in the out-of-school activities and societies, of which there were many. I opted for the Geography Society and also the Photographic Society. I recall an expedition mounted by the former on which we were all "bussed" to Talybont-on-Usk in Breconshire and abandoned alongside the Brecon-Abergavenny Canal. From there we walked up the "Seven Mile Drag" of the Merthyr Railway track into the mountains and the Brecon Beacons themselves. We made our way down to the southern side of the Beacons around where the "heads of the Valleys" road now runs to where the coach was parked awaiting our arrival. We all came limping down the lane in various stages of exhaustion and dehydration. "Geography Society" was apparently an euphemism for "Outward Bound Course"

The Photographic Society was run on far gentler lines by our German master, a mild mannered man called Christie. I remember a couple of our outings, one to Somerset's Wookey Hole and Cheddar Caves and the City of Bath and the other around Dorchester in Oxfordshire. Christie was himself a member of the Cheltenham Camera Club and arranged for us to have wall space in their Annual Exhibitions at the town's Art Gallery. We stayed behind on winter evenings when he set up a crude darkroom in one corner of the lofty chemistry lecture theatre or maybe the art room, and there we took turns at printing small whole-plate sized black and white photographs from our best negatives. I did actually get awarded a "Commended" by the judge in one exhibition, a chance snap of a whippet and cat in a confrontational pose.

Academically I found the five years at the Grammar School quite a struggle. I think I disadvantaged myself by my inward hostility and contempt. A common theme on my thrice-yearly reports was "could do better", although by some miracle, one term I was assessed third overall in class, achieving first in such unlikely subjects as French and Physics, and ended up having my name read out in General Assembly as a star pupil.

In the summer of 1963 I sat and passed eight G.C.E "O" levels and left the portals of the school forever, Its formaldehyde drenched laboratories, morning shoe inspections, obnoxious fumes from the neighbouring brewery, petty rules and regulations and bawling games masters, compulsory P.T, nightly homework, impossible Latin declensions - all behind me. But then I had by now succeeded in landing an interesting, fascinating and well-paid job.

It was to play the pivotal role as the major part of my life's career and as such merit's a detailed description in a subsequent chapter.

My early teenage years were not entirely spent lamenting my lost freedom under the authoritarian rule of the Grammar School.

Nineteen sixty was trumpeted as the arrival of the "modern age" by all the country's media. We watched Lord Boothby on our diminutive black and white television, with its twelve inch screen, presenting his series of programmes proclaiming the new age that we were all about to enjoy.

We were a somewhat depleted household by this time. My two eldest brothers were both married with homes of their own. Roland had joined the Gloucestershire Constabulary and was a serving officer at the Cotswold market town of Stow-on-the-Wold. He was destined for a peripatetic existence as regarding settling down, for in those days police officers were debarred from taking on a mortgage, or indeed incurring any sort of debt. Consequently he could, and did, find himself posted to any quarter of the County.

Brother Tony had managed to secure a far more regular niche for himself. He had enjoyed a prolonged courtship with his charming attractive girlfriend Gillian and for a number of years lived with her, sharing a large Regency house in Cheltenham with Gillian's mother, where she ran an establishment for elderly gentlewomen in their declining years. After their marriage Tony and his bride moved into an idyllic secluded thatched cottage in the hamlet of Southam under Cleeve Hill.

My two sisters, Jean and Sheila, had also married by the early nineteen sixties, but both remained in Woodmancote, starting their new lives initially in caravans.

January 1961 marks a dark period when my hitherto untroubled world was rocked to its very foundations. My mother had suddenly caught quite a nasty cold, and after battling it for a few days she reluctantly took to her bed.

Her condition slowly worsened, and I remember the sequence of events as fragments of memory which still stand out in my recollection.

We all spoke in hushed voices, for fear of disturbing her. Her bedroom door was kept closed, a very rare sight. And finally I can hear the Doctor's feet as he came through the front door and pounded up the steep staircase with his black bag, and later the cream ambulance with its darkened windows bearing our mother away to the Cheltenham General Hospital.

The following morning of January the Twenty First, in the still black hours before the dawn, my bedroom door was softly opened and my sister Jean entered and knelt by my bedside. She was sobbing. Our beloved mother had died during the night. She was just sixty one years old.

I bravely decided to go to school that day and left the grieving household, to catch the eight twenty five bus as usual. But by mid-morning, sat in class during the maths lesson, the first realisation of what had happened suddenly hit me full on, and I burst into a flood of tears. My kindly teacher arranged for me to return home again that morning. My poor father was utterly devastated. Our mother had been the strength of the marriage for nearly forty years and her sudden loss had left him bereft and bewildered.

Nevertheless he bravely knuckled down to his new responsibilities of running the home. It was really touching to see him doing the weekly shopping, cooking in the kitchen, doing the laundry wash and generally keeping the house "ship-shape".

*My mother and father walking down to St. Peter's Church,
Cleeve Hill on the occasion of my sister's wedding.*

My father and me at "Cobo" in 1963.

Perched atop Cleeve Hill during a day's expedition over the Common with the Rumney brothers.

The Rumney and Dewey brothers plus another friend 'cooking up' around the campfire, Bushcombe Hill 1960.

He had only the use of one good eye, having lost the sight of the other many years previously whilst still a young man. He had been repairing a leather satchel, and the fork he had been using to push the stiff thread through the holes of the seams had slipped with dire consequences.

In middle age he had developed diabetes and a side effect was the growth of a cataract which clouded his vision on his remaining eye.

He went into Cheltenham General Hospital for what was then an extremely delicate and difficult operation to remove the cataract. With modern laser technology today it is classed as an out-patient procedure and one is back home again within hours. But nearly fifty years ago things were very different. His eye was bandaged up for several days and he had to convalesce for a week or so at the ex-sanatorium, Salterley Grange, on Leckhampton Hill overlooking Cheltenham Town. Whilst there, my father became fond of the matron who tended him, and for some time after he had returned home they continued a correspondence. I think he was lonely and felt vulnerable, with me still a young son of fifteen to care for, and would perhaps have eventually re-married. But it was not to be.

It must have been about this time that I took an interest in gardening. My father had never bothered too much with what to him was a necessary chore. My neighbour, Martin, who with his father, maintained their own garden wonderfully and even cultivated an allotment in neighbouring Bishop's Cleeve. He encouraged my enthusiasm, and gave me a small book by Mr Middleton who had been a "gardening guru" on the wireless before the war. It inspired my efforts to even greater lengths.

I remember constructing a high wooden wheelbarrow and wheeling this construction up the hill, lifting it over stiles with the help of a companion, and filling it with cow droppings.

It was proudly trundled home and the contents strewn across the freshly-dug vegetable patch. The horse-flies and rich smell meant that one never sat out for long at Nutbridge Cottage!

To supplement this "back to the land" enthusiasm I had the offer of some hens from "Nan" Mansell of Sevenhampton Manor. She was the old mother of Nancy, my mother's lifelong friend from her early years in Guernsey. I and my brother-in-law Peter drove up there in his old Ford 8 van and collected half a dozen Rhode Island Reds.

Those hens were to become as family pets all living to what for a chicken would be a ripe old age, eventually each dying from a variety of unfortunate fowl-like diseases and maladies.

As young teenagers, I and my friends did all the things that one might expect. Girls were beginning to feature in our social lives and we used to organise extremely rustic dances in the old village hall, which acted as a "honey-trap" for the village beauties.

Our height of naughtiness was to smuggle illicit bottles of beer into the hall under cover of darkness which added a certain "frisson" to the evening.

My closest friend was Michael Dewey who lived just down the road from me. Between us we converted his father's garden shed into a den. The windows were covered with impenetrable curtains, the concrete floor carpeted and easy chairs and settee installed. We hooked up a mains power cable from the bungalow which enabled us to work the Dansette record player.

Our gang and sometimes one or two local girls spent many a happy afternoon disporting ourselves in "The Shed".

One of our number, Ian Staite, the local butcher's son, who always seemed to have more ready money than the rest of us, supplied the library of dubious reading matter. Poor Michael's father, Ted, used to mutter "I just do not know what you all find to do in there all day!". And nobody will ever know!

With the onset of Autumn and the darker evenings we would establish ourselves in the rough wooden shelter on the village playing field. During summer cricket matches it served rather euphemistically as a "pavilion" but now we youngsters took it over as a useful place to congregate. John "Willie" Williams owned a large portable transistor radio permanently tuned to Radio Luxembourg 208 and pop songs of the time could be heard wafting through the night air.

On a handful of occasions three or four of us actually spent the whole night out on the hill, in the shelter of an old quarry outside the gate into Bushcombe wood. We got a fire going of dried wood which we kept burning all night and on which we fried eggs and bacon in an old frying pan purloined from our parent's kitchen. The cold light of dawn would see us all trooping wearily back down the hill to the comfort of our own beds, and usually all suffering from acute indigestion.

A far more civilised evening was to be had at Willie's house, where we had the use of the front parlour in which we could play cards and listen to records on the family stereogram. His mother would bring us in a bite of supper and invite us into the back "snug" where we could enjoy the satirical "That Was The Week That Was" on a massive twenty-six inch screen black and white T.V.

Around this time, 1962, the Parish Council had acquired the field which became the playing field and onto which the cricket team moved from their previous pitch which they had been hiring at the local secondary modern school.

As my two older brothers, Pat and Dave, were both stalwarts of the team it was only natural that I should now follow in their footsteps.

The facilities on the new field were minimal. I helped with the construction of the aforementioned shelter, crude in the extreme, akin to a giant open-fronted wooden bus-shelter. But it served its purpose for many years.

The grass was at first kept down by a local farmer putting his flock of sheep in the field during the week. At weekends they were driven off, and a working party organised to pick up as many of their plentiful droppings as possible. Inevitably a number were missed and became a real bone of contention, with both the home and visiting sides bemoaning the skid marks on their clean white flannels and Blanco boots.

Consequently we persuaded another landowner, Nigel Organ from Manor Farm, to run over the long grass with his tractor-mounted side mower around the outfield. The square itself was cut short by the laborious pushing up and down of my father's Qualcast 12 " hand mower. On one famous occasion Dave Hatton, our demon fast opening bowler, attached this same mower to the rear bumper of his Standard 10 car and drove around the boundary with my brother Pat clinging heroically to the mower's handles trying to steer a straight course and thereby mark the boundary with a twelve inch wide cut of shorter grass.

Any watering that needed doing was achieved with great effort by means of filling a steel builder's wheelbarrow, from a helpful neighbour's outside tap and then wheeled out to the wicket. What water was left in the barrow was then slopped out onto the pitch.

Playing cricket not only provided the afternoon recreation, it was also the catalyst for the evening's socialising at the village inn, the "Apple Tree". Initially I was not old enough to enter the premises. I stood out in the yard, listening to the hubbub of excited voices inside whilst I clutched my bottle of lemonade and crunched a packet of crisps.

Periodically the latch on the bar-room door would rattle and as the door opened so would the volume of chattering and laughter increase, as a red-faced customer would leave and go happily toddling on his unsteady way home to the sound of the many farewells. I was absolutely fascinated by all this ritual, and couldn't wait until I could at last go inside, if not legally then at least by looking old-enough.

That finally came about when I suppose I was about fifteen. And I was not disappointed as it opened up a whole new social world.

For one thing there was the singing. It would only take someone to start on a certain note, ears would prick up around the bar with recognition and soon the whole company would be roaring out song after familiar song until we became hoarse. At Christmas the singing was even more rousing, if that were possible, with customers coming around to the public bar and forsaking the "posher" lounge which lay adjacent.

The landlords face would drop at this, as drinks in the upmarket lounge, with it's carpeted floor and walls adorned with hunting scenes, were a couple of pence dearer then the "public".

On summer evenings the crowds would be entertained out on the lawn by the "Isaac's Cavemen", a traditional skiffle group, complete with a wooden tea chest and broom handle double-bass and a washboard percussion.

They were a very competent band as well as being popular and were booked for local dances on a number of occasions.

The Apple Tree sported a bar billiards table in the front alcove, the latter called the "cage" on account of it's open beamed construction. You initiated the table by pushing sixpence into a slot which in turn released the balls by raising an internal bar mysteriously hidden from view. A concealed clockwork timer would be ticking away whilst you were desperately trying to pot all the balls, and finally with a clunk the bar would descend again as one's sixpence worth expired. Such was the draw of this wondrous machine that I spent most of the "free study periods" during my G.C.S.E. exams feeding my sixpences into it's steel maw!

It was in 1962 that I made my first ever flight in an aircraft. My father was still not fully recovered from his eye operation and also trying to come to terms with the loss of my mother.

My sister Sheila and her husband Peter decided that the best tonic for him would be a holiday back in his old homeland of Guernsey. He had not been back since his abrupt departure in 1940, and of course his several brothers and sisters were still living there, having stuck out the war. It was thought that flying would be the most convenient and direct way to make the journey, for the sea crossing was not for the fainthearted. The old St-Patrick mail boat was then still in service and was antiquated even by the standards of the early 1960's.

Her sister ship, Sarnia, was somewhat better, being fitted with stabilisers to counter the terrible rolling effect of the English Channel seas.

We were scheduled to fly from Staverton Airport, betwixt Cheltenham and Gloucester, and on the big day Joe Powers, our local garage owner who also ran a bespoke taxi service, took us there in his big Austin.

The aircraft was a DC3 Dakota, a twin propeller affair, holding around thirty passengers. We walked out across the tarmac and boarded the plane via a large wheeled staircase which had been pushed against the plane's doorway.

The aisle was at an extremely steep gradient whilst the plane was at rest, one almost had to clutch at adjacent seats as you made your way to your appointed place.

We finally got underway and the landscape seemed to drop away from you as with its engines roaring the Dakota steadily climbed to its cruising height of around two thousand feet. From that height one could gaze out of the windows and easily see traffic crawling along the main roads and even women pegging out their washing.

One phenomenon I had never witnessed before was raindrops tracking horizontally across the windows as we passed through a shower.

A common enough sight today with modern fast cars, but the Austin Seven's and their like I had travelled in never had the "legs" for such a speed!

A rather quaint ritual "enflight" was the stewardess coming around offering everyone a barley sugar boiled sweet, presumably to stave off air-sickness.

When we eventually alighted, we were advised to hold our noses and simultaneously swallow in order to reduce the effect of ear-popping.

The Apple Tree Inn, Stockwell Lane, Woodmancote.
An early picture from when it was little more than a cider house.

'Apple Tree' locals c. 1960. National Hunt jockey Johnny Lehane is inexplicably in female fancy dress!

Woodmancote Cricket Club 1965 I appear to be wearing suede shoes!

The local roads suffered during the heavy snowfall of the winter 1962-3.

On the return journey, at the end of what for my father was a very poignant experience, our flight made a landing on the grass airstrip at Hurn Airport near Bournemouth in order for a routine customs inspection to be made. In those days travellers could bring two hundred cigarettes or their equivalent in raw tobacco or cigars, a bottle of spirits and various perfumes back into Britain as a duty free concession, hence the stop-over, for Staverton did not then boast a customs service.

The last winter of my schooldays 1962-3 was considered by many people to have been the worst in living memory. I think it was on the boxing night when the snows fell onto already frozen ground. It fell softly and noiselessly overnight and the early morning daybreak which lit up my bedroom was heightened by the eerie unusual brightness reflected from the ceiling.

I looked out onto a white landscape, familiar objects, and the trees and shrubs, their shapes moulded into fantastically grotesque icy caricatures.

The snow was up to the window sills of the house, level snow not drifted. And then it all froze. The next few days I spent out and about helping with snow clearance, even joining our team of local Council roadmen to lend a hand to their efforts in freeing the village from it's snowy bondage.

On one memorable occasion my friend Michael Dewey and I took to his father's "NSU Quickly" moped to travel out to the working party, slithering through the rutted roads with me clutching a couple of shovels in one hand perched on the luggage rack and hanging grimly on with the other.

For the remainder of our Christmas break we lads enjoyed the novel conditions, sledging until late at night on the slopes above Woodmancote and even constructing an igloo from large blocks of frozen snow which we cut out with a sharp spade.

At home, the water pipes into the house had frozen, as deep as they were buried underground. Huge fern-like patterns grew on the inside of the bedroom and bathroom windows, for our single open fire in the living room hadn't a hope of overcoming the relentless chill. Flannels in the washbasin were solid with frost and even my father's false teeth were locked in a frozen grin in their glass tumbler on the windowsill.

Of all the worse times they could have chosen, my brother David and his fiancée had arranged their marriage in mid-January of 1963.

Our household was in complete disarray on the "happy" morning, with me and brother Patrick attempting to thaw the frozen water pipes, others arranging any transport which might be able to manage the treacherous roads leading to the church in Winchcombe, five miles away on the far side of Cleeve Hill, whilst father gazed in disbelief at his moribund set of dentures.

However, in the event everything went reasonably smoothly and David and wife Julie enjoyed a long and happy marriage until David's sad death at a relatively young age in 2005.

In the summer of 1963 my brother Patrick replaced his Vespa motor scooter for a newer and somewhat more reliable model. He offered the old one to me for I think the sum of five pounds. Even that amount had to be deferred until my financial state was improved for it must be remembered I was then still a schoolboy.

Nevertheless I took on the ownership and couldn't wait to express my new-found mobility. I took off on a day's tour of the Cotswolds - no more pedalling for me!

Unfortunately within a couple of miles the bolts securing the external flywheel to the engine began to work loose and I clanked my way regardless around the remainder of the planned journey. Miraculously the flywheel held in place and all was well. I also decided to repaint the bodywork which was still in its original shade of garish turquoise. I went to Woolworth's store in Cheltenham and purchased a pint of household enamel in a shade of powder blue and using a rather dog-eared paintbrush I had unearthed in my father's toolbox, set to and transformed "VDD832" beyond recognition.

I did many miles on that old motor-scooter for the duration of my late teenage years, falling off on two occasions, luckily both at slow speeds.

The first one I am ashamed to say was drink-related, allied to an icy road surface around by Woodmancote village green. In mitigation, I was only about seventeen at the time and it was Christmas!

The second tumble was totally unforeseen and unexpected. There is a ford across the lane near the Cotswold hamlet of Kineton, above Winchcombe, where a small tributary of the infant River Windrush flows under a stone footway bridge. Unbeknown to me the bed of the ford was as slippery as ice, due to the polishing effect of centuries of running water and the generous coating of slime that had formed there. One moment I was gaily chugging through the ford and the next I was stretching my length in the very middle, and feeling extremely wet. Luckily the Half-Way House pub in Kineton provided a welcome oasis of warmth and cheer.

In the scorching June weather of 1963 my remaining brother at home, Patrick was wed. I actually bought a suit for it, courtesy of my father, the first suit I had ever owned. It was purchased from "John Collier" in Cheltenham. They were the original "sixpenny" tailors and reasonably priced compared to other more upmarket businesses.

Within days of the wedding that suit was being dusted off for a second outing, this time for a job interview. Up until then I had not given much thought to the possibility of having to actually getting employment and contributing to my upkeep at home.

My sister Sheila had spotted a vacancy in the local paper for a junior to join the in-house photographic team at the National Coal Board's Coal Research Establishment based at the tiny village of Stoke Orchard only some four miles from home.

To her eternal credit, Sheila penned a model letter on my behalf, applying for the post.

To my amazement I was invited to an interview, and on a glorious warm summer's day my sister Jean and husband Arthur took me in their old Reliant three-wheeler car to Stoke Orchard.

There I was scrutinised by a panel of three of the senior personnel of the establishment comprising the Head of Administration, Chief Physicist and the Head of the Photographic team. Luckily I had done a modicum of reading up on the work undertaken at C.R.E and also by chance had recently seen an article somewhere on the "anaglyph stereoscopic process" which I trotted out with great aplomb. After the interview I was given my shilling bus fare as expenses for the day, and Arthur drove the three of us out to Wainlodes Hill on the River Severn, where we enjoyed a drink at the Red Lion pub.

A few days later an official-looking, buff envelope plopped onto the hall carpet at Cobo - I had been offered the job as Junior Photographer, actually classed as Scientific Technical Officer grade four.

August the Twelfth was the appointed day of taking up the position - the Glorious Twelfth.

It was to mark the start of a long and varied career for me.

COAL AND CAMERAS

The Coal Research Establishment had been in existence at Stoke Orchard since 1948, soon after the nationalisation of the British coal industry. The location was apparently selected as being roughly betwixt the South Wales and Northern England coalfields and reasonably convenient for London, although I heard some cynics suggest that the proximity of Prestbury Park racecourse at Cheltenham was an added attraction with the "man from the Ministry" who made the decision.

The principle research projects concerned the processing and combustion of coal, the mining and engineering research being carried out at the two sister establishments in the Midlands and Isleworth in Middlesex.

At the time of my appointment the Establishment had just lost Dr. Jacob Bronowski as its Director. He of course is now better known from the BBC TV "Brains Trust" panel and his ground-breaking book "The Ascent of Man". 'Bruno' had been held in high regard by his staff during his time at Stoke Orchard.

I was welcomed into the team of four other photographers who provided the services demanded by scientists and engineers working at C.R.E.

Our accommodation comprised of an office, three darkrooms, (one of which was for processing films, the other two equipped with enlargers for printing) and a large studio lit by an array of spot and floodlights. We also had a projection room situated high up at the rear of the main conference room from which 16mm films could be shown down onto a large screen at the opposite end of the hall, and similarly slides (in my early days the slides were an enormous $3^1/4$" size, sandwiched in thin glass).

The range of services which we as a team undertook was vast, covering every possible technique, and this was reflected in an array of equipment which was at our disposal. The stills camera ranged from the studio variety, cumbersomely mounted on heavy wheeled stands and taking negatives of $6^1/2$" x $4^3/4$" $^1/2$" plate format, down to the then relatively lesser 35mm cameras.

The latter were the Rolls-Royces of cameras, German Leicas, but later we went over to Japanese Nikon camera systems which were far more versatile, especially in the production of the now ubiquitous 2"x 2" colour slides.

The main workhorses for location photography were the Swedish Hasselblad kits of which we kept several. Each aluminium case, filled with a camera body, several different lenses and film magazines were always ready to be "grabbed" and taken to wherever pictures had to be made.

One of our special services was the group photography of visiting parties of V.I.P's. These usually comprised of official ministerial visits or maybe Quango-type delegations out for a day's beano. We would set-up a large impressive Sinar plate camera outside, facing the doorway they were scheduled to emerge from en route to the visitor's dining room to partake of lunch. When they appeared, we would hastily assemble them into a nicely composed group, with the more senior of them in the centre.

Two quick pictures would then be exposed and rush-processed, proof prints run-off and the names of "who-was-who- stood where" noted.

The grid of names, together with title of the delegation and the date were spliced into the better of the two negatives and 10" x 8" glossy prints speedily run off, bagged-up and presented to our by now well-entertained and often ebullient guests.

They were usually quite flabbergasted at such an unbelievably rapid gesture.

Lighting, particularly in the average dark and cavernous industrial interiors, always was a problem. We used large magnesium filled flashbulbs, each the size of a domestic light bulb, screwed into white enamelled "pudding bowl" reflectors, and by means of a special high voltage distributor box connected by cable to the camera shutter we could fire off up to six of these leviathan light sources simultaneously. Later on we went over to high-powered electronic studio-type flashguns which were triggered by means of photo-electric cells fitted to their circuitry.

On the cinematography side of our armoury we undertook conventional filming using clockwork 16mm Pathe Webo cameras and later electric French Beaulieu cameras with automatic exposure systems and permanently attached zoom lenses.

We also had cameras for time-lapse and high-speed photography, that is where by either "speeding up" or "slowing down" an event you can capture information which would otherwise be too slow or occur too quickly for the human eye to appreciate.

The high speed cameras using 16mm movie film, were quite awesome in operation.

One, an old Kodak image-compensating camera, could film at up to 3000 pictures per second. It achieved this by whizzing the film through the film gate by means of a powerful electric motor, a 100ft reel being exposed in just over one second. There was no intermittently operated shutter, instead a rotating prism behind the camera's lens was synchronised with the film drive and each frame was rapidly scanned by the projected image emerging from the prism.

As the effective exposure time per frame at full speed was just 1/15000th of a second the amount of illumination required was quite phenomenal, a bank of tungsten spotlights each of 1500 watts brightness, were regularly focussed on to the target area perhaps no larger than a man's hand.

Often rapid access to the information recorded was required so that the test or experiment would be adjusted and another film made. We then used black and white film and disappeared into the darkroom where we manually dunked all 100ft of film through the 3 gallon tanks of developer and fixers, all done in complete darkness, of course. The film was then washed and force-dried and projected on a special step-by-step analysis projector in order for the results to be evaluated.

One particular project which we filmed was the investigation of particle behaviour during the cleansing of gases using devices called cyclones. A glass one was constructed which we back-lit using an opal screen, thus silhouetting

The Coal Research Establishment 1967. The house platforms representing the deserted medieval settlement of Stoke Orchard can be discerned in the field opposite the establishment.

A typical display produced for a Career's Exhibition, here at Cheltenham Town Hall, and I have been conscripted to help 'man' the show.

A practical exercise in the use of a large format technical camera,
Gloucester School of Photography 1966.

Enjoying an informal Christmas drink with colleagues.

the microscopic particles as they were whirled about and flung to the sides of the cyclone, lost speed, and were deposited in a 'catchpot'. This technology was later commercially exploited very successfully by the entrepreneur James Dyson in his range of innovative vacuum cleaners.

A similar set-up we employed in recording coal-slurry spray patterns from a series of specially designed burner nozzles. This time still pictures were made, exposed using an extremely short-duration electronic flash which "froze" the movement of the particles with a 5 millionth of a second burst of light. The results were printed onto 10" x 8" sheets of high-contrast film and sent to Cambridge University to be analysed on their state-of-the-art "Quantimet" measuring equipment. This research into the safe disposal of slurry waste had I believe been instigated by the Aberfan tragedy in the Autumn of 1966, when an unstable tip of colliery waste had become saturated and slid en-masse down onto a little community with such awful and harrowing results.

When I had first been taken on at C.R.E. I was offered the chance to further my education by means of a day-release course at Gloucestershire College of Art. I willingly took up the opportunity, for as great a practical education I was receiving on a day-to-day basis from the teams of scientists and technicians I was working alongside, college would give me a grounding in the theory of my profession and of course a set of qualifications.

Thus I embarked on a series of courses, both at Gloucester and ultimately Birmingham School of Photography, over the next seven years, all paid for by the National Coal Board. The knowledge gained has stood me in good stead over the years, and I was granted an Associateship of the Institute of British Photographers in recognition of my efforts.

I made some good lasting friendships during those years. One in particular was made at Gloucester.

We had on our course a charming erudite man, Bill Harbor who made the journey by train from his home in Bristol every week. Bill was much older than me, in his early forties and married with a daughter. He worked as chief photographer at the H.H.Wills Physics laboratory, Bristol University. He was then currently engaged in the research into plotting cosmic particle penetration in the Earth's upper atmosphere, and accompanied the team of scientists to various prescribed sites around the world where high-altitude balloons were launched carrying large one cubic foot blocks of sensitive emulsion. When the balloon's pay loads were recovered the emulsion was carefully sliced and the sheets thus produced were then processed, showing up traces of any particle exposure.

A three-dimensional model could then be reconstructed illustrating the depth and intensity of cosmic particle penetration.

Bill and I became firm friends, and I used to visit him at both the University and at his home on weekend visits where he and his dear wife made me very welcome.

It was through Bill that the seeds of my early interest in railways and the Brecon Beacons area of Wales were sown.

To this day, as I write in the summer of 2007, we are still very much in touch, though sadly Bill and his wife Marjorie neither enjoy very good health, and are now both well into their eighties.

The two years spent in Birmingham were far less structured than those at Gloucester had been. For one thing there were only three of us on the scientific applications course, and as we all travelled together the tuition could not begin until we had arrived. My companions were Clive Davis who was for a short time my colleague at C.R.E, and Derek Hurn in whose new Rover 2000 we travelled.

Clive was a devotee of the "Swinging Sixties" and had a long-suffering girlfriend in an on-off relationship. They did eventually marry, in a monastery of all places, though sadly it inevitably was not destined to be a very settled marriage. Clive went on to set-up as a specialist in commercial high-speed cinematography, his best known work being the Quality Street TV advert where a tin full of chocolates are shot out of their tin.

The Government's attempt at curbing industrial and domestic pollution with the creation of smokeless zones had provoked research into the manufacture of smokeless fuels and also the development of "smoke-eating" heating appliances. (The technological basis of the latter had been exploited on London's Victorian underground system whereby steam locomotives were converted to run without filling the tunnels with their acrid smoke).

The field testing of these early appliances was carried out on a large scale when complete miner's estates in Nottinghamshire wholly owned by the NCB, had the stoves installed in every house. The principle of their operation was very clever, and involved a second combustion chamber where the smoke could be burnt off before the flue gases disappeared up the chimney and out into the open air. They required a particular size of fuel, the supply of coal graded to around "bean" size. This became the nub of the problem which had not been anticipated. The miners at this time were receiving a huge amount of concessionary coal every year, amounting to several tons, and unfortunately it was of an unsuitable quality for these new appliances. Consequently there was much acrimony generated, and the whole scheme became virtually a political issue.

In order to discredit the technology of smokeless combustion the householders were abusing their stoves by feeding them with garden waste and the like, and also operating them with the doors open, which defeated the principle of the combustion cycle. In the middle of all this rancour we were brought in to set up cameras and monitor the overall smoke emissions on the estates, and also do a "roving" survey with hand-held movie cameras to identify persistent individual polluters.

Word spread like wildfire among the residents as to who we were, and I felt very vulnerable walking the roads with my "spy camera".

Our work was judged of such importance that a car was sent up from

Cheltenham to transport me and the precious exposed films down the M1 motorway to the vast Kodak colour film processing plant at Hemel Hempstead for overnight service and collection the following day in order that the results could be viewed and evaluated by senior managers.

Suitable vantage points were crucial when filming on these monitoring exercises. In the case of the Nottingham housing estates we persuaded the local vicar to allow us access up his church spire, and on one job, a case of alleged pollution by a rival fuel manufacturer which was threatening safety on the M1 motorway, we sought permission and were granted access to the ramparts of Bolsover Castle in Derbyshire.

The Phurnacite briquetting plant at Aberaman in the South Wales valleys became the focus of a drive to improve emissions. The scale of these coal carbonising ovens was immense, the overall length of the site extending and filling the valley bottom for about a mile, with its own network of railways and other infrastructures. I spent the hottest few days of my working life there, up on the oven tops, time lapse filming trials of lute compounds used to seal the oven doors. The air temperature was around 140 F, and coupled with the relentless sulphurous fumes and choking dust and the steel oven tops so unbearably hot that one's feet would blister in ordinary industrial boots and wooden clogs had to be worn, the whole experience became one of severe discomfort.

I returned to the Phurnacite plant in a very different role during the National Miners' strike of 1972. Rather impetuously I had volunteered my services to join teams of men to help keep the plant running. If production had been halted, and the ovens allowed to cool, then the refractory linings would have become unusable and a multi-million pound refit made necessary. This would have compromised the viable future of the works and with it the job security of many hundreds of local men and the economic prosperity of the whole valley.

We were bussed in nightly from our base, the New Inn in Pontypridd, and had to run the gauntlet of the picket lines. Feelings were running high, and on one occasion attempts were made to turn our coach onto its side by violently rocking it. It had been the first national strike in the coal industry since 1926, and there was a grim determination on the part of the miners to succeed in their aims.

I was put on the "pitch loading" team which involved shunting thirteen-ton railway wagons into position and discharging their contents of pitch binder into hoppers. We managed to de-rail one wagon by over-zealous shunting which caused something of a delay, but overall I think our labours did us proud, and the jobs of the regular men were saved.

A mention must be made of a fascinating commission with the pollution control project team to RAF Cardington in Bedfordshire, as it illustrates just one of the many places normally denied access to the general public, that I was privileged to visit.

We hired a giant "barrage" type balloon, tethered securely to a six-wheeled heavy truck, which was sent up to several hundred feet on the end of its anchor-line. On it was attached a nifty device containing a charge of typical polluting particles, ash, coal dust and the like, which could be released remotely. All around a vast area of the airfield were placed large sticky mats on which any particles could become attached on landing and thus a "map" of distribution under various heights/wind conditions could be produced.

Cardington has a long tradition of airship operation and the enormous hanger which housed the ill-fated R101 airship still stands and is I believe the largest aero-nautical structure anywhere in the world. Its size defies description.

Whilst there I observed an impressive display of acrobatics by a modern airship made on the site by "Airship Industries". My visit here had an unfortunate sequel, as the following day my one eye was stinging unbearably and it transpired that some of the airborne material released by our balloon had found its way into my eye so a visit to Cheltenham General Hospital A and E was necessary.

One area of England with which I was to become very familiar is Rutlandshire, our smallest county, and now back on the political map having at one time being swallowed whole by its much larger neighbour Leicestershire. The object of our work was at the huge Ketton cement works and quarry operation. The latter is just about the largest working excavation in Britain and has a history dating back to the reign of Henry the Eighth. The principle ingredients of cement are limestone and clay, both of which are found in abundance in that area.

The scale of production is simply massive. Huge Euclid dump trucks carrying perhaps one hundred ton loads of the raw materials transport their burden to the plant's crushers which in turn feed a vast rotary kiln.

The kiln must be several hundred feet long and around twenty feet in diameter, roaring away day and night, providing the cement to build and maintain Britain's infrastructure.

The surrounding countryside of Rutland is charming and I fell in love with it from day one. The local limestone weathers to a beautiful honey-colour and gives all the villages a wonderful warmth. We based ourselves at the Bluebell Inn in the village of Easton-on-the-Hill and to sit on the lawn in the sunshine after a gruelling day at the works was a delight, disturbed only by the occasional sortie of RAF jets from the local base at Wittering.

I "discovered" the then comparatively unknown Empingham reservoir before it became popularised as a leisure facility and christened Rutland Water. It represents the drowned valley of Normanton Park and the parish church still defiantly stands half submerged by the risen waters. You can peer through the upper parts of its windows and see the fish now swimming where once worshippers knelt in prayer.

One aspect of the work at C.R.E which gave me the greatest satisfaction, and also usually offered the most difficult challenges, was the design and development of specialist and often innovative equipment for recording hitherto unobtainable information.

Filming and stills photography from the mountainside of the Cynon Valley overlooking the phurnacite manufacturing plant near Mountain Ash.

The drowned church of Normanton Park, Empingham Reservoir, Rutland. 1979.

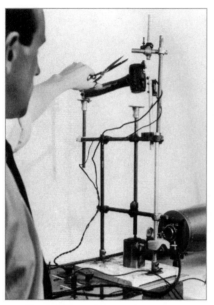

Heath Robinson 'in extremis': triggering the image-dissection camera.

Testing the 6" diameter intrascope.

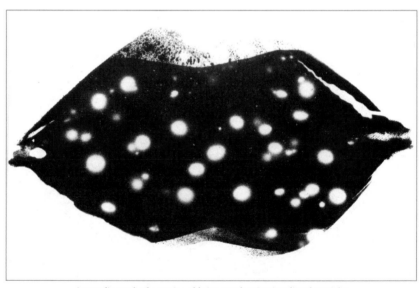

Autoradiograph of a sectioned briquette showing irradiated particles.

The following are descriptions of a few of these successful techniques which at the time of their development represented completely "one-off" projects, and were evolved before today's modern electronic technology could possibly provide a much more sophisticated solution.

A major part of the research at C.R.E in the 1960's was developing a range of fuels by means of carbonisation and briquetting processes.

One problem was the integral strength of briquettes and it was suspected that cracking was related to particle size and densities in the briquettes.

A series of miniature aspirin-sized 1cm thin discs of the briquetted material were prepared of various parameters regarding particle size etc.

Our task was to record the crack propogation produced by stressing each sample (ie hitting them a sharp tap with a hammer!)

Some years previously the C.R.E photography group had designed and had built a device called an image-dissection microscope. Basically it was a 1 metre long steel box with a lens at one end and at the other a lenticular plate of "lenslets" which could be moved extremely quickly by the release of a set of strong springs, and which produced a raster pattern of the event being recorded onto a photographic plate. When the plate was processed the image could be "unscrambled" and a moving picture observed. The equivalent frame rate was judged to be anything up to a quarter of a million pictures per second though of course only for a fraction of that time, as long as it took for the springs on the camera back to travel.

It was this equipment which I set up, Heath-Robinson in the extreme. The sample was mounted on an anvil with a mallet suspended on a string above it. The string was cut with a pair of scissors, the mallet descended, tripping a microswitch on the way down. The switch activated several mechanisms - the first was to fire a large flashbulb using mains voltage for instant combustion. This was about two inches from the specimen for maximum illumination. The second was to release the sprung-loaded camera back and also trip the camera shutter. As there was an inherent delay in all these functions it was crucial to synchronise them all by means of adjusting the position of the all-controlling microswitch, otherwise you obtained a superb picture of an intact micro-briquette sat on the anvil or else a cloud of dust as it disintegrated under the hammer blow.

A second exercise concerning investigating the relationship of briquette strength to its structure was undertaken at the pilot plant near Doncaster in Yorkshre which produced a cushion-shaped briquette christened "Roomheat".

Our work was pivotal to the whole experiment and because of the expensive consequences of mistakes we did much preliminary planning.

The scheme was to introduce radio-active particles into the raw materials used in the briquetting process. The briquettes would be carefully sectioned and the flat faces polished. We developed the idea of sandwiching each section, several hundred in total, between a thick clear Perspex block and a sheet of special auto-radiographic X-ray film. The isotope was brought up from the nuclear research laboratory at Harwell by lorry in a special thick lead walled container.

Sodium 24 was chosen as it had a half-life of only 15 hours. We worked into the night and had to work fast, making up the sandwiches, giving them a very brief flash of light in order to outline the sample onto the film, then storing them in the light tight drawers of a large plan chest for the fifteen hours. At the end of that time the films were separated and eventually taken back to base for processing. The radiated particle dispersion was graphically illustrated by ominous dark blobs where the radio-activity had worked on the film emulsion.

Another problem baffling the scientists was how to assess the temperature of tiny incandescent particles being rapidly ejected from the top of the fluidised bed furnace. The bed was bubbling and surging at a temperature of 800°c, red hot, but it was evident the emitted streams were far hotter. But how hot?

We adopted a technique known as photothermometry. The particles were photographed onto a very "fast" highly sensitive black and white 35mm film by poking the camera through the inspection port and exposing at a shutter speed of 1/1000 second. Then without changing any camera controls the appearance of a sample of the same bed material was recorded onto the same length of film using a muffle furnace. An incremental series of exposures recorded the rising temperatures at specific noted intervals, covering the range of temperatures thought to be represented in the fluidised bed. The film was then processed to a negative, taking especial care to give even regular development. Using a microdensitometer the density of the latter series of control images can be plotted onto a graph and then similar readings made of the unknown particles and "read-off" on the graph. We found temperatures, I recall, of well over 1000°c in the particles. Researchers at Cambridge University read the paper which I subsequently wrote on the technique and I hosted a visit from them in order to demonstrate more fully the complete procedure which I believe they took up in some application of their own.

One problem which had bedevilled the fuel technologists was their inability to inspect the interior surfaces of chimneys for damage, deposits or corrosion during and after testing.

There was no equipment such as "go anywhere" miniature video cameras in those days, and even if there was the optical difficulty of achieving a 360° perspective deep down a flue would still arise.

We achieved this by developing a device which we called an intrascope. At its heart were a pair of highly polished cones, made of duralium, mounted co-axially base to base.

Under the lower one was a small battery powered flashgun and above the upper cone we fixed a small clockwork driven 35mm stills camera called a "Robot". This could be wound up and on depressing the release button it exposed the film and advanced the film ready for the next shot. The negatives were 24mm square, two thirds the length of standard 35mm ones and therefore gave us around 54 pictures on a 36 exposure film. The whole arrangement was mounted in a 5_" diameter sturdy steel tube with a large cut-away area adjacent to the co-axially mounted cones. It was built for a 6" diameter round flue and by lowering it under gravity, we could take pictures every two inches and thus eventually record the whole length of chimney. Initially we fired the camera by yanking on a long piece of string but subsequently modified the camera with an electrically triggered solenoid using a thin cable secured to the lowering rope.

The whole rig was extremely successful and I travelled the country to field-trial sites putting it through its paces.

We made it even more sophisticated by converting it to motion picture with a long cable acting as an "umbilical cord" supplying power for the cameras and a powerful reflector lamp.

At this time the only commercial intrascopes for the small scale work were very short, around a foot long, and primitive in the extreme. They were also ridiculously expensive. The fibre optic system, with which anyone who had been at the receiving end of a hospital endoscopy will be familiar, had not been exploited, the problem being the inability to manufacture coherent fibres of any practical length.

We ended up developing a range of our own intrascopes, from ones for inspecting and filming 1" boiler tubes to a large one of 9" square section for photographing brick chimneys.

My boss at the time, Dr Alan Standing, seemed very impressed with all this innovative work, and when he was approached by a joint committee of the Royal Photographic Society and Institution of Mechanical Engineers with a call for papers for presentation at their forthcoming Christmas symposium, I was charged with the task. To say I was horror struck is an understatement. I had yet to celebrate my twenty third birthday and had never spoken to an audience of any size before, let alone such an erudite gathering as could be expected on this occasion. Nevertheless Dr S ignored my protestations and two papers were prepared. One covered the auto radiography and image dissection techniques plus a stereo photogrammetry project I'd been involved with.

The second paper was the "Development of Intrascopes for Combustion Research".

I went up to London on the eve of the conference to discover I had been booked into a "temperance" hotel. I still remember it, "The Vandom Place" in St James's behind New Scotland Yard.

I made my way to the venue the following morning, the headquarters of the Institution of Mechanical Engineers in Birdcage Walk near Westminster.

It was quite a thrill standing giving my talk with a huge oil painting of George Stephenson, the father of railways, gazing down on me, and before me the tiered ranks of polished mahogany benches filled with the academia of the country.

That evening the panel of speakers was invited to a "Conversazione" at the Café Royal in Regent Street, in order to chat to the delegates. It was held either in the Dubarry or the Elise suite, I forget which, but the whole setting was magnificent with its broad carpeted staircase and mirror-walled sumptuously decorated meeting rooms. To me it seemed to exude the very spirit of Oscar Wilde and his antagonistic associate the Marquis of Queensberry.

I was destined to return to the Café Royal on several more occasions over the following years.

The NCB had instituted the "Coal Science Lecture" to be delivered by an invited speaker drawn from the international ranks of scientists and academics, and the Café Royal was the chosen prestigious venue. To my disquiet I was detailed to provide and set-up any visual aids which would be required, such as slide and overhead projection facilities and undertake the sound recording of the lecture.

These occasions were destined to be the most dreaded jobs of my entire career. There was so much to go wrong and with such unforgivable consequences, the events all taking place under the public gaze of the great and famous. I would even rather have been up on the oven tops in Aberaman!

The logistics of the operation were complicated. For a start, getting all the equipment needed up to London was an exercise in itself. On arrival at the Café Royal with the screen and projector, cables and so on all packed into the estate car, we managed to discover a narrow service lane running behind the building. With difficulty you could with luck find a slot in which to park for a few minutes whilst I and my driver manhandled the kit through a rear door and into the foyer via the "backroom facilities". then we had to persuade a co-operative uniformed Commissionaire to requisition a lift in order to achieve the designated suite of rooms several srories above. The driver then had to hurriedly remove the car to the NCB Headquarters at Hobart House in Grosvenor Place, where they operated a basement garage. On one of these hurly-burly performances I nearly collided with Prince Charles as we were both making for the same doorway, me with my arms full of equipment.

My premonition of disasters waiting to happen were generally unfounded with one notable exception. On this occasion all was set to begin, the audience all in their seats, including the NCB Chairman and the Prime Minister accompanied by several of his Ministers.

I had dimmed the lights , the speaker requested his first slide and nothing happened - the projector wouldn't switch on. Like a man possessed, in the darkness of the room I frantically felt along the length of the mains extension cable I had run out earlier to a convenient wall-socket. Utter relief, somebody must have caught his foot on the cable when taking his seat and yanked the plug from the socket -"Thank you, Lord!"

I mentioned earlier that I had the luxury of a driver to get me to the destinations described . This was not a situation peculiar to myself, but just the way the NCB transport system worked. Over many years I enjoyed the services and daily company of a variety of characters. For some reason, drivers the world over exhibit that brand of fierce independence and of being "their own man" and who, having been given a journey to undertake, like to accomplish it in their own way without interference. My colleagues were no exception.

There was Ginger, an ex-heavy haulage man, a great raw-boned Yorkshireman

'Cottage industry' – lowering an intrascope adapted with a movie-camera.

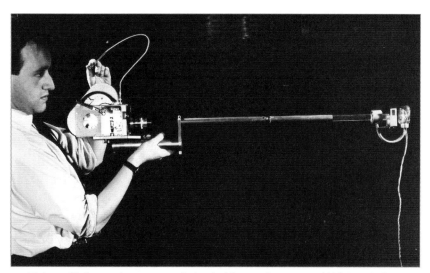

Miniature 1" diameter intrascope attached to the 16mm movie-camera and high-intensity lamp.

Skylarking with the lads at a field test station near Bretby in the Midlands.

Preparing for take-off: aerial photography using the twin-engined Beagle.

who had the disquieting habit of driving at a steady eighty or so miles per hour with his legs crossed and steering with just his thumb on the bottom of the steering wheel. I enjoyed a "night on the town" with him when we visited the Rex Hotel in Whitley Bay one evening for a "grab a grannie" experience. I felt so fragile the next morning that I nearly succumbed going through the Tyne Tunnel, but the creosote fumes belching from the Monkton Coke Works soon put me right!

When the time came to journey home, Ginger persuaded me that as it was a lovely summer's day we would return south via a tortuous east coast route which he knew, taking in such places as Whitby, Scarborough, Bridlington, the Humber Bridge and so on, down to pick up the motorway south. That trip was made forever memorable for me by Ginger calling at Bridlington and insisting on buying some fresh crabs from a stall which he knew. By the time we had reached Nottingham the whole vehicle was pervaded by an all-enveloping stink of decomposing fish filling the hot car, and I seem to remember that by Burton-on-Trent the crabs had been jettisoned out of the window!

Other men who did the honours on those trips were Arthur, ex RAF; Ted, ex-Army, who without fail always fell asleep on arrival at our destination; Bill, an ex-long distance coach driver; Mick, an ex-Army instructor and examiner, who once told me how to perform an emergency stop with a bulldozer "Just drop the blade!"

There was Nobby, a chirpy Cockney Sparrow and quietly spoken Gerry, an antique dealer when he wasn't chauffeuring; and finally old Joe, a small rather hen-pecked man who seemed to perpetually chain-smoke. He was a driver of the old school, having been in long distance haulage since just after the Second World War, but hadn't lost his eye for the ladies!

I salute all these men who provided companionship and took me safely throughout the land over many thousands of miles. Sadly for several of them my thanks must needs be made from beyond the grave.

With them I travelled the land, visiting a wide range of different sites; glassworks, hospitals, including a mental hospital (where I actually observed a patient being pursued by two male nurses in white coats across the lawns); dairies where two hundred milk tankers a day would deliver from a multitude of farms; other farms where I filmed from a moving sileage harvester as it bumped across the grasslands; the Michelin Tyre Co at Stoke-on-Trent, so extensive that they supplied us with a car and driver on arrival to transport us around the factory complex; the Tate and Lyle Sugar Refinery at Silvertown abutting the River Thames just down from the famous Thames Barrier. Here we crossed the river using the Woolwich ferry, a surreal experience for as one sat in the stationary car the whole of London appeared to be gently revolving around you; and the British Steel River Don Works at Sheffield, later to be the home of British Forgemasters with their politically notorious "supergun" scandal. Here we made many required visits whilst producing a film and stills record of the construction of a large 30 megawatt fluidised bed boiler installation. The whole plant sits on a raft of reinforced concrete, nearly ten feet thick, next to the River Don. I remember the film we produced chiefly for the absence of any crane lifting sequences of the main boiler shell, for we were in the pub that particular day at lunchtime, and the crane driver promised he would wait for us before making the lift of the huge component. Never trust a crane driver!

It was on this particular boiler that I witnessed first hand the devastating awesome power of high-pressure superheated steam. I was summoned up to Sheffield one morning urgently to record the damage caused when one of the boiler tubes had developed a hot-spot and this massive tube, some six inches across and of toughened steel nearly one inch thick, had blistered and burst outwards with an ear-splitting roar. Fortunately there was no injury suffered by any of the operators. A jet of superheated steam, invisible to the human eye, can cut a man in two, as a knife through butter.

A far more amenable boiler location was that at a Co-Operative nursery growing tomatoes in an extensive glasshouse complex in deepest rural Herefordshire. These visits, which continued over several years, I enjoyed immensely. For one thing the work was usually carried out quite leisurely and was fairly undemanding. For another, lunchtimes consisted of a fabulous ploughman's meal washed down with local cider at an idyllic pub, the Cross Keys in a neighbouring village of Withington. I'm ashamed to admit that work efficiency in the afternoons took something of a nosedive!

Finally the last examples of the unusual locations were jobs we did at Heathrow and Gatwick airports, out on the runways. The former was particularly spectacular as we had special dispensation to go out to the end of the main runway where huge jets were roaring over our heads every few minutes, literally blacking out the sky.

Air travel did not feature as a method of travel with us. A vehicle generally was far more convenient and gave us a base to operate from when on location with a load of equipment. Also, on overnight stops, one had a runabout with which to visit restaurants and so on.

I did however travel to Edinburgh using the hourly shuttle from Birmingham Airport on a couple of occasions, involving a 7am departure and arrival just one hour later. I remember phoning home from Princes Street at around 8.30am when my wife Loretta was just enjoying her first cup of tea in bed - the teapot was still warm from my earlier brew!

We were tasked with producing a series of air-to-ground pictures of the site at Stoke Orchard for general publicity use, and organised the hire of a light aircraft from nearby Staverton Airport. In the event we were supplied with quite a large eight-seater Beagle which was a little too unwieldy for the purpose. Despite taking off the door for maximum visability the underslung wings obstructed a clear view beneath, therefore the pilot had to run in with a series of sorties, banking sharply each time in order to dip the wing tip. The outcome was that the actual useful photography time was relatively short. A better proposition would have been to use a helicopter, but at around four times the cost it was prohibitively expensive.

Several years later we commissioned a private company who offered a service of aerial photography using an extremely simple but effective and reasonably inexpensive technique. They sent up a medium sized helium balloon, tethered to their Landrover jeep, adjacent to the site to be photographed. Under the balloon was a small platform to which was secured both a video camera and an electronically motor-driven stills camera, mounted "piggy back" fashion in such a way that both cameras shared a common field of view. The balloon was manipulated from the ground until the required viewpoint was achieved by observing a small video monitor linked to the aerial video camera, and a colour picture of high quality then taken, via a second electrical connecting lead, on the stills camera.

Not so much fun as hanging out of an aircraft but infinitely safer!

In the early 1970's the unrest which beset the Middle East and the ensuing uncertainty of oil supplies to the Western world served as a wake-up call regarding our dependence on imported fuel. Consequently a project was initiated at Stoke Orchard to develop a conversion process for "petrol from coal".

The technology had been practised abroad for a number of years. For example, South Africa with no indigenous oil reserves of her own, but plenty of coal, had built conversion plants, and back during the Second World War, the German Luftwaffe was fuelled mainly on fuel from coal. The big problem was that these older processes demanded a large input of energy, were inefficient, and thus very expensive.

I recall a visit from the Government Minister David Owen when I set up some publicity pictures of him pushing a motor mower apparently powered by "CRESTO", the sobriquet with which we tagged the small volume of experimental petroleum that the scientists had managed to produce. The problem was that there simply was not enough to even fill the tank of the garden mower, so we filled a can with ordinary Esso and stuck a large label on the side proclaiming "CRESTO" for the purpose of the staged demonstration. David Owen was none the wiser, and dutifully trotted up and down the lawn quite happy to co-operate for the photographs.

The Point of Ayr colliery is sited on the marshy levels of the River Dee estuary near Prestatyn in North Wales, so close to the shoreline that at times of high tides the mouth of the shaft has been sandbagged to prevent the possible inrush of seawater down into the pit. It was here in the mid-nineteen eighties that a start was made in building a large scale "petrol-from-coal" plant under the technical direction of the Coal Research Team.

I visited the site from day one to record the initial work of "piling" to stabilise the ground prior to construction, and I continued monthly visits thereafter until in fact I ceased work for British Coal. It was always a journey that I enjoyed and one which could be varied to take in many places of interest. Thus it was that I became familiar with such towns as Wem, Whitchurch, Mold, Wrexham,Flint and Rhyl, the latter in winter having to be seen to be believed, presenting as it did a spectacle of utter depression under the grey rain clouds and biting on-shore wind, with its seemingly endless rows of laid-up caravan sites.

The construction and operation of a series of rigs associated with the "petrol from coal" project at CRE made the management consider the risks involved with such volatile high-integrity plant. It was decided to form a small fire-fighting and rescue team and a call went out for volunteers. Thus it was that I ended up as one of a team of eight men drawn from various groups within the establishment.

The training was to consist of a wide-range of fire-fighting techniques, risk assessment, rescue procedures and first-aid skills, all undertaken on a "one hour per week" basis which of course put severe limitations on the level of instruction.

Initially our equipment was rather spartan, some of it inherited from the war-time civil defence era. For example, the pump for powering the water hoses consisted of a Coventry Climax engine mounted on a two wheeled heavy duty trailor, too large and unwieldy for manual handling. This was replaced by a Reliant alloy engine and integral pump with an extendable handle at each corner and therefore transportable by four men. We then purchased a second-hand long wheel-base Landrover and had a bespoke body fitted to include special equipment, lockers, hoses and of course the main item, the pump.

Eventually a redundant Dennis fire appliance was acquired from the County Fire Brigade which was a much more acceptable proposition and great fun to drive. It boasted a powerful six litre engine and could really shift. There was a four hundred gallon tank of water mounted "amidships" for immediate "first aid" fire fighting and several four inch hose outlets at the rear for pumping off the main hydrant system using the vehicle's engine via a power-take-off. Such was the suction generated that precautions had to be taken in order not to collapse the mains pipework.

All in all the several years I spent with the team were most worthwhile and educational. We enjoyed day-training sessions with both the Gloucestershire and the Hereford and Worcester brigades. The former put us through their breathing apparatus training centre, a specially built "derelict" house with blacked-out windows and which could be filled with thick pungent smoke at will. We had to make our way through the building, in pitch darkness and swirling smoke, ascend wooden staircases with whole treads missing and even squeeze through a two feet diameter mock sewer pipe, whilst wearing full kit and carrying the forty pounds weight breathing apparatus. None of it for the faint hearted!

A somewhat more passive "jolly" was a visit we made as guests to observe a fire-fighting demonstration on Filton Aerodrome, near Bristol. Prior to the main event the extinguisher company who sponsored the demonstration regaled us to a buffet lunch and seemingly unlimited supplies of wine. We were then transported on a six-wheeled Range Rover across the vast airfield to a remote spot as far as one could reach away from the office complex.

In the heart of the Nottinghamshire coalfields: Welbeck Colliery.

On site with a gleaming brand-new Ford Cortina in 1981.

The fire and rescue team, May 1985.

'Scotching the serpent' – high pressure hose practice.

It was one of those days in high summer of pure blue skies and brilliant sunshine, and the heat beat up relentlessly from the white concrete runway.

The two men running the show donned silvered asbestos suits and set-up one spectacular feat of fire-fighting after another, each succeeding one more "gung ho" than the first. It culminated in our two fearless showmen actually creating a firestorm by the device of strapping half a dozen large capacity propane cylinders together and knocking the valves off whilst igniting the gas which came roaring out as a raging inferno. Such a violent conflagration demands so much oxygen that the storm effect is generated by the surrounding air being drawn in as if by a giant unseen vacuum pump. The combination of too much wine coupled with the burning sun made me delirious with thirst. I couldn't concentrate on the matters in hand but instead was mentally willing the time to pass until we could get back to base and assuage that awful torture. It was by far the greatest thirst that I had ever endured.

Occasionally we set up a fire and rescue exercise at C.R.E, sometimes involving the County brigade. We had moments of high humour on these, for example when I and a colleague were stretchering a volunteer "victim" to the ambulance and I lost my footing pitching the poor unsuspecting casualty off onto the ground. The lesson there is never to walk backwards whilst carrying a loaded stretcher.

On another occasion we were all gathered on the top of a huge empty six hundred ton fuel silo, and practising lowering a fully equipped member of the team through a small hatch into the dark cavernous interior. He was securely strapped into a harness on the end of a strong nylon rope. When we "retrieved" him back up through the hatch he had become inverted by the weight of his top-heavy breathing apparatus and emerged into the bright daylight looking like a joint of meat in a butcher's shop window, much to our unrestrained amusement.

High-pressure water and hoses are a combination guaranteed to produce a potentially comical situation, especially when two of us were struggling to hold the pulsating nozzle and inadvertently let go. Immediately the four inch heavy hose, still gushing water at enormous velocity, became a writhing giant snake, drenching everything and everybody within a huge radius, with nobody feeling brave enough to "scotch the serpent" by grasping at the flailing brass nozzle.

Our first aid sessions were often fraught with unintentional comedy, for example when practising our bandaging techniques on each other I ended up rendering my poor colleague completely immobile, looking akin to a festive turkey ready for the oven! Conversely when my partner came to examine me, prior to treatment, he needed to check my carotid pulse by pressing on my neck. Now, I have had a lifelong aversion to anybody touching me anywhere under my chin so our encounter degenerated into a wrestling match as I tried desperately to fend him away.

On a more serious level, the experience and knowledge I gained during my time served on the team have stood me in good stead, and I feel better equipped to handle any emergencies which may face me in everyday life.

We should all develop a healthy respect for the dangers of fire and smoke inhalation, for having had the consequences demonstrated at first hand I can confirm that they are to be taken very seriously indeed.

In the mid-nineteen eighties it became evident that British Coal was becoming a contracting industry with privatisation finding a foothold in its more viable and thus potentially more profitable activities. There were a series of damaging strikes and walk-outs accompanied by protest marches supported by many people of various persuasions. There was a general lowering of morale amongst the general workforce and this was reflected to a degree at Stoke Orchard. Many old established and long serving employees saw the red light and offered themselves up for redundancy. By this time I too was becoming unsettled, not only because of the work run-down but also the tremendous changes which were happening a-pace in the photography and film professions. For some time we had been operating computers and video equipment as useful tools in our armoury of facilities, the former to store records of the many thousands of slides and negatives on file and also to generate simple coloured "pie-charts" and the like, via a coloured electronic paint box palette.

But now the whole ethos of photography was caught up in the computer and video revolution and I found that the craftsmanship which I enjoyed so much was being eroded from my chosen profession. So it was that in the autumn of 1988, I offered myself up for redundancy. I was then not yet forty two years old and would have to wait over eight years before I could enjoy the benefit of an occupational pension of sorts.

Nevertheless I did my sums based on the financial figures which were on offer and decided that in the very worst scenario I could just cover life's basics for the next eight years. So I grasped the nettle and with very mixed emotions accepted a predicted departure date in April the following year.

The next few months were so surreal. Under the terms of redundancy you were not supposed to know officially for more than four weeks in advance therefore I had to keep up a charade of feigning interest in the job whilst inwardly knowing I was not going to be around any longer after early April.

My heart was heavy as I went mechanically about my work. I remember in the February of 1989 travelling to a job at Sutton Bonnington in Leicestershire and on a road adjacent to the M1 motorway near the East Midland Airport seeing the embankment strewn with wreathes of flowers. It was at Kegworth, the scene of a tragic air disaster which had recently occurred. Somehow it characterised how I too was feeling, the portent of a period of ones life drawing to a close.

My very last assigment of any significance was the Joint European Torus project "JET" at Culham in Oxfordshire. This was an attempt to harness the vast unlimited amounts of energy released by nuclear fusion and involved the construction of a huge circular "torus" which would require a prodigious input of energy to operate, something like the total output from the neighbouring Didcot power station.

It has struck me as somehow apt that such a far-seeing project, arguably the "power of the future" should have occupied my final days with the coal industry. I had been involved with the whole gamut of energy-related matters from the early Victorian coal-fired Lancashire boilers through to twenty-first century state of the art technology. And what a fascinating and varied journey it had been.

As a final postscript to this chapter in my life I was invited back in 2003 to the old site at Stoke Orchard. It turned out to be an extremely poignant and emotional visit for me. Half of the site was derelict and empty. My old quarters were stripped bare, everything gutted out, even the power points from the walls and all the floor tiles gone, the whole complex of rooms barely recognisable. As I write there are attempts in hand to gain consent to develop the site as housing.

The ghosts of the buildings hung heavy about me, the ghosts of my younger days and of the men whom I had worked beside for so long, as if none of it had ever existed except in my imagination. I came home feeling strangely affected by a deep melancholy bordering on depression.

Life goes forwards, not back and it is sometimes as unwise to revisit past once familiar places as it is to rekindle long-over relationships.

LIVING ALONE

Early in January 1964 a family tragedy occurred which marked a "sea-change" in my own life.

Late one gloomy afternoon my boss came into my office, looking even more po-faced than usual, to say my brother-in-law Arthur wished to see me. When Arthur arrived he merely mumbled something about there having been an accident, and he had been asked to return home to Woodmancote and take me with him. He almost seemed to imply that he assumed I knew what was going on. Looking back I think the responsibility of breaking the news proved too much for him to express.

We were met at the door of Nutbridge Cottage by a red-eyed Jean, my sister. I think I knew by then what she was to blurt out to me in her grief. Dad was dead, killed in a freakish accident at his place of work. At the G.P.O stores depot which he managed in Cheltenham, a lorry was in need of unloading and he had offered to assist. He had only the one useful eye, which itself was of poor sight, and consequently he had missed his footing on the lorry platform and fallen onto the hard standing, striking his head and rendering himself unconscious. Anybody present with a modicum of first-aid knowledge would have put him into the "recovery position" and thereby saved his life. As it was, he lay on his back and choked to death on his vomit.

The following days became a blur of people and events. The house was full of family including several of Dad's line from Guernsey, over for the funeral and to pay their last respects. I cannot fully recall my own feeling at that time. I suppose at the age of just turned seventeen a boy inhibits what raw emotions he may possess. When finally the last visitor had gone, and the house was now empty except for myself, did the realisation hit me that I was on my own, responsible to no-one but me.

As time went on my family in the village, brothers and sisters, uncles and aunts, were a great support and comfort to me. My older brother Pat was a rock at this turbulent period in my young life. He had been appointed executor of our father's estate, as slender as it was, and he arranged for me to continue living at Nutbridge Cottages and keep up Dad's mortgage payments in lieu of rent which otherwise could have been enjoyed by my other six brothers and sisters. It was a fairly complicated scenario, as of course I too was a benefactor, but still technically under the age of majority. It was anticipated that on reaching the age of twenty one the house would be sold by the family to me, my share becoming effectively my deposit, and I would raise an affordable mortgage on it. As Father's mortgage was with the Cheltenham Rural District Council they hopefully could advance me the money for my mortgage, making adjustments for the difference in values. When the time came that is what we negotiated.

Everyday living was helped considerably for me by the loving attention of the family. They arranged a weekly rota amongst themselves to give me Sunday lunch, and my sister Jean took in my frugal laundry, made sure that I had clean bedding and generally kept a motherly eye on me, God bless her.

On Guernsey with 'Willie' Williams, June 1964.

Cobo Bay, Guernsey: the Rockmount Hotel, to the right of picture, still under Curr ownership in 1964.

Woodmancote Chapel Harvest 1965.

My lone figure recording the last days of the Somerset and Dorset railway in 1966.

In the June of this same year, 1964, my friend "Willie" Williams persuaded me to join him on a holiday to Guernsey to which suggestion I enthusiastically agreed. It would be my first visit back since the one with my father two years earlier.

So it was that early one Summer's morning Willie's father delivered the two of us to St James's railway station in Cheltenham, all squeezed along with our luggage into his little black upright Ford Popular saloon car. I cannot remember the route down to Weymouth port in Dorset but I like to think it was at least in part on the now long defunct Somerset and Dorset line. The sea crossing was made on the "Sarnia", owned and operated I think by British Railways, and quite a noticeable improvement in comfort to the old "St Patrick" steamer.

The two of us had a wonderful week, the weather perfect and staying in a friendly family-run guest house at Rohais near the centre of the Island. It was just the tonic I needed, after the traumas of earlier in the year.

Around this time I had started revisiting the Woodmancote Chapel for the Sunday evening services, mainly at the urging from my sister Jean. She was secretary at the Chapel, quite a pivotal role, for not only was she responsible for booking the many lay preachers from the surrounding area but also often in collecting them from their homes and delivering them safely back after the service, courtesy of Arthur, her long-suffering but patient husband, in his small fibre-glass bodied three-wheeled Reliant car.

Harvest time was perhaps the highlight in the Chapel's calendar, for then the altar was adorned with all kinds of produce, groceries and fruit and vegetables, all donated by local people, and symbolically the display was set-off with a large lump of coal and the whole crowned with a sheaf of corn.

Jean traditionally made up an enormous hanging display of woven flowers and greenery which was carefully suspended on a hook securely fixed to the ceiling high above the heads of the worshippers.

On one of these festive occasions I set up my tape-recorder and recorded the entire service. The microphone was secreted amongst the flowers which adorned the preacher's pulpit and the actual recording machine was on the floor by the little harmonium behind its screen of velvet curtains.

Here I briefed the "resident" lady organist, my dear friend Jane Mills, on how to set the recorder going and also how to turn down the recording level during the more tumultuous hymns. (I still have that precious seven inch reel of tape although by now, after well over forty years I would expect the magnetic signal has decayed quite appreciably).

I have never considered myself particularly religious in the spiritual sense believing that God, if he exists at all, exists amongst us in our day-to-day lives and not exclusively in man-made churches. However those evenings spent sitting with that tiny congregation of villagers, and sharing their simple faith, was a source of comfort and companionship to me.

Adolescent boys, and probably girls too, can harbour strange aspirations and ideas of self-importance in themselves and I was no exception. In 1965. I developed the notion of taking up the writing of novels and enjoying all the trappings that successful authorship can bring. The first step would be to learn to type so that I could sit at my desk rattling off page after page of literary expression. I therefore enrolled on an evening course at the Comprehensive School in neighbouring Bishop's Cleeve.

It was a disaster from the first lesson. I turned up with my shiny new leather briefcase, notepad and pens, bubbling with enthusiasm. For a start, I was the only male in a room full of young girls. They all seemed experienced typists and our tutor, an old spinster lady, brooked no nonsense from her class. There was to be no talking or banter as we each bent industriously over the black iron typewriters tapping out interminable A.S.D.F's and Q.W.E.R.T.Y sequences all evening. I suppose my expectations were rather too high. A comparison might be to undergo piano lessons and come away after the first one able to regale an audience with Rachmaninoff's No 2 piano concerto. My enthusiasm evaporated into thin air and any intentions of writing best sellers forgotten.

1966 turned out to be quite unforgettable for me due to two totally unrelated experiences, the first one being my first ever stay in hospital as a patient and the second, later in the year, was the meeting and start of what turned out to be a long on/off courtship with Loretta, my future wife.

The hospital confinement was the result, albeit indirectly, of a car accident. The date March the sixth, is remembered as the last day before closure of the Somerset and Dorset railway. I had accompanied an old school friend and neigh bour, Olly, (of whom I shall write more fully later), in his father's new Morris 1100 car to Bath. There we enjoyed a run down the line from Bath Green Station to a small halt named Cole, as far as our slender resources could fund, and back to Bath on the next train. It was on the car journey home that disaster struck. We were descending the A46 road into Nailsworth town when poor Olly took one of the many sweeping bends rather too wide, slid and struck the high nearside kerb with his rear wheel. Unfortunately the impact damaged the wheel and punctured the tyre. He carried no jack and yours truly nobly offered to attempt to lift the back of the car whilst he changed the wheel. Of course it was futile and after gathering our senses we decided to contact his father, despite it now being around midnight. We left the car by the roadside and walked down into the town where by an amazing stroke of good fortune we discovered the police station actually lit up with an Officer on night duty. We would today search in vain for a police station in Nailsworth. We explained our plight and the end result was Olly's father being roused from his bed and making the mercy trip up to rescue us in his other car, and bring us back to Woodmancote.

The following morning I awoke with a persistent dull ache in my groin which increased as the day wore on. By the evening a pronounced bulge had developed, which became even more protuberant after a couple of pints of beer.

A visit to my Doctor confirmed that I had succeeded in giving myself a ruptured gut, a hernia in other words, and he arranged an operation for me. By accepting someone else's cancelled "booking", I was admitted to St Paul's Hospital in Cheltenham within a few days of the diagnosis. The hospital is no more, the site now having been developed for housing, but in 1966 it was principally the maternity unit for the town. The actual building was far older, having its origins as the Cheltenham workhouse.

A hernia today is an extremely routine operation and the patient can be home the same day. But there was to be no "Keyhole" surgery for me. In total I spent ten fretful days in that ward. The utter relief on being finally discharged was indescribable, and such pleasure taken in doing everyday activities again that one takes so very much for granted. My day under the knife actually coincided with a general Election and as I lay sedated under the "pre-op" injection a most surreal thing occurred. The sitting M.P. Dodds-Parker came around the ward on a last ditch attempt to canvass a final few votes and for some reason he was accompanied by the Dean of Cheltenham in his full regalia. I opened my eyes to see them both gazing down on me from behind and therefore "upside down". The effect was quite startling!

Both my eldest brother Roland and my sister Sheila lived at this time in the village of Marshfield, a community betwixt Bristol and Chippenham straddling the main A420 road. Roland had been posted there as the village policeman some years previously and when Sheila and her husband were looking for a house nearer to his area of work they settled on Marshfield. After my operation Sheila kindly invited me down to spend a week or so with them in order to convalesce. I had, of course visited both my siblings on a number of occasions previously, in fact it was the furthest that I had ventured on my Vespa scooter.

Roland had a huge area to patrol and generally be responsible for, including the notorious crossroads where the A420 intersected the Cheltenham to Bath road at Cold Ashton. One "perk" of attending many accidents which occurred there was the benefit of various items of groceries or drink which had been jettisoned from damaged lorries onto the roadway. His transport in those days was a little black Velocette motorcycle with its valve radio and aerial bolted over the rear wheel. Before the luxury of the Velocette his sole means of getting aound was the standard police-issue bicycle with it's sturdy tubular frame and high handlebars.

There was an approved school for errant girls called St Catherine's which nestled a few miles away in the Valley of the Rocks, and it was here that poor Roland had his bicycle stolen by the inmates whilst on a call-out there. Such call-outs were a regular feature of his duties for the girls were forever escaping from the confines of the school into the surrounding countryside and Roland was expected to round them up single-handedly using nothing more than his trusty bicycle.

The police station was actually on the main Chippenham road and became a favourite stop-off for a number of tramps and itinerants who regularly passed through. Both Roland and his wife Peggy were an extremely generous and compassionate couple and offered hospitality to any down-and-out who happened to call. I recall one morning being advised not to go near the garage as "the tramp was not up yet". They had made a rough bed up for him the previous evening using the emergency stretcher kept there.

During my stay in hospital I had been visited by several colleagues including two or three of the girls whom I was acquainted with, and who worked as clerical or secretarial staff. They told me, with a knowing look on their faces, that a secretary in the office had wanted to visit me but was too shy. This naturally roused my curiosity and on my return to employment I made a point of meeting the lass in question and ended up inviting her out on a date.

To my surprise she immediately accepted which threw me into a state of near panic. I had taken a number of girls out before on a sort of casual ad-hoc basis but never on a formal date. Suddenly what to me had been a flirtation to "test the water" became reality.

Loretta seemed far more mature than I was, which intimidated me somewhat. But looking back I was totally misguided. She turned out to be every mans dream with her soft voice, honey colour hair and big blue eyes which exuded warmth and affection. She was, and still is, the most caring, generous and selfless person that I have ever met, and I bitterly regret that I gave her the most despicable run-around in our early days. With hindsight I was simply immature and ill-equipped to deal with any sort of emotional relationship. However it did not daunt dear Loretta and she eventually won the match!

Our famous first date is still remembered with affection by us both. We decided to go into Cheltenham and see the recently released film "Alfie" adapted from Bill Naughton's stage play and starring a very young Michael Caine. My brother-in-law Peter, affectionately nicknamed Noddy, had just purchased a brand new Vauxhall Viva and he offered to drive us into town posing as a taxi driver. We picked Loretta up from Sunnycroft, where she lived with her parents and resident grandmother in nearby Bishop's Cleeve. She felt so flattered on my hiring a cab for our very first date!

During the interval of the film I think she expected an icecream, but instead I produced a half-bottle of rum from my pocket, which a colleague had brought back duty-free from Germany, and we both enjoyed a cap-full. At least I thought she had enjoyed it, but later learnt that she hated the taste and has never touched a drop of rum since!

Loretta was undeterred apparently by all this fandangle for she accepted an offer of being taken to our village show the following Saturday. Our early dates were bedevilled with wet weather and this second one was no exception. The rain was coming down like stair-rods, driven by a bitter northerly wind. And this the end of June! Nevertheless I called at Sunnycroft on my Vespa and went in to meet "mum and dad" whilst at the same time dripping water from my drenched clothing all over the carpet and furnishings. The final seal was put on the meeting by the family Alsatian making a bee-line for me and sending my cup of tea flying over both me and the armchair.

In the freezing fog exploring the hills around Marshfield on my Vespa motorcycle.

Loretta at the time of our first date, 1966.

Boarding the DC3 Dakota at Guernsey Airport, 1966.

'Willie' Williams, Len Williamson and me: encamped near Torquay 1967.

76

Loretta and I had not been seeing each other for long when I made another trip over to Guernsey. This was a holiday arranged some time previously with my friends Len Williamson and Michael Dewey. We flew from Staverton airport, as I had with my father years earlier, but instead of the old Dakotas passengers now enjoyed the relative greater luxury of Viscount Turboprop Airliners.

We were booked into the same guest house at Rohais where I had stayed during my two other holidays on the island. As Michael had been a late booking the landlady fixed him up with a metal framed folding bed next to Len and my two divans. My enduring memories of our vacation were of Mike on our first night suffering a nightmare and standing on his ricketty put-u-up desperately trying to escape from the bedroom over the top of the picture rail at three o'clock in the morning. The second night I was awoken by a crash and a cry of anquish from Michael as the safety catch on his bed broke and with a great twang the springs contracted him into a ball, imprisoned in the iron bed frame. He was none too happy and expressed as much to our landlady the following morning.

The holiday the following year was one of a very different kind. I and my two friends "Willie" Williams and Len Williamson decided to embark on a camping tour of Devon and Cornwall. Willie was then a young police constable and managed to borrow a massive green Icelandic ridge tent which was usually used for outward bound courses. It was designed to sleep twelve bodies!

This, plus all the other camping paraphernalia, was strapped to the roof of Willie's tiny Austin A35 saloon car and off we set. I can remember our route to this day, down into Somerset and the excruciating drag up Porlock Hill for the long-suffering little Austin, then on down following the coast to Bude. The trip was somewhat dampened by an accident which we came upon at Stratton. We actually heard the collision and rounded the bend to witness the result of an old Ford Popular having overshot the corner and hitting a car head-on. The tragic aspect to the incident was that the innocent second car contained a honeymooning couple. I had never before seen a man so distressed and in a state of shock, running witlessly about with his shirt hanging off his body in tatters. Willie did what he could in the way of first aid and generally directing matters and then we continued our journey, naturally all three of us feeling very subdued.

That summer of 1967 has gone down as the "Summer of Love" and nowhere was it better demonstrated than on those hot sunny beaches of Cornwall. Everywhere we went the strains of "San Fransisco" and "Whiter Shade of Pale" assailed our ears from tinny sounding portable transistor radios, overlayed with the sound of the breaking surf and squawking seagulls.

The Autumn of this same year saw me enrolling on an evening course, one of many offered by the Bristol University's Extra-mural department, to study the history and lives of birds. It was a positive move on my part to help break the cycle of work and socialising that any young man adopts.

Our tutor was Christopher Swaine, a master at the private Rendcomb College, and something of an acknowledged authority on birdlife.

We enjoyed several field trips under his tutorage, one in particular to that narrow strip of "no-mans-land" which lies betwixt the River Severn and the Berkeley Ship Canal south of Gloucester. It was easy to see how Peter Scott, the son of the Antarctic expolorer Robert Falcon Scott, became inspired to found his now world famous Wildfowl and Wetlands Trust at nearby Slimbridge.

This same Autumn I developed an interest in numismatics, mainly because the prospect of the phasing out of the British system of pounds, shillings and pence had become a reality.

The Government planned to introduce initially the new ten and five pence coinage which would eventually replace the florin and shilling pieces. Ironically, the florin had its origins in a very early attempt to "go decimal", there being just ten to the pound. Its milled rim was a reminder of the days when it was worthwhile for unscrupulous people to file appreciable amounts from such coins as they were then minted in sterling silver.

Until starting collecting the range of extant British coins I was blissfully unaware, for example, that there were two different designs of shillings, Scottish and English, and pennies had been minted not only at the Royal Mint but also, around the time of the First World War, at two private mints, Heaton's and King's Norton. The latter are identifiable by a minute "H" or "KN" alongside the date, barely visible to the naked eye.

The "holy grail" of the more modern coins, to me, was the 1952 sixpence. A total of just over a million were minted, which may seem a large number but in coin circulation terms is quite low. I was thrilled to be given one in change at a tea bar, for it filled a prominent gap in my collection, although I am loath to admit that most of my acquisitions were gathered during transactions at my local ale house.

In the course of my evening's socialising at the Apple Tree Inn I became acquainted with, and in time became firm friends with, a charming character by the name of Arthur "Puffer" Walker. Although probably then only in his late forties he came across as "one of nature's" gentlemen of the old school. Puffer actually had a very humble background. On his discharge from the Army after the war, where he served in Poona in the Northern Indian territories, he came back to a job as a dustman and later as a painter with a maintenance team working at the Smiths Watch and Clock factory. He lived with his elderly parents in a council flat at Prestbury on the outskirts of Cheltenham, having been a lifelong bachelor.

He delighted in what he would call "connections" making friends with people of somewhat higher social standing than himself. Every evening he would scrub himself up and don his Harris tweeds, take the maroon double-decker bus, which then ran to the top of Cleeve Hill and walk down to the Apple Tree. He would stand there puffing on his cigar, beaming benignly at the little circle of associates who habitually gathered around him.

It was through Puffer that I became interested in what was destined to become a consuming passion. Knowing of my involvement with photography, one evening he produced from his top pocket a grubby postcard sized picture of a rural scene portraying a group of village worthies in a harvest field. Could I make a copy from it for its lady owner, a near neighbour of Puffers?

It had such an interesting local connection and poignant background. One of the young men portrayed in the photograph had fallen in battle during the First World war and the small picture had been retrieved from his tunic pocket. He must have carried that little memento as a symbol of earlier happier times in his native Gloucestershire. I copied the photograph with great care and did myself a copy at the same time. I was hooked, and it was to be the first of many hundreds of local scenes and characters which I was to collect over the next forty years. The eventual result is manifested in two bulging albums crammed to capacity with mounted and annotated copy photographs with their corresponding negatives filed and contact printed for ready retrieval.

As the summer of 1968 drew to a close two wildly different activities engaged my attention. The first was fairly short lived, when I joined a men's skittle team. The form of skittles played in North Gloucestershire is actually of a local nature, for as one travels outside the area then so the game changes and eventually becomes unheard of. But not so around Cheltenham where several skittles leagues for both men and women of varying abilities thrive. I am sorry to say that I did not enjoy the season with the side. Most of the games in those days took place in cold dismal echoing alleys, usually stuck away behind a back-street urban pub. You had to attend every match, for failure to do so meant you became a reserve the following week, still having to attend but not actually playing. Women were "persona non grata" on these occasions and the men-only assembly did their best to "out bawl" one another with constant barracking. All in all it was not an experience that appealed to me and I quietly withdrew as a member of the team after that first winter.

The second activity involved me with a group of very different people, articulate, cultured, humorous and good natured, in short, enjoyable and stimulating company. They were the Bishop's Cleeve Players, a talented society of amateur actors and actresses supported by an enthusiastic team of back-stage and front of house volunteers. They were in need of somebody to photograph their forthcoming production of Richard Brinsley Sheridon's "The Rivals". The pictures would be used for a variety of purposes; a front of house display, press publicity and to make up the Player's albums chronicling their twice yearly shows.

I was approached to see if I would undertake the task to which I readily agreed, and went along to the first dress rehearsal. I was very cautious in my handling of this commission. I used my Rolleiflex roll film camera on a tripod and set-up a selection of posed tableaux involving as many of the performers as possible, and lit with the stage spots and floodlights. Whilst technically satisfactory they lacked the spontaneity of shots taken "live" during actual rehearsal.

For later productions I switched from using the Rolleiflex to a hand held Pentax 35mm camera loaded with a "fast" black and white film and was able to take pictures discreetly during the rehearsal under the stage lighting.

One aspect of these plays was the "late night party" which was held on the Saturday evening in one or other of the member's houses. The uninhibited revelry which ensued was a sure sign of another successful production "put to bed".

I was involved with a total of thirty three plays over the years, finishing with very mixed emotions in 1984. The principle reason for my decision to sever my links was the move from the cosiness and informality of the medieval Tithe Barn in Bishop's Cleeve to the Playhouse Theatre in Cheltenham where it seemed things were handled far more seriously.

I was touched to receive the present of a signed card and book token from the whole assembly at my final party. The token was converted into J.B.Priestley's "English Journey" which had then just been republished as a golden anniversary edition and continues to give me pleasure to this day.

Two years ago out of the blue came an invitation to join a party in the Cheltenham Racecourse hospitality suite, celebrating fifty years of the Player's continuation. It was a delightful evening, meeting so many old friends again, all some twenty years older than when we last met but still equally charming and full of "joie de vivre" and without exception they all greeted me as a long-lost fellow thespian.

I cannot recall now what it was that led me to join the Cheltenham Camera Club. Possibly I was inspired to do so after visiting one of their Annual Exhibitions held at the Art Gallery in the town.

The club claimed to be the oldest established club in the country, if not the world, with a history stretching back to 1865. There is a charming period sepia-style print of the members posed amidst the ivy-clad ruins of Raglan Castle on their very first field outing in that same year.

When I joined the club they used to meet every Thursday in the lecture room at Cheltenham's Y.M.C.A. It was run on fairly formal lines with we, the audience, sat in rows of chairs awaiting the introduction by our Chairman of the evening's speaker. Most of the talks were illustrated by a non-stop succession of coloured slides, and covered the typical output of your average amateur photographer - holidays, scenery, autumn tints, portraits and so on.

In the over-heated darkened room with both the drone of the projector's cooling fan and the drone of the speaker we frequently "lost" several of our older members into the Land of Nod, one old boy who always sat in his same seat at the front giving a wonderful aural display of nasal impressions!

Occasionally the meetings some weeks were enlivened by a top-class

Loretta with 'Puffer' Walker.

The first of many: this picture started off my collection of historic local photographs.

81

At an 'after-show' party with the Bishop's Cleeve Players in 1984.

Cheltenham Camera Club Cotswold outing: lunch stop near Stowell Park, Northleach, 1973.

stimulating talk given by a doyen in the particular subject. For example I still remember with pleasure Maurice Rowe the well-known motor sport photographer who had for many seasons followed the Grand Prix "circus" around the world, recording the feats of such great names as Fangio and Stirling Moss.

Other speakers of note whom I can recall included J.S.Lewinski the portraitist, Sir George Pollock F.R.P.S a leading exponent of colour photography; a fascinating old couple, Jack and Grace Cotton of the "Rough Stuff" cycling club and local characters such as Fred Rowbotham who wrote the definitive book on the world famous Severn bore and Bill Bawden of Eagle Photos who was responsible for those marvellous black and white photographs of Cotswold landscapes and stone villages with massive cotton-wool clouds billowing across the sky, pictures which seemed to adorn every Cotswold calendar and guide book of the time.

The club held a "running" competition throughout the season consisting of a series of heats each with a specific subject, for example men at work, people at play, or an abstract theme, such as "time" or "speed". We were invited to submit prints or slides to be judged by a visiting "expert" on the night, and at the end of the year a winner was declared, based on the best overall result, and presented with a plaque.

I used to bash off two or three 20"x16" prints from negatives fished out of my files and to my astonishment actually was awarded the coveted plaque on my first attempt! I like to think that I won it by default, being sufficiently keen to enter every heat.

As a result of this unexpected fame I found myself appointed as organiser of the studio group. "Studio" is rather a euphemistic description for what in effect was a damp cheerless basement below a large Regency house in the town's Priory Street. Not only was I expected to entice members along once a month but also to lure unsuspecting females along to pose for us, take the subscriptions from participating photographers, make the tea, ensure the model had transport to and from the studio and even supply her with a set of gratis prints of the evening as a way of thanking her. People were generally quite happy to turn up, do their "thing" and enjoy the evening then disappear off into the night. I kept the studio going for a couple of seasons until I understandably became rather jaundiced with the whole scenario. The final straw was the battle I had with the Club committee to splash out some money for a new roll of white background paper. The old roll of the nine feet wide sweep had become torn, creased and covered in dusty footprints with barely enough paper left to reach the floor. It was a cheap variety when purchased new, with the quality of Izal medicated toilet paper. In my professional work we used a "cartridge" paper quality Colorama paper which was replaced after every session and we had a special rack made holding a selection of colours plus white and black, so having to struggle with the tattered flapping remnants of the Camera Club's idea of background material drove me to desperation, and finally resigning with great personal relief, from running the whole fiasco.

I actually participated in a couple of outings which the Camera Club organised.

The first was quite a civilised affair when we travelled as a party by coach to the Birmingham Botanical Gardens. The second occasion was not so leisurely. We all assembled in front of Cheltenham Town Hall with our own private cars and what ensued was more like a motor rally, when our leader, who had organised the afternoon, took off at speed on what turned out to be a whistle stop tour of the Cotswolds. Somehow we all managed to stay in convoy long enough to reach a picnic stop, a muddy lay-bye under some dripping trees near Stowell park at Northleach. The only photograph I could muster that day is a colour slide of our party trooping en masse across an enormous bleak bare field like some group of travel-worn refugees desperately trying to gain the shelter of a sympathetic land.

Nevertheless, despite all the aforementioned vicissitudes, on the whole I enjoyed my eight or nine years as a member of the club. The old order there has long gone, of course, and the club enjoys new premises under a new generation of keen young enthusiasts. I occasionally visit their Annual Exhibition at the Cheltenham Art Gallery and marvel at the immaculate computer-generated digital photographs, perfect in every detail, and I inwardly chuckle at my bitter-sweet recollection of struggling with that recalcitrant roll of background paper so long ago!

For some time Loretta had been taking driving lessons, official ones through an accredited driving school supplemented by taking the wheel of a colleague's car for their journey to work. Before she came to take a driving test an opportunity arose to purchase a car for herself. It was a Morris Minor Series Two 1955 saloon, powered with a proven "A" series overhead valve 803cc engine, and finished in glossy black cellulose paint. It was on offer privately at just ninety pounds, quite a tidy sum in 1967. When she told me how undecided she was I managed to persuade her that buying it would prove the necessary spur to apply for, and hopefully pass, her driving test. It turned out to be the case, her perseverance paid off and with great jubilation she informed me that she had passed.

We now had a means of independent travel - no more missing the end of a film at the local cinema in order to dash for the last bus home.

Between us we planned a short touring holiday together, heading into Wales, an area for which I had already developed a great affinity.

There is nothing quite like being thrown together with another person as a test of compatability, and I think it was on both our minds that a successful week in each other's company would decide once and for all any future plans we may make.

So it was that on a glorious autumn morning of late October 1969 the two of us set off ensconced in "Dumpy" as our little round Morris had now been christened.

Wales is delightful as summer turns into autumn. There was a stillness over the land as the landscape seems to gather its strength to face the forthcoming rigours of winter, laying a golden carpet of leaves to adorn the woods and river banks.

We made our first stop at Brecon, finding a reasonable "bed and breakfast" at the Watton on the approach to the little market town. The following day we headed north through the Epynt forest to Builth Wells and on up to Rhayader, the gateway of the Elan Valley. The gallant little Dumpy didn't miss a beat as we slowly climbed the narrow deserted road linking the vast sombre reservoirs, Caban Coch, Penygarreg and Craig Goch, lying still and grey under the lowering autumn skies. The power locked up in those awesome masses of impassive water was unimaginable, power that was tapped via the ingenious device of the massive pipe which bore its precious cargo flowing entirely by gravity into the heart of the English midlands some eighty miles distant.

Here I must say that Loretta performed heroically in transporting us safely on our journey. I did not posess a driving licence other than a provisional one for my long defunct motor scooter, so all the driving was down to her. They do not teach you how to negotiate treacherous hairpin bends on Welsh mountain passes when schooling you for the driving test, so it was something of a baptism of fire for poor Loretta, which she came through with flying colours!

We headed out from the top of the Elan Valley to Devil's Bridge, pausing on the way to view the haunting complex of lead ore processing buildings at Cwmystwyth. The wind was clanking the broken corrugated iron cladding which hung from the derelict deserted empty sheds, the only sound, apart from the tinkling of the stream which once drove the ponderous over-shot water wheels used for grinding the hard won lead ore.

The whole place was imbued with the spirits of long-dead workers and we were both glad to carry on our way and leave the ghosts of the past to their undisturbed peace.

Our next port of call was Aberystwyth where it was necessary for me to visit the branch there of my bank. It was the end of the month when I knew my account would be replenished by my monthly salary cheque and I could withdraw some essential extra funds. In those days before the now ubiquitous cash point machines were dreamed of, it was an incredibly complicated and cumbersome procedure to organise a withdrawal directly over the counter at any branch other than one's own. Before our trip I had supplied my branch with a specimen of my signature which was then mailed to their Aberystwyth colleagues before my arrival at the counter there. I passed over my cheque made payable to "self" and had the cash counted out to me once the signature had beeen scrutinised. It certainly seemed a hard won ten pounds!

As we headed on northwards, through Machynlleth, Dolgellau, Ffestiniog, into Snowdonia and up and over the Llanberis Pass with Loretta still clinging doggedly to the wheel, we crossed the Menai strait by Telford's magnificent suspension bridge and at Beaumaris, in the shadow of its castle, Dumpy's game little engine finally was switched off, and we decided to find accomodation for a couple of nights.

Loretta had lived as a young girl at Rhosneigr on Anglesey's western coast for two years and was anxious to return there for her first visit since leaving to settle in Gloucestershire. My lasting two impressions of the village were the relentless on-shore wind and the ear-splitting screams of RAF jets flying sorties from their base at nearby Valley. We did not linger there for long.

Our eventual return south was via the historic A5, Telford's visionary route from London to Ireland. We crossed over the River Conway and on to Llangollen and the iron canal aquaduct of Pontcysyllte soaring 127 feet over the valley of the River Dee. Here we paused and took time to walk across the structure on the narrow towpath. It was plain to understand how it earned the description of one of the World's Wonders when it opened for boats at the dawn of the nineteenth century.

Commercially it never fulfilled its intended purpose as the branch of canal linking it to the rich coalfields around Ruabon was never constructed, so instead Telford's masterpiece merely served as a water conductor, replenishing the remainder of the Shropshire Union canal system.

We broke our slow progress homewards with an overnight stopover in Shrewsbury and the following day made a visit to the fledgling railway H.Q. of the Severn Valley revival scheme at Bridgnorth.

Since those early days the S.V.R. society has gone from strength to strength and is one of England's oldest established and best known "volunteer" railways, providing a regular schedule of services to Kidderminster, some twelve miles south.

I have described this particular journey with Loretta in some detail, not only because it was such an enjoyable and interesting experience but also because it consolidated our relationship and established a new depth of understanding between us both.

Loretta had been beside me constantly for those last five blissful days, and when at last she said goodbye outside Nutbridge Cottages and drove away, disappearing around the bend in Dumpy towards her own home, I think she had finally decided in her heart of hearts that I was the man with whom she wanted to spend her life.

Loretta with 'Dumpy' at the Penygarreg dam in the Elan Valley, October 1969.

Amusing sign spotted on the Menai suspension road bridge, Anglesey.

Leading our guests from St. Peter's Church up the treacherous pathway.

Leaving for our wedding reception aboard the 1930 Alvis tourer.

MARRIAGE

Early in 1970 Loretta contacted me to ask if I was free on March the Seventh. She had decided that if she did not make a positive marriage arrangement then the two of us would go on drifting from year to year ad infinitum. I was caught completely off my guard and went along with her plans quite passively. To this day I do not know why March the Seventh should have been the prescribed date when there was the whole of the forthcoming spring and summertime to enjoy.

To her credit, Loretta arranged the complete schedule of events, starting with our little "pep-talk" from the rector of Bishop's Cleeve, Canon Kenneth Edmunds in the back-room "snug" in his Rectory, and all the rest of the minutiae that go to make up the traditional procedure of an English wedding day.

We didn't see each other for several days before the actual date, the last occasion being when Loretta delivered my one and only dark suit back to me from having had it dry-cleaned. I later was to find a small black moulded plastic cat in the jacket's breast pocket which she had placed there for luck.

The ceremony was to be held in St Peter's Church on Cleeve Hill, where my two sisters and brother Tony had previously wed. I decided to book a room at the Rising Sun Hotel, vitually opposite the Church, for the Friday night, so all I had to do was cross the road the following morning, take my seat in the front pew and let the chain of events unfold about me.

Thus I spent a very convivial evening in pleasant company, becoming the butt of much well-intentioned humorous advice from everyone and even engaging in a game of darts before finally making it to my last night's sleep as a single man.

I was greeted the following morning by Eileen Davey, the genial and kind-hearted landlady of the Rising Sun, as she brought my breakfast up to my room "as a special treat". She pulled back the curtains, flooding the whole bedroom with a dazzling white light. To my alarm it had snowed heavily during the night and the ground lay blanketed several inches deep.

When I eventually had breakfasted, and made myself ready for the day, I went outside and shuffled my way across to St Peter's. The steep path down from the road to the Church doorway looked treacherous but as I had neither the guile nor the inclination to do anything about it, I made my way back to the lounge of the hotel where I had arranged to meet my brother Pat, who was officiating as "best-man", and any other early birds who fancied a couple of "stiffeners" before events got underway.

In due course we all made it down the slippery slope (symbolic of marriage?) back to the church where we sat and waited. Suddenly there was a slight disturbance behind us, the organ burst into strains of Handel's "Entry of the Queen of Sheba" and there was Loretta, looking absolutely radiant on her Father's arm, beside me. She was later to confide that it was the biggest surprise to see me there at all! All along she had harboured the secret fear that I would have second thoughts at the eleventh hour, and even her own Father's words to her as they were leaving the family home that morning were "If things don't work out, Liz, you can always come back here"

I still cherish the hilarious movie film of the shambolic progress of the wedding party back up that death-defying pathway. People were hauling themselves using the iron handrail, Loretta was sandwiched between my brother Pat and the organist in an effort to keep her upright and I am seen, legs whirling like pistons in a desperate attempt to maintain my balance, before sliding back on my stomach virtually between organist Brian Basham's legs.

Apparently that morning the Rector had wanted to transfer the entire ceremony to the Bishop's Cleeve parish church of St Michael at literally a few minutes notice, which was obviously totally impracticable.

Our party of invited guests eventually regrouped at the High Roost Hotel half a mile away, Loretta and I enjoying the journey in a vintage open Alvis tourer belonging to a friend of mine. In the few minutes it took to arrive at our reception poor Loretta had turned blue with the cold and had to be wrapped in a padded anorak to revive her senses.

The reception thereon passed very enjoyably, enhanced by ending with a general display of singing "in the round" a repertoire of many Apple Tree Inn old favourites. My dear friend and mentor Bill Harbor, honourary photographer for the day, observed that it appeared and sounded like a traditional tribal wedding custom peculiar to this part of rustic Gloucestershire.

As a consequence to this "carousalling" my bride and I were late leaving, much to the consternation of the more elderly contingent of Uncles and Aunts who felt bound by etiquette to wait and bid us their farewells and bon voyage for our honeymoon.

By some means "Dumpy" our Morris Minor had been delivered to the door of the High Roost, but not before several nameless individuals had done the obligatory doctoring to Dumpy's décor and also placed handfuls of pebbles in her hubcaps. Thus we rattled and slid our way through the snowy landscape over the hills to the city of Bath, our first planned stop. Originally the general plan was to embark on a tour of Devon and Somerset, coming home on the following Saturday, but the widespread weather conditions were to confound our proposal.

We spent a pretty dismal night in Bath, starting with a modest supper in a small café where Loretta unwittingly shook out all the confetti which was lodged in her coat over the floor. We then retired to our digs for the night, a pub I have long since forgotten the name of, near the Avon Bridge. Here we suffered an endurance test of slipping and sliding around under wretched thin nylon bed linen until the blessed arrival of morning. Things were relieved somewhat by an inebriated guest blundering into our room in the middle of the night, bumping and crashing around until even in his witless state he realised that perhaps his own bed lay elsewhere.

We left Bath early on the morrow and headed on down into Somerset. Loretta was still the only one of us with a full driving licence and was decidedly nervous at negotiating the icy lanes which did not appear to have been gritted. Having circumnavigated the Chew Valley lake we thought it prudent to head slowly back towards Gloucestershire and home.

We made a second overnight halt at Alveston on the main A38 trunk road, for incredibly thick fog had started closing in as evening drew nigh. We found a charming period farmhouse owned by Squadron Leader Loder and his wife. Mrs Loder, I recall, was one of the organising committee for the Cheltenham Music Festival.

We bid them farewell the following morning and in the bright early Spring sunshine pulled off the main road and into the canalside village of Frampton-on-Severn. It was here that Loretta did her first grocery "shop" for the two of us, the start of her new life as Mrs Curr.

We arrived back at Nutbridge Cottages that afternoon and Loretta parked Dumpy on the broad grass verge outside. It was to be our home for the next fifteen years.

A FRESH BEGINNING

After over six years of bachelorhood it came as something of a shock to find another person sharing one's home, taking up space which previously had been exclusively one's own. I suppose the most obvious change was suddenly having somebody other than yourself to consider. You simply couldn't just come and go as you pleased, eat when the fancy took you, even watch or not watch the television. Conversely, there was somebody, your chosen partner, who also considered and cared for you.

I have never forgotten that first thrill of experiencing the warm glow of home comfort that Loretta brought into our home, the joy of being greeted by the delicious smell of home cooking on returning from my work on a gloomy winter's evening, a clean and tidy house, regular changes of laundry, in other words my cold cheerless dusty and drab house had been transformed into a welcoming home.

Heating had never been top of my list of domestic priorities and one of Loretta's very first actions was to order half a ton of coal from our local fuel merchant. The fireplace grate in our sitting room was in a terrible state, the iron grate itself had collapsed and the supporting refractory bricks had long disintegrated, to the extent that any fires I had bothered to light were actually on the bare concrete plinth level with the hearth! I perforce had to effect some sort of repair, but Loretta decided that we really ought to install a central heating system. As fortune would have it I had recently inherited a small sum of money from my late grandmother's estate. She had actually died a few years earlier but there was a long period before her house and orchard could be sold for development, and then a contention had arisen over who of her surviving family qualified to benefit under the terms of her will. Eventually what would have been my late mother's share was divided equally between we seven siblings and my portion funded the central heating project.

The saga of its installation over the coming months would be a book on its own.

Arthur Withers, "Art" as he was affectionately known, was my brother-in-law and a master plumber of the old "measure twice and cut once" school. When he learnt of our plans he somehow took on the job without us actually asking him if he would do it. One evening his little white Reliant three-wheeler drew up outside Nutbridge Cottages (little did we suspect what a common familiar sight it would become over the ensuing months) and Art came to the door, tape measure and notebook in hand. At the finish of his survey I was given a long shopping list of piping, pumps, fittings, taps, ballcocks, tanks, and so on, which I was expected to source and get delivered.

Thus began the long period of domestic upheaval that drove Loretta to distraction and me to despair. In my innocence I judged maybe a week or two of work would see the task completed, and purchased a small case of bottled beer so Art could refresh himself after the evening's work. A week later only the radiator brackets were in position, screwed to the wall in their allotted places and the beer had disappeared.

Early married life at Nutbridge Cottage.

Arthur Withers – master plumber.

Central heating installation in progress – utter chaos reigns at Nutbridge Cottage.

A welcome break at Dolgwartheg cottage in Merionethshire.

Art would settle himself down, pour himself a glass of ale and regale us with stories of long ago, usually prefaced by the words "before the war", whilst all about us lay the detritus of Yorkshire fittings, pipe benders, gas cylinders, rolls of solder, odd lengths of pipe, wrenches, blow torches, all scattered in every room of the house. Carpets and floor coverings had all been rolled up and we were living on the bare boards where they themselves had not been prised up. The final straw was when Art drilled the plaster ceiling in the kitchen and deposited a dusting of Gypsum like newly fallen snow over a lemon meringue pie which Loretta had just taken out of the oven.

Needless to say, the job was finally completed and was a monument of fine craftsmanship. We were certainly never to feel the cold in Nutbridge Cottage again. On the contrary, when a fresh wind would get up, the "draw" on the solid fuel closed stove in the lounge was phenomenal and it would begin to sing like a giant kettle, its interior resembling a white-hot fireball. Then the copper cylinder in the airing cupboard above our heads would start to rumble ominously and to alleviate the situation we would recourse to turning on the circulation pump. This was a massive affair; Art evidently was one of the "you cannot have too big a pump" school. When running it caused the water pipes to oscillate and chatter, giving a fair impression of the start of the Manx Motorcycle TT.

We had managed to save some money out of my bequest and decided that we owed ourselves a short holiday away. My old friend and near-neighbour Ted Dewey had rented a traditional Welsh cottage not far from Dolgellau in mid Wales, and recommended it as a very good base for excursions or walking. He introduced us to the owners, a local couple, and so it was that we started what was to be a long association with that part of the country.

We loaded Dumpy with enough stores for the week, groceries, everything we could anticipate needing for the duration of our stay.

With careful planning it is possible to cover much of the one hundred miles or so to Dolgellau using lesser roads, travelling from Gloucestershire by way of small towns such as Leominster, Presteigne and Knighton through the delightful border Marches.

Our cottage "Dolgwartheg" or "meadow of the cows" was unbelievably remote and difficult to locate on this first visit. As the metalled lane turned into a stony track and we had crossed two fast flowing streams through unchartered fords and opened several gates, it seemed impossible that we were on the right road. But as we rounded the breast of the hill there below us was "Dolgwartheg" looking like Snow White's cottage nestling under a wood, with meadows beyond sweeping down to the River Wnion. It was just the tonic we both needed as an antidote to the rigours of the "central heating traumas" earlier in the year. The sun shone unceasingly and new-born spring lambs gambolled around our cottage. We took our meals outside, under the shade of an apple tree, to the sound of a rushing stream which sped by on its way to the Wnion. When night closed in I would light the huge open fire which served to heat the entire cottage, fuelled with the limitless supplies of wood which abounded outside. We had no need to venture far from this idyllic spot for the duration of our stay. Besides it was such a palaver gaining the public road with the gates and fords to assay and the nearest inn being several miles away at the quaintly named "Cross Foxes".

We resolved to return again to such a charming retreat before the year was up, and so once again that October Dumpy brought us over the mountains of Mid-Wales back to Dolgwartheg. This time we were more adventurous, discovering the gold mines at Clogau up in the hills above the Barmouth road, and one day I persuaded Loretta to climb to the summit of Cader Idris, Penygadair, at 2,927 feet. She grumbled and complained every muscle-aching step of the way! As a recompense for her efforts we later that week drove down past Tal-y-llyn Lake to Towyn and enjoyed a run on the historic narrow guage railway. This little railway has the distinction of being the first of Britain's preserved lines and the one with the longest unbroken service. When the author and engineer Tom Rolt with several other stalwarts took over its running and revived its flagging fortunes, in 1950, the tiny rake of coaches had already been trundling up and down the valley continuously for the previous eighty four years. Tom has immortalised those early pioneering efforts in his entertaining and informative book "Tal-y-llyn Adventure".

Before the onset of winter, and "pulling up the drawbridge" at the end of the previous eventful months, Loretta and I had one more rather stressful experience ahead of us.

We had spotted an advertisement by our local coach company, Black and White Motorways, now part of the National Express group, for an inclusive trip to Weston-Super-Mare where we would embark on the White Funnel ship "Balmoral" and enjoy a sea cruise to Lundy Isle. It was to be the very last such cruise of the season, before the weather worsened. Lundy Isle is situated in the Bristol Channel, off the Devon coast with Ilfracombe being its nearest mainland contact. It is famous as a bird sanctuary and also has several interesting and unusual buildings which have been restored and converted into holiday homes for letting by the Landmark Trust. There is a resident population on the island of around fifty souls. We didn't hesitate on booking our seats and early one dark morning in late October saw us catching the coach in Bishop's Cleeve.

We were taken to Birnbeck Pier just to the north of Weston town and awaited the Balmoral's arrival. Our little group of intrepid voyagers stood huddled on the end of the historic Victorian pier, straining our eyes across the grey expanse towards Penarth on the Welsh coast. Gradually a plume of black smoke could be distinguished and then the shape of the boat itself, rising and falling as she crossed the swirling muddy waters. The pier shuddered as the Balmoral was made fast to the massive timber mooring structure, and we all made our way warily up the narrow gangplank.

The boat was heaving heavily on her ropes and when I glanced at Loretta, her face had turned a ghostly white. The next moment she had grabbed my handkerchief and was being violently sick. This became the defining moment for the whole journey, as one passenger after another succumbed. I was fortunate in as much that I revelled in the exhilarating crossing, bracing my feet across the bow's deck and "riding" the boat as the prow rose up high and crashed down again into the boiling waters.

A boat develops a pattern of pitching and rolling under these circumstances which you can anticipate. The worst thing a queasy passenger does is hide away below deck where there is no point of reference to the boat's movement and the brain interprets wrongly that the boat is steady and thus cannot calculate what is happening, so runs amok, with the inevitable consequence to one's sense of balance.

However explaining this to poor Loretta was small comfort and she proceeded to endure the worst experience of her whole life from which only a sudden and merciful death could release her.

By the time we eventually dropped anchor off Lundy we were hopelessly behind schedule and there was barely time for even the most brief of landings, let alone any prospect of exploring. The first mate was walking around the decks, calling out last orders for lunch whilst nonchantily sluicing down the floors with buckets of water. He must have seen it all before many times.

We set off back in the autumn gloaming and as darkness fell so did the wind, and the sea was becalmed at last. All was still, the only sounds the gentle throb of the boat's engines and the splish-splash as her bows cut their way through the black waters. The scene was transformed, seaward the lighthouses and beacon buoys winked out their warnings whilst towards land there blazed a myriad of twinkling lights from the small towns and coastal villages which lie betwixt Ilfracombe and Weston. I sensed that such a poetic scene was somewhat wasted on Loretta who was still huddled below, looking extremely sorry for herself, willing the minutes to pass when she could step once more onto "terra firma".

Altogether it had been a memorable day for each of us, albeit in somewhat different ways!

In January 1972 my sister Jean's Jack Russell bitch presented her with a late Christmas present in the shape of a litter of adorable cross-breed puppies. Jean suspected that they were a result of a clandestine coupling with a neighbour's poodle and, as endearing as they were, homes had to be found for each of them. Loretta was very taken with one of the puppies, a delightful little woolly bundle who squinted at you from under eyelids not yet fully open, reminiscent of a T.V cartoon character. Thus it came about that "Mister Magoo" established himself in Nutbridge Cottage, and became a much-loved member of our household.

It is said that cats belong to places but dogs are loyal to people, and this was certainly true where Mr Magoo was concerned. He became our constant companion, always by our side and making it plain that he did not wish to be left out of things. He adopted Dumpy as his kennel and would happily spend his days and nights in her which was a great convenience to us when away on holiday. He was certainly a great character with some infuriating as well as engaging habits. Of the former I suppose cocking his leg up anything and anywhere was the one we most despaired of. Nothing was sacred, bad enough at home but a nightmare when we were out visiting or staying away somewhere. Apart from this little trait Mr Magoo was to be a loyal and true companion for the next seventeen years until when in 1989 he finally was laid to rest in a secluded corner of the garden.

Mr Magoo had not been long with us when Loretta announced that a fourth member of our family was expected. A baby was on the way and due to arrive in September. I cannot remember my reaction to the news but it was probably along the lines of "I wonder where that came from?"

We decided to enjoy a Spring holiday whilst we still had the freedom and opportunity to do so, therefore we once more booked "Dolgwartheg" and headed westward in our trusty Dumpy. We had reached a point on our journey about six miles west of Newtown in Montgomeryshire when we suffered the first ever mechanical problem with our transport. Water droplets started appearing on the windscreen and investigation revealed a badly leaking seal on her water pump. Coolant was being blown by the fan out through the radiator grill and our slipstream was taking it up and onto the windscreen.

We were at the small village of Caersws, a settlement with Roman origins on a crossing point of Roman roads with the River Severn. Incredibly, the local rural garage actually found a spare water pump amongst their stock, for even then a Morris Minor 803cc engine was obsolete and specialist parts were becoming hard to locate. We left Dumpy with the garage, still loaded to her roof with all our requisites for the week, and were told to return in a couple of hours. We killed time with a walk out towards Llanidloes, following the track of the long defunct Van mineral railway which at one time served the lead mines up in the hills to the north. Caersws was the junction of this railway with the Cambrian main line, the latter beginning its long ascent westwards over Talerddig summit via Machynlleth to Aberdovey Junction. Here the line splits southwards to Aberystwth and northwards following the coast, and crossing the mighty Mawddach estuary at Barmouth en route to Pwllheli. The two of us plus of course Mr Magoo, spent a pleasant relaxing week preparing ourselves for the certain change of lifestyle which the Autumn would bring. It was to be a change of which no amount of planning can truly prepare you!

As the time drew nearer towards Loretta's confinement in September we started making preparations for our new expected addition to the family. Money

"Balmoral" at Birnbeck Pier, Weston-super-Mare.

"Balmoral" arriving off Lundy Island.

*The Mawddach estuary: view across the Cambrian Railway viaduct
against the backdrop of the Cader Idris mountain.*

The new pram arriving.

seemed forever in short supply and balancing our monthly budget became a regular juggling act. Loretta scanned the second-hand classified advertisements in the local paper and the village notice board for our requirements and item by item we slowly built up the various necessary "baby equipment". We bought a sturdy wooden playpen which was spruced up with a coat of fresh white gloss paint and my sister Sheila handed us down a wooden high chair which received similar treatment. Somebody in the village had a marvellous coachbuilt traditional pram for sale and I recall with amusement Loretta self-consciously wheeling it back home whilst our neighbours looked on with intrigue.

In anticipation of the big event I had booked a week off from my employment so as to be around when things started "happening". With hindsight this was rather ill-conceived as my week off had come and gone before there was any sign of Loretta's big day.

I was actually taken completely by surprise when it came. The arrangement was for Loretta to go to her parents and I would turn out to take her into hospital when the time came. We had no telephone at home, so the local shop would relay any messages to me.

This came about on that Tuesday morning of the 3rd of October 1972. The breathless lady shop assistant hurried up to my front door with the news that Loretta had started. Dumpy was with Loretta as I had not yet taken a driving test and was still displaying the "L" plates which I had put on for our honeymoon. Therefore I ran the long mile to Bishop's Cleeve via the field path and the railway level crossing, in the process managing to fall over a stile and wrench the heel off my shoe. When I eventually reached "Sunnycroft" panting and sweating, hardly able to speak, there was Loretta sat serenely enjoying a cup of coffee and reading the newspaper. She calmly informed me that it had been a false alarm. When my adrenalin surge had subsided I made my way back home and resumed normal activities, that same evening having to go into Cheltenham and organise the Camera Club studio group.

Returning on the last bus I decided to drop in to see Loretta only to be greeted by my Mother-in-Law beaming an enormous grin "Congratulations, you have a lovely baby daughter". Loretta had been rushed into St. Paul's hospital that evening and all our waiting was now over. Life as we had known it would never be the same again.

The summer of 1973 saw Dumpy once more taking the familiar route west and the Welsh border. She was somewhat more loaded down this time, as we now had the addition of Louise Fife as our new offspring was christened, and all the accompanying paraphernalia that a nine month old baby requires. We had arranged to share a rented bungalow with Loretta's parents at Saundersfoot, the small harbour village on Wales's west coast near Tenby, and for once I was able to go off exploring on my own.

There had been a thriving coal industry, albeit on a small local scale, around Saundersfoot and Kilgetty, and I resolved to explore what tangible features still remained.

The carboniferous limestone bands in this area exhibit two of the more famous landmarks in the world of geology. They are both to be found on Saundersfoot's coast. The one is a huge fold in the strata, like an enormous inverted "Vee" and the other nearby is a circular swirl of sedimentary rock as if a giant carpet had been rolled up and then petrified. This latter formation is aptly named the "Elephant Ear". On the shore at neighbouring Amroth can be traced the vestiges of a vast sunken forest when the tide is at low ebb.

The bay at Saundersfoot is named Coppet Hall, a corruption of "Coalpit haul" and gives a strong clue concerning the area's long extinct coal industry. There are a series of tunnels hewn through the solid rock linking Wiseman's Bridge to the harbour, through which the horse-drawn trams delivered their burden of coal to waiting boats. There are also signs of old railways, including an incline, around Thomas Chapel and the remains of Broom Colliery and Stepaside. It was altogether a fascinating part of Wales, and a welcome diversion for me on what would otherwise have been a purely family affair.

The success of this summer holiday spurred Loretta into organising an autumn break for just the three of us, plus Mr Magoo of course, in the same area of West Wales that same year. She succeeded in booking a cottage through the "Lady" magazine reader's holidays service. It was in the hamlet of Brynberian at the foot of the Prescelly mountains. From the tops of Mynydd Preseli the thirty three dolerite stones were taken and transported by some mysterious means to Salisbury Plain for the building of Stonehenge around four thousand years ago. It was as if that long dead race left their curse upon these brooding hills, for the stage was set for what was to be the most traumatic of weeks we were ever to experience.

We received an omen of what was ahead when within a mile of setting out from home Dumpy's engine started fluttering and cut out completely. I had recently been given the chance of stripping an old Morris Minor, due to be scrapped, of any spare parts I wished to recover. Amongst these was an electric fuel pump of a later design to Dumpy's original one, so before our trip I fitted the newer pump despite the old one being perfectly satisfactory. By some incredible chance I had left this older pump in the tool box, as if I had an uneasy premonition of potential problems. Sure enough, the offending article was hot to the touch indicating a burnt out coil so there and then on the roadside, I replaced Dumpy's original fuel pump. It was to give perfect service for the next thirty years!

As we drove deeper into Wales the cloudscape had become more threatening, and by Carmarthen the rain was sweeping across our bows, driven by a strong easterly wind. Without warning a particularly violent gust caught us and carried away the windscreen wiper on the driver's side. Another emergency stop whilst I transferred the sole remaining wiper, and for the remainder of our journey poor Loretta could only gaze through a blur of besmeared raindrops in front of her.

On the back seat Louise was sat, propped up on cushions and wedged against the dog basket in which Mr Magoo was sleeping peacefully. Around them both every available space was fitted with bags and boxes, all our requisites for the week's stay away from home, groceries, dog food, clothes and a huge supply of very essential nappies - no disposable ones in those days!

When we finally arrived at our destination the delightful cottage as described in "The Lady" was in fact a tin hut up a muddy track half a mile from Brynberian hamlet, the latter being up the hill on the far side of the main road to our residence. That night the rain really closed in, drumming incessantly on our tin roof like machine-gun fire. Even more disturbing was the accompanying electrical storm which flickered about us, lighting up the deserted landscape, with the thunder echoing off the encircling hills. Poor Loretta was demented, clutching our twelve month old daughter, trapped in a steel box whilst bolts of lightening played all about us. In actual fact we were probably in the safest place under the circumstances, protected by the earthed steel cocoon, but it was not easy to assure Loretta at the time. We survived the ordeal and had recovered our humour by breakfast time. We were visited by a mangy little tabby cat which I fussed over and even gave her a saucer of milk. It was then I noticed we had neighbours, for further up the lane was a ramshackle stone cottage with an equally ramshackle old van parked outside. It turned out they were a group of hippies, squatting in the empty property. We saw nothing whatever of them during our time at Brynberian, no coming or going, the only tangible sign of occupation being their emaciated cat.

Louise was in the process of teething and this had given her rather loose bowels. Loretta's holiday was turning into a non-stop cycle of washing nappies and endeavouring to dry the laundry on a ricketty clothes horse in front of the smouldering open fire which I did my best to keep going. By mid-week I was despairing of being cooped up in such a bleak dreary landscape. Every day the pattern had been the same, the menacing lowering clouds over the Prescelly mountains thickening to release the saturating drizzle, backed with a freshening wind. Louise was irritable and grizzly constantly with her teething and diarrhoea, so with Loretta's blessing I decided to set off on a day's hike leaving her to baby sit.

There was marked on my ordnance survey map the site of a Cromlech called Pentre Ifan, a megalithic stone chamber tomb, about three miles away up in the hills towards the coast and I made this my destination. I set off, kitted out in anorak and my new tweed cap with my camera safely tucked under my coat in an effort to keep it dry. The lane up through Brynberian was deserted as I doggedly plodded on through the steadily increasing rain. Then suddenly, there it was, Pentre Ifan, a huge stone structure standing alone in a field, with its enormous capstone balanced on the points of its vertical supporting crude columns. I stood captivated by this monument which had been placed there by a primitive people perhaps four thousand years before. In that lonely place wreathed in a swirling mist the "genius loci" was overpowering. No glossy colour photograph in a guide book could ever hope to capture the evocation of that moment. Thus uplifted I pressed on with my walk towards the summit of Carn Inglis, a bare rocky height overlooking the small town of Newport and Cardigan Bay.

The whole area is studded with stone hut circles which have lain undisturbed for millennia, and pausing there, bracing myself against the raw never-ceasing wind, I was uplifted by the spirituality of my surroundings. Unfortunately my new cap was also uplifted and went swirling away over the cliffs like a Frisbee propelled by some invisible hand. In high dudgeon I started my homeward journey back through the dismal lanes to "Brynglas" as our tin shack was euphemistically called. Loretta was awaiting me anxiously, for Louise's condition had worsened and giving cause for serious concern. Fortunately we had details of local doctor's and their surgery times so we all bundled into Dumpy and drove on what was now a mercy mission through the darkening lanes over the hills to Newport where Louise was able to receive proper medical treatment for her delirium.

The following day we had visitors. There was a loud rat-tat at the door and two shifty looking characters stood on the step, with their decrepit unmarked van parked in the lane. They were the infamous "Knockers" of Wales, unscrupulous dealers who circulated around the remotest rural cottages in the hope of duping the witless occupants out of prized antiques, dressers and the like. I gave them short shrift and sent them on their unwholesome way.

We had noticed Mr Magoo was scratching and licking himself even more than usual and on examination I discovered he had several large lumps which had erupted out from under his flesh. He had picked up sheep ticks, small predatory arachnids which attach themselves to an animal's skin and burrow into their flesh. Here they gorge themselves on its blood and swell up, trapped under the skin, hence the distended hideous pustules. I had read somewhere that they could be removed by the device of a glowing cigarette butt, although as I was a non-smoker I tried using a match instead. Unfortunately I merely succeeded in causing poor Magoo even further distress and nearly setting his coat on fire in the process! We were subsequently faced with an expensive vet's bill for a course of canine injections which killed off the tenacious little parasites.

Mr Magoo wasn't the only one of the family to have suffered at Brynberian. On our return home a week later a colleague of mine casually pointed out some bizarre red circles on my neck. I had contracted ringworm from that wretched cat that I had fussed over! My doctor prescribed an ointment which eventually eradicated the loathsome symptoms. One can imagine our relief at finally turning our backs to that miserable tin hut crouched under the glowering Prescellys, although there was one more sling of misfortune awaiting us, en route back to Gloucestershire. Pulling up at a set of traffic lights in Lampeter Dumpy's engine suddenly, without any warning, died. One glimmer of luck was that there was a garage actually within sight and I persuaded a couple of the mechanics to push our ensemble into the workshop, where they diagnosed a faulty electrical contact breaker in the ignition system. It was a thankfully straightforward task to get us on our way once more and it was a very tired but

Saundersfoot: tramway tunnel hewn through solid rock towards the harbour quayside.

*Brynberian: our holiday cottage under the Prescelly mountains
(the larger building in the foreground housed the local telephone exchange).*

Pentre Ifan cromlech.

Brent Knoll 'services' on the M5 motorway. July 1974.

relieved little family who finally pulled into the driveway of Nutbridge Cottage that evening.

By way of recompense for such an awful test of stamina in Wales we were invited by Loretta's parents to join them for a week the following July down in Cornwall. They had the use of a traditional cottage at the small hamlet of Treknow near Tintagel which we had visited three years before. Then all four of us plus their family Alsatian dog had squeezed into Father-in-Law's Vauxhall Estate car for the journey.

This time we had Louise and Mr Magoo as additions so Dumpy made the long journey south, two hundred miles being the longest single trip she had ever undertaken.

The north Cornish coast is far more rugged than that on the south side of the peninsula and has been the setting for innumerable unfortunate shipwrecks down the centuries. The tombstones in the Tintagel and Padstow churchyards bear witness to the sad fate of the drowned mariners, many of foreign origin. It is also striking to read of the deaths abroad of English sailors struck down with exotic fatal diseases and their remains returned to their native shores for a Christian burial in their home graveyard.

Whilst in the area I wanted to discover the Delabole slate quarry which at one time was the deepest man-made hole in the world. It is immense, with its own internal infrastructure of roads which zig-zag down the precipitous sides, bearing the giant Euclid trucks loaded with slate returning to the top with their weighty burdens. Such is the scale of the surroundings that these huge vehicles looked like yellow insects in a sand pit.

At the end of a relaxing week, when the sun smiled down on us almost every day, we reluctantly started home joining the fairly-recently constructed M5 motorway at Taunton. A break was taken at Brent Knoll near Weston-Super-Mare, now a fully equipped service station, but in those days just a gravel pull-off with a portakabin-style toilet and a picnic area.

The summer of 1974 brought with it a tinge of sadness to our family. My brother Tony had been unwell for several weeks and had been reluctant to seek medical advice. Eventually his conditioned worsened to such an extent that it became obvious he was a very sick man and for the next couple of months he had to endure exploratory operations in Cheltenham Hospital and the Frenchay Hospital at Bristol. He was diagnosed with cancer of the oesophagus and returned to his home as being an inoperable case, dying peacefully in his bed that October.

His death had a profound effect on me and I started brooding on the transience of life and worrying irrationally about my own health. It became an eternal circle from which I could not free myself. The worrying caused a tightening of my solar plexus and this discomfort in turn caused further worry. In the end I visited my doctor who was very sympathetic but could do little more than prescribe a course of valium tablets. I knew they were not the answer, and eventually, with time my distressing condition lessened. It was a period when the support and love of one's close family are crucial and in that I was so fortunate to be blessed with Loretta's unfailing understanding and concern.

Apart from this particularly unhappy period the seventies were a time of contentment and what amounted to the start of a new life style for me. Socially there was never a lack of local venues to enjoy where I could guarantee meeting up with friends and acquaintances. At the end of a demanding week "workwise" Friday nights became a haven when I would walk up to the Golf Club on Cleeve Hill for a chat and a game of the then popular pub game "pool" and then down to the nearby "High Roost" Hotel, the scene of my wedding reception some years before, for a convivial couple of hours with another group of good friends before toddling home down the lanes and so to bed.

The Golf Club had been taken over by the Tewkesbury Borough Council and the course itself administered by them. Before then the licence had been the property of the Cotswold Hills "parent" club who as a concession allowed the local "artisan" club use of their course and that of a wooden shed as a base for changing in and storage of kit.

Once a year the artisans were able to hold their Annual Dinner and prize giving in the clubhouse as guests of the Parent club and although I never played golf or joined either club I always contrived to get myself invited to these occasions, and what memorable ones they were! They were gentleman's evenings in the true sense of the word, highly respectable, with good food and drink, affable company, and entertainment in the form of comedians or singers thrown in for good measure. We even had a coach laid on to transport us half a mile up the hill to the Clubhouse and one year a helpful passenger suggested to the driver that he could turn his vehicle around on the Common, with the inevitable result that the coach became stuck with its rear perilously close to the "Milestone" quarry. The morning light revealed the large bulk of our conveyance outlined against the sky for all in the vale below to see and wonder at.

The other establishment which I visited regularly on Cleeve Hill was the Rising Sun Hotel. It had its origins going back to when the new road, following the line of the present modern main road, was constructed in around 1825 and thereby bypassing the original coach road which took a tenuous route across Cleeve Common en route to Winchcombe and beyond from Cheltenham. When I was patronising the Rising Sun it was owned and run privately, and one of its residents was the old uncle of the landlady. His name was Frank Stride and I looked forward to our weekly chats when he would regale me with stories of when he was a young man up in London. Frank had spent his early days working in aspects of the infant motor industry, first with London Transport and later on his own account, at one time as a chauffeur driving Rolls-Royce motor cars.

I have a copy print of him and one of his charges, an enormous landaulet-bodied Rolls dating from 1913, with young Frank in his smart livery standing proudly alongside. One of his prized possessions was an aged oil painting of a ballet scene which Frank claimed was by Hilaire Degas. He had acquired it many years before in settlement of a debt and one evening he brought it down from his bedroom in order that I could photograph him with it. It certainly looked genuine to my untrained eye, and had been painted on ship's canvass, as Frank had claimed. I wonder to this day what became of this potentially valuable artefact on Frank's death in the late 1970's - perhaps it is gracing the gallery wall of an affluent American businessman in New York!

The Woodmancote, Southam and Cleeve Hill branch of the Royal British Legion had thrived in the area for many years and were responsible for the early village summer shows and later the Cheltenham Searchlight Military Tattoo. The money raised had been used to support beds for ex-servicemen in certain hospitals, but then in the late nineteen sixties it was decided funds should be invested in a local clubhouse for the Branch, which until that time had no tangible base to operate from. Accordingly land was acquired at the redundant goods yard on the Bishop's Cleeve side of the Honeybourne to Cheltenham railway line and a modest pre-fabricated concrete building was erected to serve as a clubhouse. I started going to the Saturday night "bingo and dances" as a guest of my uncle who was a member. Ex-servicemen could join immediately but people such as myself had to wait their turn on the ever-burgeoning list of local folk wishing to join. Eventually I was admitted as a member in my own right and enjoyed many a Saturday evening there, later taking my daughter when she became of that 'certain age', old enough to dress up and do a turn around the dance floor, usually with a reluctant father as a partner!

Since those early years the club has gone from strength to strength in the true tradition of its motto "Service not Self".

One morning in the spring of 1975 I overheard a colleague eulogising with great enthusiasm about a guest-house he and his family had stayed in at Weston-Super-Mare. It all seemed too good to be true, spacious comfortable rooms, a garage for one's car, first rate food served in embarrassingly large portions, all presided over by the most charming and personable of ladies. It sounded just the antidote we needed after suffering some of our endurance tests and an ideal location for our young toddler of a daughter, where she could play in the sand and paddle and splash about in the shallow water. We lost no time in discovering the address of this dream location and succeeded in booking a week there in that coming May. We were not disappointed and the blissful week we spent at Gifford House, Uphill, was the start of a long and happy association with the village and with Joan Exon, our most hospitable landlady, a friendship which has endured to this day.

Uphill village is on the southern fringe of Weston town and a community in its own right. It lies at the mouth of the River Axe, which flows down out of the Mendip Hills and enters the Bristol Channel betwixt Uphill and the Brean Down promontory. The Down is perhaps only half a mile away as the seagull flies but around twelve miles by road via the lowest bridging point of the Axe on the Bleadon Level. There is a small ferry for walkers at Uphill half hidden amongst the sane dunes, enabling walkers to reach Brean Down, but it seemed unmanned for most of the time we were there and I thought there was a good chance of becoming stranded on the far shore when the time came for the return journey. The boat was reached by a narrow wooden walkway laid across the mudflats of the tidal Axe, and at low water one could simply walk onto one end of the moored-up ferry and off the other end as one would cross a bridge, with scarcely any effort on the part of the ferryman.

One of the many channels, or rhines, which were constructed long ago to drain the Somerset Levels, passes through Uphill village in its deep cutting and forms a tidal creek leading off the River Axe. The wharf on this little creek has a history reaching back to when the Romans worked the lead mines at Priddy on the hills above Cheddar and brought the material for export down to Uphill and thence onto trading vessels. It has even been said that Joseph of Arimathea landed here on his pilgrimage to Glastonbury, where he planted the legendary Glastonbury Thorn.

Standing on the broad high downland above Uphill are two landmarks which have guided sailors returning to the port of Bristol for centuries. The one is the stone stump of a derelict windmill, the other being the shell of the Church of St.

Nicholas with its burnt-out roofless nave, and dedicated to the patron saint of mariners. Over the churchyard wall on the seaward side there is a sheer drop of a hundred feet or more, forming a vast face of bare stone. At its base there is a cave system penetrating the hill in which have been found the bones of long-extinct creatures such as the woolly mammoth and wild bear, along with signs of occupation by primitive man. It is a fascinating area to explore and represents a totally different landscape to that found a mere half a mile or so away in the town, where the usual mix of tawdry shops and fast-food outlets abound to cater for the day trippers who spill down from the Bristol conurbation on fine summer weekends.

We were doubly-fortunate with our first visit as a family to Weston in that it heralded the beginning of two consecutive abnormally hot dry summers in England.

The second year, 1976, was even hotter, and longer duration of unrelieved sunshine, than 1975 had been, triggering alarm and concerns of drought in the countryside. That summer I played my last season of cricket with Woodmancote and experienced first hand the relentless heat endured whilst fielding under the

Across the River Axe towards Uphill cliff and the roofless church of St. Nicholas.

The open-topped 'Coastliner' service turned around here at Uphill Wharf. May 1975.

An early-morning round by Artisan Golf Club members on the highest green of the Cleeve Hill course (note the Ordnance Survey's triangulation pillar).

Frank Stride with his 'Degas' painting. June 1972.

pitiless sun. The grass pitches became as brown coconut matting, and huge cracks opened up in the turf down which one's boot could disappear.

As the water table sank lower, so water courses dried up, along with the wells and boreholes from which people had drawn water for generations. This caused acute problems in rural areas as it became evident just how many country folk relied on such sources for their everyday supplies.

I remember with great clarity the day in September when the drought broke. Loretta, Louise and myself were out enjoying an autumn walk by the Avon in Evesham's riverside park when almost without warning the clouds started bubbling up out of a clear sky and immediately huge raindrops began plopping onto the parched ground, faster and faster until we were hurrying through a curtain of water in a desperate but futile attempt to get back to Dumpy parked on Merstow Green four hundred yards away.

The smell of wet earth and sensation of all pervading wetness after so many arid months was unforgettable and, despite us all becoming literally drenched to the skin in that four hundred yards sprint, we were too excited with the sheer exhilaration of the experience to care.

Ironically when we had regained Dumpy and started for home, her windscreen wipers failed to operate after laying idle for so long!

It was a memorable end to a memorable summer.

Loretta and I had been married for seven years and the "L" plates I had fixed to Dumpy for our honeymoon were still fixed firmly in position albeit looking somewhat tatty after so many thousands of miles. It was becoming inconvenient for Loretta to accompany me as the "qualified driver" for my every journey so I decided to purchase a motorcycle which had been offered to me. It was a single cylinder 175cc. CZ of Czechoslovakian origin and about six years old. It cost me just £70. I had not driven on two-wheels since the demise of my trusty old Vespa scooter over ten years earlier and had forgotten what a potentially perilous undertaking motor cycling could be. Nevertheless it gained me a much needed measure of independent mobility and relieved Loretta of the total responsibility of being the household's transport 'workhorse.

I constructed a capacious top box on a frame of aluminium angle strip, cladded with plywood, the box then covered with thin aluminium sheeting. The latter consisted of old off-set lithographic plates trimmed to size and mounted "image inwards"!

Although my newly-acquired machine was used mainly for local journeys I did assay a trip down to Chepstow at the mouth of the River Wye to visit my eldest nephew Terry, who was stationed there with the Gloucestershire Constabulary.

One embarrassing feature of my bike was its lubrication system. The two-stroke combustion cycle demands that oil is introduced directly into the engine cylinder and usually this oil is mixed with the petrol when refuelling. The CZ used a separate oil tank, the contents of which were squirted into the carburettor in direct proportion to the throttle opening. If one's speed was not commensurate with the throttle setting, for example when ascending a steep hill, then the surplus oil would be burnt off in the engine and in one's wake a smokescreen of dense light blue smoke swirled about the unfortunate following traffic. I used to glance back over my shoulder and see nothing but a complete "white-out" of the scenery behind me, whilst inwardly praying for the next level section of road ahead!

The machine seemed chronically underpowered, requiring a gear change down from top when coming to the slightest of gradients, until on one occasion it underwent a serendipitous moment.

I was going up Gamble's Lane, a one in four gradient leading from Woodmancote village to the main road atop of Cleeve Hill when a small securing bolt which actually passed through the exhaust pipe became loose and fell out. The old CZ had never accelerated so quickly in its life, it took off like a rocket up that hill with me clinging for dear life to the handlebars. The reason for this new-found performance was that either a blockage in the exhaust's silencer box, or maybe simply inherent poor design, had been causing back-pressure in the exhaust system which can cause chronic power loss in a two-stroke engine. Needless to say, I never did replace that bolt!

One evening when I was idly flipping through the evening paper, the Gloucestershire Echo, my eye was caught by a modest notice in the "Situations" classified colomn. The Gloucestershire College of Art and design were seeking a lecturer in photography, technical background preferred. I felt drawn to that little advertisement and decided to apply for the post. It was against all logic for me to do so, I was in an interesting, well-paid and secure job already, but with hindsight those were perhaps the very reasons why I needed a change.

The College invited me for an interview at their Gloucester campus and the spring of 1977 saw me back in the familiar surroundings that I had last seen ten years earlier as a part-time student. It was quite surreal being shown around on a pre-interview tour and shaking hands with the few tutors whom I recognised from those early days of my career. As to the interview itself, as it progressed I started to suffer massive withdrawal symptoms - what was I doing committing myself to a life-changing move which, when logically compared with my present position had virtually nothing extra to offer and many disadvantages?

I came back home bearing very mixed feelings and after much heart searching telephoned the College the following morning to inform them I was not able to take the post if offered it. As it transpired the position went to a person who was already employed at the College on a part-time basis, and I suspect his recruitment was a "fait accompli". This suspicion was borne out by the inconspicuous initial advertisement inserted for one night only, and the fact that as far as I was aware I was the only other interviewee. It was a total relief to have had the decision made for me, and I took up my existing job thereafter with a renewed vigour!

Since the previous year my sister Jean had been enthusing about a holiday cottage, which she had taken with my other sister Sheila and their respective families, in the Pembrokeshire Coast National Park near St. Davids. They had again rented the same "cottage" actually a large farmhouse called "Cerbyd" and sleeping upwards of twelve people,, for the coming July, and we were cordially invited to join them all. So our long-suffering little Morris Minor, Dumpy, was loaded to her gunwales and made the long journey westwards. I could not face such a tortuous trip without a break so we decided to stop overnight around midway and arrive fresh at Cerbyd the following morning, a plan which worked out very well.

Sister Jean had not exaggerated the quality and spaciousness of our accomodation. Cerbyd was one of several properties in the area which had been developed into luxury holiday homes by local businessman Leonard Rees. They were fitted out in grand style and every consideration had been given to all aspects of providing comfort and convenience in a traditional Welsh setting.

Our new home was set in its own grounds abutting the River Solva and a mere few minutes drive down the valley to the charming coastal village of that name. Three miles west of Solva is the village of St.David's. considered by many people to be technically a city by virtue of its medieval masterpieces, the Cathedral and Bishop's Palace. The former is the third church to stand there, the present edifice started in 1180A.D and taking nearly three hundred and fifty years in the building. Of particular note is its ceiling of black Irish oak, one of the last embellishments to have been constructed in 1500 A.D.

The coast hereabouts is fascinating, with its secluded rocky inlets and harbours studded with the remains of innumerable lime-kilns used to roast the limestone which, when slaked and crushed, enriched the acidic soil of the fields and also provided the essential ingredient of mortar for building work.

There are nearby the tangible reminders of the huge quarrying industry once extant until well into the twentieth century. Just south west of the harbour village of Porthgain is the quaintly named Ynys Barry, Barry Island, where the sea has broken through into the hole left by this quarrying and formed a sinister deep inlet by the name of the Blue Lagoon.

The granite won from these works was crushed in mechanical plant constructed on the cliffs above Porthgain and stored in huge stone-built hoppers on the harbour side there, to await transhipment around the southern coast of Britain, mostly to London. Here the chippings went into the road construction and development of that growing city.

Continuing north-eastwards the town of Fishguard is reached. In 1907 an enormous breakwater was built out across the bay at Goodwick and quays were put in, large enough to accommodate ocean liners. The idea at the time was to cater for the Transatlantic trade where passengers could disembark and be whisked by fast express train up to London. Alas, the scheme never materialised and the port now only serves the ferries which ply the Irish Sea to Rosslaire as evidenced by the Irish money which freely circulates around the shops and bars in the town.

Altogether our stay with the family at Cerbyd was wholly enjoyable. The week was rounded off by Leonard Rees entertaining our whole party to lunch at the St. Non's Hotel at nearby Porth-Clais. Here I had the pleasure of meeting the artist Graham Sutherland who was a frequent visitor to the area, staying at Picton Castle where the gallery there featured regular displays of his work.

Our stay with the family at Cerbyd was memorable and judged a real success, so when my sister asked us if we would care to join them the following summer we did not hesitate to accept. It was to be a memorable stay also, but not in the way we would have wished.

Before leaving I gave Dumpy a short service including replacing her points and condenser in the distributor. It was to be a salutary lesson in the maxim that "when a thing is not broken then it does not need fixing". Our disappointment was that the family could not secure the Cerbyd farmhouse, as hoped, but instead were offered and accepted a somewhat smaller property. The outcome was that Loretta, Louise and I were booked in for bed and breakfast with a local family that sister Jean had befriended, and we would join our family for their evening meal before returning to our digs. The arrangement seemed reasonable so we agreed to the idea.

The journey westwards, as long as it was, passed uneventfully except for the occasional "hiccup" from Dumpy's normally reliable little engine. I was not unduly concerned as once we had reached the Pembrokeshire coast our mileage would be quite nominal for we had accomplished all the sightseeing trips the previous year. Our host, Benny, was the local coach driver and I noticed the elderly Bedford twenty-seater parked under what was to be our bedroom window. The house in which Benny and his wife and children lived was on the main coast road and fairly busy with the seasonal holiday traffic.

Our first night there established the pattern for the remainder of the week. The din from the regular traffic gradually diminished as we settled into our beds when suddenly a dog would start its prolonged yapping into the early hours from somewhere in the vicinity. Just as at long last you imagined it had barked itself hoarse, and silence fell, then a cursed cockerel would take up the chorus, heralding the dawn for which we had long been praying. In case our torture had not been sufficient there came the whirr of a starter motor under our open bedroom window and the ear-splitting clatter of Benny's coach as he warmed up

Llandinnog farmhouse, Cerbyd.

Porthgain Harbour. July 1977.

117

Longhouse Cromlech, Abercastle, Pembrokeshire with a very young Louise. July 1977.

Examples of lime kiln remains which abound on the western Pembrokeshire coastal harbours.

its engine ready for duty. As if the noise was not enough, clouds of pungent diesel fumes came rolling in through the window, which called for a rapid sprint out of bed in order to shut them out. Needless to say, an alarm clock was quite superfluous when residing with Benny.

Rather embarrassingly the toilet and a wash basin were actually directly off the small kitchen downstairs, and Loretta and I self-consciously used to say our "good-mornings" to the family assembled at breakfast around the kitchen table, and perform our necessary business not six feet from where they were all sat, every slightest noise which we made sounding as if it reverberated around the whole house.

Our breakfast too was something of a procedure. "Clingfilm" had not long been introduced and it had obviously captured Mrs "Benny's" imagination completely. Everything was shrink-wrapped in the stuff, the butter, the pots of preserve, even the cereal boxes, all cocooned in its sticky grasp. As soon as we could decently take our leave, we would go off in Dumpy and join the family wherever they had planned to be that particular day. The favourite venue was down the valley to the harbour at Porthgain where the "Sloop Inn" became the main focus of enjoyment.

Even here was not immune from problems. My brand new beach-casting fishing rod and reel, bought especially for the holiday, proved virtually unusable, every cast resulting in the reel spinning wildly and over-running the rapidly playing line, until the whole lot jammed in a solid mass of nylon gut. I spent more time endeavouring to untangle the mess after each cast than actually fishing, until my patience became exhausted and I jettisoned the complete tackle into the deepest recesses of Dumpy's boot, never wishing to see it agin.

Poor Louise did not escape from this catalogue of misfortunes. On her first day she pitch-poled down the steep rocky ledge above the harbour side and as a result sported a "duck-egg" of a lump on the side of her head. It could have had far worse consequences, for another couple of feet would have seen her disappearing over the side into the water. That same day she decided to have a paddle and without warning started bawling uncontrollably. By a stroke of incredibly bad luck she had picked up a discarded fish-hook in her tiny foot, and the cruel barb had lodged it firmly under the skin. There was further high drama and protestations as we carefully attempted with eventual success to extract it. From the hubbub the local population must have imagined that we were committing violent murder in their midst. Louise's problems were not yet over. A couple of mornings later, following yet another night of relentless caterwauling dogs and cockerels we awoke to see her already out of bed and standing in front of the large dressing-table mirror, clutching at her face with both hands. We could scarcely believe it, she had somehow contracted mumps. Already her worried little face had swollen up like some comical caricature.

What with Louise's worsening condition and my uncertainty regarding Dumpy's state of health I was not sorry when the morning came to get underway and head for home. The day dawned bright and sunny, but we were to have no eyes for the beauty of the scenery in the hours that followed. Louise was installed on the back seat as comfortable as we could make her, surrounded by the usual clutter of holiday paraphernalia. Almost as soon as we started off Dumpy began coughing and jumping and as the miles passed so did it become more of a struggle to keep going. I carried out a roadside check as best as I could, remaking the high tension connections on the ignition and cleaning the points and so on, but to no avail. The problems were at their worse when any demand for power was made on the engine, such as the slightest uphill ascent, or pulling away from traffic lights. Loretta nearly became hysterical when we had to climb out of Carmarthan away from the river, bucking and jolting sandwiched between two enormous honking juggernauts, with our five and a half year old daughter lying ill on the back seat. The sunshine which we had enjoyed all week now became our enemy as it rose to its zenith and we were ensconced in the ever-hotter interior of our ailing little black car.

I remember calling a halt at Llandovery and climbing to the top of the shady castle mound in that small market town where we sat and relished a brief respite from the nightmare which we must soon renew afresh. And so we continued, through Brecon, Abergavenny, Monmouth and Ross-on-Wye when at Churcham, a small hamlet on the main road near Gloucester, I spotted a garage, a proper one, not merely a petrol station, and pulled into the oasis of its yard.

By now it was late afternoon and the mechanics were locking up for the day. They were persuaded to stay and sort out our difficulties but did not show much enthusiasm for the task. They fitted a new distributor head on the engine and gave the petrol pump a sharp rap with a spanner as if by magic that would be the "open sesame" signal for everything to burst into song. Then having relieved me of my remaining cash, they all disappeared off to their respective homes and the prospect of their Friday night's socialising, leaving one still sick car containing an equally sick child and two distraught parents alone on the forecourt. I forced my brain into thinking rationally and decided to phone our good friend and neighbour in Woodmancote, Roger Tallis, and as we slowly set off once more until by good fortune came upon a roadside public call box. It was out of order. By now what wits I still possessed were rapidly evaporating and I blindly went to the only house we could see nearby and rang the bell, intending to throw ourselves on the occupant's mercy. It was answered by a woman whom I can only describe as "having learning difficulties" and she could not comprehend my distress and, by this stage, rather wild demeanour.

As I write now, nearly thirty years on, I simply cannot recall how it came about that Roger, our knight in his shining armour, not on a snow-white charger, but instead in his Rover car bearing his emergency tool-kit, did arrive on that long-ago errand of mercy. I only know that he did, and by the simple expedient of removing that wretched "new" condenser I had fitted before our ill-fated holiday, a component the size of my thumb nail, he rescued us from our plight and earned my life-long gratitude. I still see Roger from time to time and he is as cheerful, willing and helpful as ever, with that enviable charisma of confidence and optimism which is so reassuring in a person.

I cannot recall what it was that moved a famous wit to remark "it focusses the mind wonderfully" but it could easily have been marriage and married life. It certainly spurred me on regarding turning Nutbridge Cottage, in which I had spent the previous six years enjoying the happy squalor of bachelorhood, into something more like a home into which to bring one's bride. Over the next fifteen years I put in hand several projects, large and small, one or two which I tackled myself, the others entrusted to the professionals.

The first task was to get Dumpy, our Morris Minor off the road. Therefore I applied to the Local Planning Authority for permission to have the pavement kerbstones lowered and a hard driveway built across the broad verge to our property. This was duly granted and as the next step I contacted Gloucestershire County Council who at that time undertook private contracting. A personage in the shape of no less than the Divisional County Surveyor visited the proposed site of works to assess the scheme, and in due course a team of workmen with road making equipment and materials arrived, dug out the verge and rolled in large quantities of hardcore, lowered the kerbs and finished the whole job off with a smart dressing of hot asphalt. The total bill came to an unbelievably low twenty five pounds, a figure to which one could easily add two noughts today.

Having now a proper vehicle access I decided to treat Dumpy to a garage, although despite standing in the open for the past twenty years she looked none the worse for it. I ordered a steel-framed asbestos fire-proof building which was delivered as a "self-assemble" kit of components. The base which I put down myself was a raft of concrete onto which the garage frame was bolted, sixteen feet by eight feet. It was the most demanding physical job I had ever endured, as all the wet mix of concrete was made up by me, from the huge piles of raw aggregate and sand and bags of Portland cement I had purchased, using just a hand shovel. To achieve a seamless finish the whole raft had to be laid in one session and laboriously tamped level with a long heavy plank of straight-edged wood.

A second most useful addition to our house was a lean-to conservatory which replaced a tiny porch my father had built many years earlier. Again, I forged ahead and did it all myself, as ready money was in short supply during that first period of our married life together.

The concrete base taxed my muscles once more and on it, block by block, rose the shell of the planned structure. The steel window frames I purchased second-hand and, after carefully measuring their apertures, purchased the glass panes, cut to size by the supplier. I discovered "puttying" glass into window frames is not as simple a job as it looks. If the putty is too moist it will adhere to everything but the window frame, so I ended up with it stuck stubbornly all over my hands, or of the mix is too dry it merely crumbles into pellets and falls on the floor! However I persevered and finally we had a splendid useful ten feet by eight feet "utility" room, complete with table and chairs for summertime meals, and a well-used old settee on which I spent many a sunlit afternoon, curled up with Mr Magoo tucked against my back.

The biggest project of all was the construction of an upstairs bathroom and toilet in the largest bedroom and removing the archaic downstairs one, extending the kitchen into the space thus created.

I approached my brother David, who had gone "self-employed" as a general builder and carpenter and he agreed to undertake the whole job. David was a skilled craftsman and a cabinet-maker of the highest order. Probably because of his other work commitments the first problem was getting a starting-date out of him. After some twelve months we eventually secured the pledge of an anticipated starting time. Meanwhile David had commissioned his retired father-in-law to visit us in order to draw up the necessary plans, so at long last things were appearing to be on the move.

In my innocence I suggested to David that Loretta, Louise and I could go away for a week whilst he did the job in order that he could have a vacant house and not have to work around a family's day-to-day muddles. I was to realise what the quizzical grin that he gave me at the suggestion signified!

When we returned from our break away David had barely started, so we decided that Loretta and Louise, with Mr Magoo, should install themselves at her mother's for the duration. It was just as well, as even in my worst imaginings did I consider what an upheaval there would be once the work got underway.

The upstairs bedroom had a disused fireplace and chimney breast which had to be removed, along with the kitchen internal-wall, and the amount of dust generated was incredible. It found its way everywhere, into our clothes, stored carefully in drawers and wardrobes, into the larder, over the décor in the lounge; everything not sheeted over was anointed with a thick film of mortar dust.

The outside wall had to be breached in order to provide a window for the new bathroom, and I would lie abed at night listening to the temporary sheet of polythene covering the bare hole flapping wildly as the wind caught it.

I have since realised that self-employed craftsmen, be they builders, plumbers, electricians or car mechanics, will not allow themselves to be pinned down to any deadline or time schedule. They never wish to turn work away, so they will always agree to undertaking the work initially. Then, of course, a situation develops where they are working for several customers simultaneously, who are probably unaware of each other's existence, so they become like a juggler spinning a row of plates on poles. The trick is to act as the plate which starts wobbling before the others, thereby claiming the attention of our erstwhile man. In my case it was actually Loretta doing all the wobbling, as she was impatient to return back home and be mistress in her own house once more.

All's well that ends well, and David eventually completed his work and left us with a superb result having transformed a drab ex-council house into a home we could now be proud of.

The new conservatory taking shape at Nutbridge Cottage, 1973.

Order is restored at Nutbridge Cottage: the new roomheater stove neatly installed.

Astride my new bicycle.

Yew Tree inn, Conderton with landlord Dick Cranton. July 1982.

1980: I marked the start of the new decade by purchasing for Loretta and myself a bicycle each. We had neither of us ridden for many years, in Loretta's case not since she was a teenager. They were acquired from a newly-opened discount cycle shop in Cheltenham's Lower High Street, and Loretta bore her machine, a "shopper" style with small diameter wheels, back home in Dumpy. I elected to ride my "tourer" for the four miles or so back to Woodmancote, and what a shock the experience turned into. I had forgotten how slowly one travels in relation to other traffic and the amount of anticipation needed to judge one's manoeuvres, and allow for the arrogance and ill-consideration shown by certain other road users to whom a cyclist is an unnecessary nuisance.

Familiar stretches of road which previously you regarded as level became relentless interminable gradients against which you had to battle, and the slightest headwind exacerbated your discomfort into muscle-wrenching agony.

I arrived home in a lather of sweat to be greeted by Loretta with a sheepish expression on her face. She had contrived to catch the brake lever in Dumpy's interior roof lining whilst unloading her "shopper" and tear a great slit in the hitherto pristine "Rexine" material. Undaunted we decided on a trial spin a few days later out to the Yew Tree Inn, a rustic pub in the hamlet of Conderton on the lower slopes of Bredon Hill about seven miles away. We arrived without incident and even managed a walk on the hill itself, leaving our two cycles chained to a fence. We then made the fatal error of adjourning to the Inn and indulging in several glasses of a most potent brew of perry, cider made using pears, before commencing our return journey home. The gradient was initially in our favour as we sailed down the narrow ominously named Crashmore Lane with its many blind corners and hump-backed railway bridge crossing the long-abandoned Midland Railway branch line. Loretta performed valiantly on that tiny bicycle, sweeping around the Teddington Hands roundabout on the main trunk road, with huge juggernauts bearing down on her from all directions, and then making an all-out thrash down the straight of Poplar Row, legs going like pistons. On arriving back at Nutbridge Cottage we both collapsed exhausted into bed and fell into an immediate and deep sleep, the perry and the unaccustomed exercise having worked their magic!

I still possess my trusty bicycle and calculate that I have since ridden it probably the equivalent of twice around the "Earth's" equator over the intervening years. Loretta is proud to be unable to make a similar claim!

In the springtime of this same year I replaced my well-used "CZ" motorcycle with an "MZ" machine, again of Czechoslovakian manufacture, but a twin-cylinder model with the larger capacity of 250cc. The increase in power and torque coupled with the overall smoothness of the transmission was quite dramatic and gave a performance more akin to that experienced when driving a car. My enjoyment was destined to be relatively short lived, for in the spring of 1983 I took a car driving test.

Two factors conspired in the making of this decision. The first was that we had purchased a second Morris Minor the previous Autumn, a 1960 model and in superb general running order, for a bargain price of £300. Loretta started using this Morris in preference to Dumpy, so our faithful old workhorse was finally rested after giving an unbroken service of twenty eight years on the road. She was actually parked up on the front lawn of Nutbridge Cottage and suffered the ignominy of being used as a bird table over the winter months!

The second reason for abandoning two-wheels in favour of four was a recently passed law restricting learner motor-cycle riders to low-performance machines and also having to take a test within two years of holding a provisional licence. In my case I had held a provisional licence for twenty years, the last thirteen of them for driving Dumpy. I reckoned that if taking a driving test was to be compulsory then it may as well be with a car. So it was that on April the Fifteenth 1983 I reported to the Cheltenham driving test centre, whilst Loretta disappeared off into the town centre to do some shopping.

Things did not get off to an encouraging start as the examiner started groping for his seat belt and I informed him that, being exempt due to the age of the vehicle, they were not fitted. Out came his book of rules to check out my claim and he eventually begrudgingly agreed to continue the test. Thereafter I breezed around the course that he dictated as if I was going on holiday. The three point turn in the narrow side street was just that, two quick forwards and reverses and away. At the finish of the test, back at the test centre, my examiner looked up solemly from his sheaf of notes and uttered the memorable words "I do hope that I am doing the right thing, Mr Curr, but I have decided to pass you, although I trust you do not normally drive like that!" With that, he got out and walked up the path to his premises, turning briefly back his head towards me, still sat alone and bemused in the driving seat. He had a broad grin on his previously dour face!

Loretta had for many years been keen on involvement with local activities and from our early days together she had acted as the Honourable Secretary for the Bishop's Cleeve Old Folks Club. They met every week in their clubhouse, a pair of ex-wartime prefabricated asbestos huts at the back of Eversfield bakery on Priory Lane. On several occasions I had helped out by taking along my 16mm sound projector and entertaining them with selections of hired films. When she moved to Woodmancote Loretta soon joined the village Women's Institute and it was not long before she undertook the running of their "Village At-Home", a mid-week afternoon tea for locals to enjoy a "cuppa and a chat" amongst themselves.

This regular get-together provoked a demand from the older visitors for their own club, akin to the Bishop's Cleeve Old Folks, and so it came about that Loretta and a friend between them established and ran the "Woodmancote Senior Citizens Club". As part of their regular entertainments programme I was asked if I could put on the occasional slide show to which I readily agreed. I had a fairly wide-ranging collection of colour slides covering such things as rural scenery, interesting places and so on, but by far the most popular show was the

A halt at Chew Valley reservoir, Somerset, with our second Morris Minor en route to Weston.

Loretta and Mr. Magoo outside the Bishop's Cleeve Old Folk's Association clubhouse in Priory Lane.
August 1975.

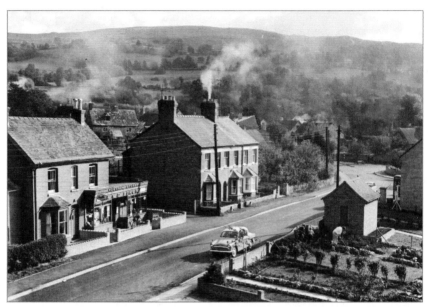

Towards Cleeve Hill, from the chimney stack of Nutbridge Cottage, 1964.

England's Glory Ladies Morris perform outside Nutbridge Cottage.

one I assembled from my burgeoning archive of historic local scenes.

Initially I produced the black and white copy slides by laboriously reduction-printing the monochrome negatives in the darkroom onto two-inch square pieces of high contrast film, processing each tiny sheet by hand under the red safelights. I subsequently evolved a far easier and more straightforward technique of producing my slides. I simply loaded my single-lens reflex Nikon camera with colour slide film and copied the photographs directly from the album pages. Using a daylight-quality film and tungsten illumination the "warmer" light quality conferred a sepia-type appearance on the projected pictures and added a "period" ambience to them.

It became evident to me that local speakers prepared to talk to groups and societies are in great demand, and over the next few years I received invitations to give my "Old Woodmancote and Area" slide show to a variety of local organisations, such as the Women's Institute, Probus Clubs, church groups and the Royal British Legion Ladies! It is said that the finest way to learn ones subject is to give a talk on it and in my experience that is certainly true. I mentally researched each picture and evolved in my mind a brief entertaining and informative spiel about them, embellishing some of them, I must confess, with a degree of journalistic licence! An interesting consequence to all this publicity was a visit from the "Gloucestershire Life County magazine journalist Diane Alexander accompanied by freelance photographer Michael Charity to Nutbridge Cottage where I was interviewed, and photographed leaning on my front gate, for inclusion in a forthcoming article about Woodmancote. For a second article, this time exclusively about me and my collection, I was honoured with a visit from the editor of the magazine in person, John Hudson.

He was a delightful man, and for a short time after we corresponded on various bits of information he had unearthed and thought may have been of interest to me.

Such publicity often generates yet further and wider interest, an example being the totally unexpected raising of a ghost from the past. My mother, whilst yet a teenager, knew a Dr John Henry Garrett, who resided on Cleeve Hill, as a friend of her family and a frequent visitor to their home in Bushcombe Lane, Woodmancote. In fact, her brother Leslie worked under Dr Garrett in the latter's role of Chief Medical Officer of Health for Cheltenham until he, Leslie, enlisted for service in the Great War and sadly lost his life in its closing weeks on the battlefields of Belgium. John Henry is remembered today for the classic local book "From a Cotswold Height" a rather flowery account of his many perambulations around Cleeve Hill and District.

A few years ago I received a letter from a Dr John Garrett, also of Cleeve Hill, who turned out to be the son of John Henry and had recently retired to his native area and now proposed writing a book covering a similar topic to that of his late father, viz: Cleeve Hill. I wrote back giving what little help I could with his researches and of course mentioning our family's association from all those years ago.

Dr Garrett Junior was possibly in his late seventies when we corresponded and has now passed on, but nevertheless I wondered how old his father was when he sired his offspring. I made a couple of enquiries and apparently J.H.G married "late in life"!

OLD FRIENDS

It is said that the average person makes the acquaintance of some twenty thousand other souls in the course of their lifetime. Remarkably only just a handful of this huge number are ever destined to remain, and it is to my own small group of faithfuls that I dedicate this chapter.

The Dewey Family

Around the time of the second world war Edward Dewey came to Gloucestershire and took up a post as design draftsman with the fledgling Dowty Rotol aerospace company. As a young man Ted had been involved with the legendary Sir Alan Cobham on an early air-to-air refuelling project. These trials called for such a high degree of "hands on" skilled pilot expertise that it was considered only the aces who performed for Cobham's famous Flying Circus would be capable for the task. Ted related with amusement how on one such manoevre they lost a heavy steel counterweight at several thousand feet over Bournemouth on the English south coast, and never did discover where it landed or if any serious damage was caused.

Ted met his wife to be and subsequently married in Cheltenham and moved to a bungalow "Algoma" in Woodmancote with his new bride, Adele. Here they raised their family of two boys, Michael born in 1946, a couple of months before my birth and Robert in 1950.

Thus came about my life-long association with the family, as I grew up and attended school with both the boys, and together with a couple of other village lads we formed an inseparable "gang".

Father Ted was a man of extremely wide-ranging interests and he had the happy knack of imparting his enthusiasm on others in his company.

His own father, whom I met only on one occasion, was a very free spirited character right up until his death at an advanced age. Mr Dewey Senior had been an early pioneer of the British Caravan Club in its early days, and I think Ted had inherited much of his father's vigour. He had an innovative outlook in all his many and varied interests. I used to visit "Algoma" and marvel at the television pictures, the first I had ever seen, and certainly one of the original T.V sets in Woodmancote.

There was a large glass heated fish tank in the sitting room teeming with exotic tropical fish of bright shimmering iridescent colours. In the kitchen there was installed a refridgerator which Ted had constructed himself, although I did not appreciate the fact at the time.

I certainly remember his exotic taste (for that early post-war period) in motor cars. He drove very spiritedly an early Fiat Topolino and later the Hitler Volkswagon with its rear-mounted air cooled engine and christened the "Beetle".

Ted also at some time owned a Citroen "Traction Avant" an extremely rakish and sporting design, in many ways ahead of its time. I was often invited to join family days out in one of these vehicles and these were the first trips that I ever enjoyed in a motor car.

Ted had been an enthusiastic touring cyclist when younger but in the years I knew him walking had replaced the former interest to a degree. This was reflected in his appointment as a Cotswold Warden and he became involved with the establishing and way marking of the "Cotswold Way" long distance footpath. Locally Ted served as a member of the Cleeve Hill Board of Conservators, a body which had been founded at the time of the Common's Regulation Acts in the late 1890's. One of his crusades in that role was in the prevention of widespread vehicle access to the Common and the subsequent damage which this practice could cause.

I accompanied Ted on several memorable walks, two in Gloucestershire, the first following the bed of the long-disused Thames Severn Canal from Stroud up the Golden Valley where the canal and fast flowing River Frome jointly served the many cloth mills which once operated in the "Five Valleys". The canal was opened for traffic in 1788 but never fully developed its trade, due partially to the later competition from the Great Western Railway which accompanied the canal, but mainly from the problems of supplying the relatively short summit level at Sapperton with sufficient water. The climb up the Golden Valley via a series of locks demanded huge volumes of water and this demand was exacerbated by the porosity of the Cotswold limestone through which the canal was driven. The mighty tunnel which pierced the summit at Sapperton, at the time of its building the longest in the world, also was the cause of time consuming and operational expense. In an effort to keep the canal open it was taken over by the Gloucestershire County Council just before the First World War, but despite further heavy investment it finally closed officially in 1925.

The second local walk was along the seventeen miles of the Berkeley Ship Canal, starting at the Sharpness docks. The chief engineer of this waterway was none other than Thomas Telford whose influence can be admired in the exquisite bridge keeper's cottages with their classical Doric facades. The canal opened in 1827 and enabled sea-going craft to reach Gloucester avoiding the treacherous tidal passage up the River Severn. Thus the docks at Gloucester made the city England's most inland port, and they became a staging post for goods which were transhipped onto smaller barges and narrow boats to continue the journey into the conurbations of the English Midlands.

The day Ted and I did our walk was one of high summer, with the sun beating down relentlessly from a cloudless sky. We were accompanied by Ted's two faithful little whippets and it was typical of their owner's thoughtful kindness that he knelt and dipped his empty camera case into the waters of the canal in order that the dogs could assuage their obvious thirst. Ted and I did not wish to indulge ourselves in the same way and therefore had to patronise the several excellent traditional pubs en route. Two that stay in my memory are the Ship at Purton, and the Bell which borders Rosamund's Green at Frampton-on-Severn. The cool of their stone-flagged interiors was a welcome relief for two very hot and weary travellers, and a quart of refreshing amber-coloured ale completed our recovery!

At the Sapperton tunnel entrance on the Thames-Severn canal in 1971.

*Gloucester - Berkeley Ship Canal: the tug 'Speedwell' heading south
with a string of three barges. April 1975.*

Llanfoist Wharf on the Brecon-Abergavenny canal.

Ted Dewey walking the course of Thom. Hill's 1825 tramroad towards Garndyrus and Blaenavon in June 1974. Note the line of stone blocks.

On occasions our explorations took us further afield. I remember once tracing the route of the old horse-drawn tramway which linked the blast furnaces at Blaenavon with the Brecon Canal at Llanfoist near Abergavenny.

Starting from Llanfoist Wharf the slopes of the Blorenge Mountain were ascended by means of a steep rope-worked incline down which the loaded wooden trams were lowered and up which the empty ones would have been hauled on their journey back for refilling at Blaenavon and the mountain top forge at Garndyrus. This dramatic eighteenth century industrial landscape has been vividly brought to life and immortalised in the writings of Alexander Cordell with his novel "The Rape of the Fair Country".

The Severn, Britain's longest river, rises in the Plynlimon mountains east of Abcrystwyth in Mid-Wales. What perhaps is not so well known is that the River Wye also has its source there, barely a mile or so from that of the infant Severn. Incredibly the two rivers go off on two wildly different courses in opposite directions, diverging by the best part of one hundred miles before finally being re-united and converging once more near Chepstow on the Monmouthshire/Gloucestershire border.

In the September of 1972 I joined Ted and his elder son Michael on a hike to discover the source of the Wye. We drove to the hamlet of Eisteddfa on the main A44 trunk road which was as near as we could get before pulling on our boots and taking to the hills. The peaks of Plynlimon (the five fingers) rose up ahead of us to a summit of nearly two and a half thousand feet. A couple of miles from the road we came across the ruins of lead mines, the skeletal remains of long-disused buildings and spoil heaps slowly returning to nature and melting into the rugged landscape. In one hundred years time probably only an experienced eye will be able to detect their previous existence. Our destination, the actual source of the Wye, was rather insignificant, barely more than a damp patch in the grass, but an embryonic symbol of what it was to become in its passage through rural Radnorshire and Herefordshire.

After a desultory few minutes viewing the Wye's official source we continued upwards to the summit of Plynlimon hoping to be rewarded with a spectacular vista across to Cardigan Bay with the Llyn Peninsula beyond. Unfortunately the visibility closed in as we reached our goal and the limit of our view was the Nant-y-moch reservoir, a mere two or three miles to the west.

Ted was an ardent amateur photographer and an 8mm cinematography devotee. He recorded aspects of many of his varied interests especially during the last days of steam power on British railways. The two of us made a long drive up the M6 motorway in May 1968 and again later in August the same year to enjoy the sights and sounds of steam working on the railways in the Lancashire area, especially the Settle to Carlisle line. I have some pleasing records taken on my Rolleiflex roll film camera of a pair of Stanier Black Fives double-heading an express train through Whalley in Lancashire and also some pictures of the "Oliver Cromwell" locomotive hauling its long train across the bleak Pennine landscape near Ribblehead.

Ted originally used to work with black and white film, which he processed and printed as enlargements in a large wooden shed behind "Algoma", but with the general advent of colour film he converted his equipment in order to carry out his own colour printing. He very cleverly based his processor on a "daylight" film developing tank which he adapted to take the sheets of exposed colour paper. The tank was mounted on electrically driven rollers and set in motion for the prescribed times demanded by the sequence of chemicals used, of which there were several. The whole paraphernalia was immersed in an electronically heated thermostatically controlled water bath for constant processing. This novel apparatus worked surprisingly well and Ted was asked by a number of photographic societies in the County to perform demonstrations of his technique at their club meetings.

I offered to assist him on these occasions, and with practice we perfected a double-act worthy of Laurel and Hardy!

We set everything up in front of our audience, even lugging in a huge twenty five litre polycontainer of water for the washing part of the process. With the assembled onlookers all agog at our antics, Ted would set the timer going, the drum started spinning and like some alchemist of old, with me as his youthful accolyte, he would deftly empty and replenish the drum anew at each stage of the procedure. When the timer's buzzer sounded off would come the lid of the tank and Ted would whip out the completed print like a conjurer producing a white rabbit out of a top-hat, and amid a rousing round of applause there would be the photograph, in its full Technicolor glory, held aloft by Ted, dripping stabiliser solution all over both himself and the floor!

Allied to his interest in railways was the wider one of Industrial Archaeology and Ted invited me to join him on the monthly meetings of the Gloucestershire Society for Industrial Archaeology of which he was a member. These were fairly erudite gatherings held in Cheltenham at Parmour House, a large Regency property owned then, I think, by the Cheltenham Civic Society.

These evenings comprised of presentations, usually illustrated with slides, of all aspects of Britain's industrial and commercial heritage, given by speakers who were often the acknowledged experts in their particular subject. Many of the society members were likewise extremely knowledgeable and we enjoyed several "members" evenings.

Two of the latter most memorable talks were given by the Rev. Wilbert Awdry, who, of course, was internationally known as the author of the famous "Thomas the Tank Engine" books.

He was a tall, angular, elderly gentlemen with a mop of white hair and thick-lensed spectacles. He possessed a loud and commanding voice and his presentations sounded more like sermons.

Wilbert's knowledge of railways was extensive and he told me how frustrated

*Ted Dewey and son Michael on the summit of Plynlymon mountain
near Aberystwth in September 1972.*

*The last days of steam traction on British Railways: "Oliver Cromwell"
at Hellifield, Lancs. in the summer of 1968.*

Guiting Power Stone Pipe Co: remains of flawed pipes embedded in nearby walls.

Ted and son Michael at the sources of the River Wye on Plynlymon mountain.

138

he became when the producers of the "Thomas" animated cartoon films ignored the basic authentic railway practices which he had incorporated into his books, causing him to protest to them that "such and such shunting" and so on, would never have been permitted under the Railway Operating Manual!

One talk Wilbert gave us was the problem at Gloucester during Brunel's Broad Gauge era when all Great Western goods coming up from the south-west had to be transhipped into regular standard-gauge wagons to enable their transport to continue northwards over the Midland metals. You simply could not make up such a tale of high comedy and farce!

His second talk concerned the network of the General Wade military roads in Scotland, a fascinating story concerning the first planned road construction in Britain since the days of the Roman Invasion some eighteen hundred years earlier.

I became friendly at these meetings with a character by the name of David Bick who was well-known to Ted. David was a man of many interests, by profession Chief Designer for the Dowty Group's railway division, and intensely keen on promoting an awareness of our own local industrial heritage. To this end he wrote two books which became classics of their genre. The first was entitled "The Cheltenham and Gloucester Railway", a horse-drawn tramway enterprise for passengers which also witnessed one of the first attempts in the world to steam-power a railway.

The second book, called "Old Leckhampton" was a stirring tale of the triumphs and vicissitudes of the quarrying industry on Leckhampton Hill, above Cheltenham Town, and the associated wide system of tramways and later railways which served the quarries. I was very pleased to be able to help David in copying original material which he had acquired for both books and producing glossy photographs suitable for publication.

He regularly came over to our village local "The Apple Tree" and joined me and Ted and the rest of our little late night coterie for a "noggin" and a "natter". David later set-up his own publishing house, albeit on a modest scale, "Pound House Books" at his home in Newent, and I was to help him on several further occasions with his illustrations. One evening he exposed to Ted and myself what he described as an outrageous Georgian fraud, based on the formation of the "Cotswold Stone Pipe Company", set up to manufacture and supply Manchester Corporation with flawed porous water pipes, made by drilling out blocks of local stone, near Guiting Power above Winchcombe. This set Ted and myself off to investigate "in situ" and sure enough we found the quarry, much overgrown, which was the site of this bizarre enterprise from one hundred and fifty years earlier. Everywhere there were discarded stone formers which were to be drilled out to form crude pipes and many had been subsequently incorporated into the dry stone walls which abound the Cotswolds.

Such is the satisfaction to be gained by 'hands on' practical industrial archaeology, although sadly progress has obliterated so many interesting sites in all but remote rural areas such as at Guiting.

It was a pleasure and a privilege to have known and make a friend of Ted Dewey. His life ended in tragic circumstances in 1990 when he was involved in a fatal car crash. I still miss his unique company, he was irreplaceable.

Ted's elder son Michael was my contempory, being a mere three months older than I was. He was very different in temperament to his younger brother Robert, for whilst they were both delightful companions, Michael had inherited more of the character of his mother's Irish background. We both started our schooldays together at the neighbouring Bishop's Cleeve school, in the shadow of the Parish Church, sharing the same little iron-framed wooden desk with its twin seats.

Our academic paths were destined to diverge later as Michael went on to attend a private school in Cheltenham, Leckhampton Court. I was invited one Christmas to their annual party and dance there and my recollection of the evening was of being turned down by a girl of around fifteen years old when I asked her to dance. She said I was too young for her, which battered my confidence indescribably and established the pathological fear of rejection which has haunted me ever since.

My other memory of that night was the hair-raising journey home through thick fog in Ted's Citroen, via the Highwayman pub, high up on the Cotswolds at Elkstone. Here we dropped off Ian Coley, one of Michael's companions. As an aside, Ian went on to achieve international distinction as Britain's representative in the sport of shooting.

After leaving Leckhampton Court, Michael was taken on at the Army Apprentices College in Harrogate, where his greatest achievement appeared to be playing the trombone in the Regimental band. From there he was posted abroad to S.H.A.P.E the Supreme Headquarters of Allied Powers in Europe, initially in Paris and later to Brussels.

Throughout this period we regularly corresponded, and I was fascinated by his accounts of his latest activity, car rallying, in which he represented the Army in local events. In view of Michael's unfortunate tendency to be accident prone, perhaps this pursuit was an incautious choice! I was highly amused by the somewhat apocryphal story of how he was aboard an army helicopter on manoeuvres and directed the pilot to land rather too close to the Command caravan, with the result that the whole caboose, containing his General and other senior ranks, was blown over onto its side by the downdraught of the aircraft's rotor blades!

After several more years of roaming the globe, including a prolonged stay in Hong King, Michael returned home to England and we resumed our friendship. I recall with pleasure the trips we made in the sporty cars which he had purchased abroad and bought over the Channel. The first was a Citroen DS, a design in many ways ahead of its time, with its self-levelling adjustable suspension, and swivelling headlamps which turned with the steering wheel. It

Michael Dewey and myself circa 1951.

'Holidaying' on Guernsey, Michael and me sixteen years on in 1967.

Michael Dewey competing in Newport Car Club rally on a special stage in the Royal Forest of Dean. January 1972.

Brunel's SS Great Britain in her Bristol dock soon after her return from the Falkland Islands in the South Atlantic. September 1970.

was a surreal sensation at night to have the two beams of light track your passage around a bend, and initially ones reaction is that of a second vehicle trying to overtake. I recall a day out in the Brecon Beacons in the Citroen, with its wide-body filling the narrow lanes with their high banks, and inwardly hoping not to meet with other oncoming traffic.

Michael's other potent choice of vehicle was a BMW two-litre saloon which went like the proverbial rocket. It is clear, with hindsight, how this Bavarian car manufacturer went on to monopolise that sector of the British high-performance market. They had moved a long way from the days of producing Austin Seven's under licence and later the "Isetta" bubble cars.

We travelled down to Bristol one weekend to view the S.S. Great Britain, which had recently been towed back to her home port from the Falkland islands in the South Atlantic ocean. She was in a piteous state after many years of utter neglect and abuse. The Falkland Island company had cut a huge hole in her hull, and used the iron shell as a warehouse for bales of wool. The constant buffeting of the waves as she lay beached had broken her back and, altogether, the project to retrieve her presented a formidable task, one of political sensitivity, and enormous expense. Thanks to the dogged determination of all the interested parties involved, including crucial financial support from that great patriot millionaire businessman Jack Hayward, Brunel's magnificent creation is now berthed back at the Charles Hill dock where she was built, a testament to the vision of Victorian engineering.

When Michael was established back in England with a job in "civvy street" he took up car rallying again, this time in a BMC Mini which he had purchased prepared ready for competitive events. I went out with his father on several of these events to give Michael moral support, and make a photographic record of the occasion, the latter not always an easy undertaking. We would stand waiting for hours at a time, perhaps atop the windy Ridgeway down in Wiltshire, or maybe huddled under the trees along some woodland ride in an extremely wet and dank Forest of Dean. The marshalls whistles would sound, and out of nowhere high-performance cars would breast the rise, or slide around the corner in a blaze of headlights, and with a blast of their air-horns would be gone, and silence would once again reign. Our cameras had to be continually trained on every competitor as they approached to ensure we had our particular target covered. "Sod's Law" decreed that the moment one relaxed a little, and lowered our cameras, then Michael would go shooting past unrecorded in a blur of flying gravel.

Due possibly to his rather impetuous temperament Michael's driving techniques were carried over into his normal travelling on public roads. I remember on one occasion Loretta, then about eight months pregnant, imprudently accepted Michael's invitation to join us on a visit to the famous Roman Villa complex in Chedworth Woods near Cirencester. We lurched and bumped through the narrow Cotswold lanes, swinging around the bends with a gay abandon, and by the time we were ascending Chedworth Hill it had all become too much for Loretta's finely balanced constitution, with the inevitable result. Mr Magoo, our little terrier, performed likewise almost simultaneously giving us two messes to clear up. It is only by good fortune that our daughter, Louise celebrates her birthday in October and not a month earlier in September!

Michael embarked on most new interests and distractions with his characteristic zeal, so when he met Gillian his enthusiasm knew no bounds. It was quite a whirlwind romance and when they announced their forthcoming marriage I was honoured to be asked by Michael to officiate as his best man. It turned out to be a match made in heaven with Gillian supporting her husband wholeheartedly in his many and varied activities.

One of Michael's most durable interests has been topography, and geology in particular, with its roots going back to when we were both children scrabbling about for fossils in the disused quarries which abound on Cleeve Hill. I recall Michael, at the tender age of eleven, investing his pocket money in a special geologist's hammer which accompanied us on all our expeditions.

One of his and Gillian's projects was to assay as many two thousand feet summits in the United Kingdom as possible, and I was privileged to view one of his many slide shows which he developed illustrating their spectacular climbs. The pictures were quite breathtaking. Michael tabulated the results of his exploits in the form of a topography survey and they were taken up by the publishers Constable and Co. and released as a book, which Constable described as "highly important" and should be on the shelves of every library.

I experienced one of Michael's climbs first hand when a group of seven of us motored down to the Carmarthen Black Mountain range with the intention of climbing the peak of Fan Foel. Michael led the way up to the summit, 2632 feet above sea level, and had equipped himself for the role with maps and compass and even lumps of Kendal mint cake should any of us suffer fatigue. I am ashamed to admit we underlings did not take things quite so seriously and Mike's brother Robert and I were more concerned with getting back to the local inn before it closed!

Ten years ago Michael relocated to Kendal in the English Lake District where he has since earned a deserved reputation as an amateur geologist. He has even discovered hitherto unknown rock formations in the area and won the distinction of having them named after him.

Sadly a few years back, Michael and his wife were conducting a geological tour in the U.S.A when they were involved in a serious road accident, being fortunate to escape with their lives. They both continue to make steady progress returning to good health, and I wish them well for the future.

Robert Dewey, affectionately known by everyone as "Rob" is nearly four years younger than his brother Michael and me, and thus was regarded as the baby by our small gang of chums. We used to tease him mercilessly and cruelly,

Loretta and Michael Dewey at the Chedworth Roman villa in Yanworth Woods. September 1972.

A successful ascent to the summit of Fan Foel at 2,632 feet above sea-level. August 1978.

Rob Dewey and me with the 'Glam Cab' girls, Goodwood Revival Meeting. September 2007.

Midsummer Day's sunset and the start of the Sun Race from atop Cleeve Hill.

but he doggedly stuck with us undeterred by such abuse. He really was an endearing placid little boy, with his large soft brown eyes and curly black hair he won the hearts of the villagers and became their darling. The tradition of "first footing" on New Years Day was still observed in Woodmancote by the older inhabitants, when it was necessary for the first visitor of the New Year to be dark haired and enter the house by the front door bearing a lump of coal and glass of water, pass through the domicile and leave by the rear exit. Rob was in great demand for this ceremony and my mother was usually in a state of high anxiety in order to secure his services on this particular morning.

Considering what such firm friends we were to become in adult life it is ironical that I saw very little of Rob throughout our teenage years and beyond. There was an age gap of course and whereas I attended Cheltenham Grammar School, Rob went to the private school of St. Kenelm's at a much later date. On finally leaving school Rob went into the insurance profession and for some years worked for the Eagle Star company in Norwich. He used to come home most weekends making a long tedious journey in his tiny Hillman Imp car and later in a bright red Citroen 2 CV, which he drove with great verve and panache. When Rob eventually returned permanently to Gloucestershire and we met up again, it was in this Citroen that we made our evening forays out to various hostelries in the area. I am convinced that remarkable car could have gone anywhere. One favourite destination we headed for was the Craven Arms pub at Brockhampton, hidden in the hills above Winchcombe. One winter's night after a heavy snowfall, we literally ploughed our way through and over the massive drifts which filled the Cotswold lanes and arrived to a near-deserted pub - even the local villagers had been deterred from turning out in such treacherous conditions! Such handling was truly amazing and inspired Rob, with a handful of other fellow 2 CV owners, to found the "Flying Dustbin Preservation Society", their intention being to promote the extraordinary feats which their vehicles could perform by organising various trials and rallies exclusively for that marque. To sit passively in the passenger's seat as I did whilst Rob took a bend without seemingly diminishing speed, was an alarming experience. It was akin to yachting, with the car tilting further and further over until you are convinced that the wheels must have left the ground, never to return to an even keel. But your fears are proved groundless, the horizon appears level once more as the car straightens up and you continue on your way unscathed.

Rob's interest in motor sport extends way beyond that offered by the 2 CV society and he may be found frequently at any one of a number of well-known venues, such as Donington Park in Leicestershire or the Castle Combe circuit down in Wiltshire, steadfastly videoing whatever action may be unfolding out on the track. Clips from his work, featuring the sort of incidents that often enliven these events, have been incorporated in several nationally distributed productions.

Only this year, 2007, Rob and his partner Patricia invited me to join them both in a trip down to the historic motor racing circuit at Goodwood in East Sussex, the home of that great motor sport afficiando the Earl of March. The occasion was the Goodwood Revival meeting, an amazing re-enaction of the heyday of Goodwood during its years of activity, 1948-1966. Visitors are encouraged to dress in the fashions of that period and are regaled with displays of extremely spirited racing by machines typical with that age and meticulously restored and preserved in "full-fig" racing order. Added attractions included fly pasts by the R.A.F Battle of Britain Flight and even a parade of vintage caravans marking the Centenary year of the Caravan Club of Great Britain.

For many years now Rob has indulged in the hobby of model making and has produced a series of exquisitely crafted 1:43 scale cast metal models of exotic racing and rally cars and several larger scale 1:25 similar models of commercial vehicles. These all used to be displayed in Rob's previous home, along with a gallery of prints and posters which he had framed himself, his tropical fish tank and shelves of interesting collectable books, the whole expressed in that delightful informal muddle of contented bachelorhood!

This all had a subtle influence on my own collecting habits, to the extent that I invested in two kits of cast white-metal traction engines, one an Allchin Agricultural engine and the other an Aveling and Porter Steamroller with living van. The Allchin model I put together whilst at home recovering from influenza, and it turned out to be the ideal therapy for recouperation. All the rough-cast metal components had to be first carefully fettled to remove the extraneous metal and "knobbles" then the engine is built up in much the same way as a real-life one would have been except in my case it was a job for tweezers and "Supaglu"!

Finally the fully assembled model is finished in coats of special model-makers enamel paint and any transfers floated into place.

To complete the display, I mounted my two models each on a wooden varnished plinth, and commissioned a local glazier to cut bespoke sheets of thin glass to a size which enabled me to construct a glass dust-proof case to sit over the plinth containing the model. The final touch was to engrave a small brass plate with my name and year of construction and details of the engine, which I stuck on the plinth's rim. It was certainly a labour of love and one which could not be hurried. It became clear to me how model makers can spend many years fabricating and constructing those fabulous large-scale live-steam models which they delight in displaying.

Rob and I continued our weekly outings for a noggin' and a natter for many years. One of our early venues was the Plough Inn at Longdon, a small village on the edge of Longdon Marsh, so beloved of Sir Edward Elgar and his famous bicycle perambulations. My memories of the Plough are two-fold. The first is the enormous range of two hundred and forty whiskys and forty real ales that they carried.

The second and perhaps more enduring memory was the night in 1980 when the news broke that John Lennon had been murdered. There was a subdued hush enshrining the Plough Bar that entire evening, broken only by the jukebox playing Lennon's "Imagine" over and over, like some mournful requiem.

On one of our weekly evening excursions, whilst actually en route to our regular destination, for some inexplicable reason we decided, by common accord, to turn off at the next junction and discover a fresh hostelry as a change.

That it happened to be the Gardener's Arms in the village of Alderton, a community lying a quarter of a mile back from the main Stow road, was pure chance but one which was to enrich our circle of dear friends and lead us both into new fields of interest for many years ahead. It must perforce mark the beginning of a future chapter in my story.

Rob has always displayed a lively and competitive disposition and enjoys taking up any challenges which may be thrown at him.

So it was that he found himself entering for the first "Sun Race" back in the mid-1980's. The now famous race was devised by a good friend and ex-colleague Peter Sutcliffe, aided by my brother-in-law Peter Medhurst.

The object of the race is to assemble atop of Cleeve Hill, the highest point of Gloucestershire's only mountain at 1083 feet above sea level, on the evening of the Summer Solstice. As the sun sinks below the rim of the Malvern Hills, some twenty miles distant, the competitors set off on foot and attempt to reach the summit of the Worcestershire Beacon before the dawn, when the sun reappears in the east above the Cotswold Scarp. My vision of that very first race remains, of the small band of stalwarts coming down off the crest of the Cotswold ridge, their day-glow tabards catching the last vestiges of the evening sun, and hurrying past where I stood towards the Rising Sun Hotel and on down Gambles Lane towards their destination twenty four miles away. They achieved their aim with minutes to spare, for as the dawn broke they ascended the peak of the Worcestershire Beacon, a muscle-wrenching final excertion to the 1394 feet summit.

Rob's great passion for many years has been "cappella" singing. My first experience of hearing him was around 1978 in the public bar of the High Roost hotel on Cleeve Hill. He entertained us with all six verses of that rustic ballad "twice daily" delivered with great gusto in his distinctive rich deep voice that has since become so familiar to us all in the intervening years.

It so impressed me that I set out to learn the same song in order to be able to accompany Rob on future occasions, and thus it has come about that between us we have developed a repertoire of airs ranging from comic whimsy to the more sentimental expressions of the Celtic cultures. I did hear us described somewhat uncharitably as "rough and raw" but hopefully we make up for any musical shortcomings with our boundless enthusiasm!

Rob continues to be a loyal friend and a lively stimulating companion, and an associate whom I value and cherish most highly.

The Autumn of 1959 heralded the start of my second year at Cheltenham Grammar School and on the morning of the first day of term I stood waiting in

Station Road, Woodmancote for the regular 8.25am Kearsey service bus. There was a new face amongst the small clutch of familiar ones, a little boy decked out in his pristine school uniform, short grey flannel trousers and shiny new leather satchel, all ready for his first day at his new school. He introduced himself as David Aldred and had moved down from Lancashire the previous year with his parents, both teachers, and a younger sister.

He lived in Greenway off Chapel Lane, barely one hundred yards across the gardens at the rear of Nutbridge cottage. We became immediate friends. I cannot recall when or how he acquired his sobriquet of "Olly" but that is how I have known him down the years to this day.

Even as a young lad Olly had a lively enquiring mind and enormous self-initiative. He would go off alone for day's outings on a train, satchel on his shoulder carrying a flask and sandwiches plus of course his trusty camera. Railways have endured with Olly as his first love, particularly those to the west, the Welsh Marches and beyond.

I shortly became involved in these peregrinations myself, not always because of a direct interest in the objectives but more from the enjoyment of a day out as Olly's companion.

I can remember our early morning perambulations, often before going off to school. There would be a quiet rat-tat on my front door just as the Summer's dawn was breaking and there would be Olly stood on the front step, all aglow with the prospect of a tramp over Cleeve Hill to the Wash Pool and Padcombe Bottom.

One occasion, during the final days of the Ashchurch to Barnt Green branch railway in April 1963, we both cycled out as far as Ashton-Under-Hill photographing the early morning local milk train as it made its way from station to station, returning wearily home to a much anticipated breakfast after the twenty miles round cycle trip.

It fascinated me to observe Olly, after every photograph he exposed, record the details of the picture meticulously in tiny home-made notebooks each no bigger than a matchbox.

It transpired that his father produced these in a seemingly endless supply, and indeed Olly continued his habit of using them for the next forty years until some time after his father's death, when the stock of little notebooks finally dried up!

As soon as he was legally entitled Olly took and passed his driving test, enabling us to go further afield on our railway expeditions. These were undertaken in Mr Aldred's elderly little grey Morris Minor which Olly handled with great caution through the highways and byways. Our furthest trip was down into Somerset where we enjoyed the sight and sounds of the magnificent "9F" steam locomotives during the final years of the Somerset and Dorset railway, as they thrashed over the steeply graded metals of the Mendip Hills.

Nearer home we visited the Royal Forest of Dean with its network of mineral lines. These lines had their origin as a means of transporting the coal and iron-ores which were won from the many private workings which then abounded in

Early morning milk train at Hinton-on-the-Green near Evesham,
with myself hidden behind signboard. April 1963.

West Somerset Railway, Minehead. March 2005.

The course of the long-defunct Hay tramroad.

Hay-on-Wye: the view from my tent.

the Forest, and when the trackbeds and tunnels were first constructed many were actually carrying horse-drawn tram roads. These tram roads consisted of lengths of iron-plates, bent to form a flange or raised lip along their length and pinned down on individual stone blocks set in the ground along the course of the tramway. The wagons themselves resembled large farm carts with iron wheels, holding perhaps two tons when fully loaded.

Olly and I walked the course of several of these old tram roads, the best preserved of them, Bixslade and Whimberry Slade, still marked with the regular double-rows of stone blocks along much of their way. Dotted throughout the Forest are hidden long-abandoned iron-workings, first dug by the Romans two thousand years ago, and the later coal-pits worked by the Forest free miners. A handful of the latter are still active although sadly the inherited birth-right to be a free miner and claim "gale-ownership" has been gradually eroded over recent years.

(Some thirty years ago I spent a profitable afternoon in the archive of the deputy-gaveller's office in Coleford from where the ancient mining rights of the Forest were administered, and copied many original maps and documents appertaining to this by-gone activity. I marvelled at the extent of potentially what could easily have become devastating industrialisation of the Forest, akin to the Black country in the English Midlands)

On one expedition Olly and I investigated the long-disused harbour at Bullo Pill on the River Severn near Lydney. This was the terminus of an early tram road from Cinderford where Forest coal etc. was transhipped onto barges for distribution via the river to the Midlands or southwards to Bristol.

A coalfield associated with the Forest is that at Newent a few miles to the north-east. This was served by the Gloucester to Hereford canal, a short branch being constructed to the White House colliery. Olly and I "field-walked" the area and were disappointed at how little tangible evidence now remains to be seen. The canal arm can just be traced as a shallow depression, curving around a slight rise in a meadow, and it was astonishing to think that, a little more than one hundred years before, loaded canal boats pulled by straining horses were gliding through that same field where cattle now graze.

The town of Newent conceals yet another ghost from its past. In the early nineteenth century certain entrepreneurs promoted Newent as a Spa-town featuring an ornamental spring and associated fashionable walks. There is not a trace left now to show of this Georgian enterprise, just a tangle of undergrowth and a muddy patch in a neglected field indicating the possible location where once ladies and their beaus paraded themselves so ostentatiously in all their finery.

It was on the occasion of discovering the trackbed of another tram road that I was first introduced to the small Borders market town of Hay-on-Wye, near Brecon. The Hay Tram Road ran as part of a larger network which linked up with the Brecon to Abergavenny Canal to the south and northwards towards Kington, Eardisley and Hereford. On this particular day we sought out the town from curiosity as it had apparently laid claim to possessing the world's largest bookshop. The man behind this enterprise, Richard Booth, resided in the dilapidated rambling Norman castle which was perched atop the town overlooking the market square, and he had converted the disused cinema in Hay into this mammoth undertaking, filling it with books which he had garnered from all quarters of the world.

This visit took place some forty years ago when Hay was still principally a work-a-day market town catering mainly for the agricultural district of the Radnorshire border. Today the name has become synonymous with books on a global scale, with some thirty two bookshops purveying all manner of publications from cheap paperbacks and publishers remainders to rare antiquarian first editions, and the town hosting its International Literary Festival every springtime with wide acclaim. Hay-on-Wye is also twinned with the desert township of Timbuktu in Mali in Central Africa, a strange partnership at first consideration, but apparently the latter place was once a world hub of ideas and learning and still houses hundreds of thousands of important ancient texts on every subject from philosophy to poetry.

Since that first early visit I have been back to Hay on countless occasions, frequently pitching camp at the Boatside Farm campsite overlooking the town on the Radnorshire side of the River Wye and spending a thoroughly relaxing weekend browsing my way slowly through the many thousands of titles which the bookshops offer on their shelves.

There is a narrow lane on the outskirts of Hay, an insignificant turning off the Brecon road, and this is the route to the Gospel Pass and fabled Vale of Eywas. I first went that way one cold April day with Olly and three of his acquaintances. As we climbed steadily up the flank of Hay Bluff the view behind us unfolded with breathtaking grandeur. The patchwork of a myriad of small fields and enclosures which patterned the hills beyond the Wye were dusted with snow, and dappled with the bright spring sunlight. This was the way taken by the Victorian diarist the Reverend Francis Kilvert, curate of Clyro near Hay, who made many visits to the valley of the Honddu beyond these mountains. The magic and mysticism of the area thereabouts captivated him and he was moved to write "an Angel satyr roams these hills". Kilvert was not the first nor the last being to feel drawn to the valley for as we descended through the far lusher pastures to the south of the Gospel Pass we paused to view the small ancient church at Capel-y-ffin and opposite, up a narrow lane, half hidden amongst the trees, the ruins of Capel-y-ffin monastry where under lie interred the mortal remains of its founder and builder, Father Ignatious. Many years later the sculptor and artist Eric Gill came and settled here, attracted no doubt by such ethereal surroundings as these. Continuing on down the valley we arrived at the jewel in its crown. Llanthony Abbey, its roofless arches soaring magnificently heavenwards in their eternal proclamation to God. A more enchanting spot for such an edifice would be difficult to imagine, that early order of Austin Canons chose the site of their community with great perspicacity, and yet they subsequently moved their Order to the second Llanthony just south of the City of Gloucester.

Capel-y-ffin church. *The final resting place of Father Ignatious,*
Capel-y-ffin monastery.

Llanthony Abbey in the Honddu valley.

155

Skenfrith Castle, one of the great 'Trilaterals.'

Abbey Dore, the "church in a farmyard."

It was through Olly's own enthusiasm that I too became fascinated with the southern Marches of the Welsh border country. Olly himself had pursued an acedemic career in history with a particular penchant for that of Wales and the Welsh people. He had attained his qualifications via Bangor and Swansea Universities and studied local history at Leicester University where one of his tutors was the doyen of the discipline, Professor W.G.Hoskins. Olly had even acquainted himself with the Welsh language, attending a summer school at Harlech, on the coast of mid-Wales.

Nearer home he gained his M.A. with a momentus dissertation on the Winchcombe Poor Law and also found time to act as honourary archaelogist with the Tewkesbury Borough Council's archaeology unit.

With this background, coupled with his boundless energy and undiminishing enthusiasm it is clear just what a knowledgeable and inspiring companion Olly was and continues to be still, and explains also why we more often than not took the roads west on our regular "Olly days".

I accompanied him on a memorable day's visit to those three castles which comprise the Trilateral of defence set up by the Norman Lords Marcher to secure their hold on the Welsh border-land of Gwent, on the present line of the Monmouthshire-Herefordshire boundary. They are at Skenfrith, Grosmont and the White Castle, the former, being on the River Monnow, has outside its walls a water-mill which at the time of our visit was actually grinding crops for animal feed. We spoke to the miller, an old man well into his eighties, who owned the business, and we gathered that on his demise the mill-stones sadly would turn no more.

This district of the Marches abounds with interesting ruins, secular and religious, and over the years Olly has introduced me to many of them. I recall Tretower Court, a semi-fortified medieval manor house, with its ancient custodian who pounced on us as we arrived and proceeded to regale us with such stories and colourful fables concerning Tretower that we were left imagining that the old boy owned the property personally.

Then there was Abbey Dore, the church in a farmyard, and Kilpeck Church, adorned with row upon row of intricate Norman carving, and the buildings exterior girdled with a freize of grotesque caricatures, including a pagan-style green man.

Naturally, we continued to indulge Olly's first love, railways, on our journeys into Wales, and it was the unique narrow gauge systems which drew us the most frequently. The Ffestiniog railway, climbing its tortuous way from Portmadoc Harbour across the great bar spanning the Dysenni estuary and on upwards through the hills to the grey slate quarrying town of Blaenau Ffestiniog, is carried through defiles so narrow and winding that special articulated steam locomotives were designed and built by the railway company.

Further down the coast another narrow gauge line ascends from Towyn to the village of Abergynolwyn, again built with the purpose of bringing down the cargoes of slate for transhipment. At the latter place Olly and I rode to the terminus and then continued on foot beyond where few of the many thousands of tourists and holidaymakers ever venture, to the quarries themselves at Bryneglwys. It is a fascinating complex of ruined stone buildings and abandoned structures, one in particular, a huge square stone arch completely baffled us as to its original purpose until we subsequently came across some contemporary photographs of Bryneglwys. The arch held a massive winding drum in its maw by which means loaded wagons were lowered down a railed incline to a wharf, where steam locomotives continued the journey down to the coast.

Perhaps the most exhilarating trip Olly and I made on the narrow gauge was the Welshpool to Llanfair Caereinion Line. It was a Victorian enterprise constructed not as a mineral railway but principally for the agricultural produce of this rural region and for conveying passengers between the two communities.

The particular occasion on which we travelled was a high summer's day of relentless heat and we took the opportunity of standing on the small hand railed open platform which was a feature of the wooden-bodied coaches. The little train rattled and swayed its way up the steep valley as we both stood gripping the handrail, and looked down through the bucking couplings to the metals shimmering in the heat below our feet. Every so often the train would squeal to a halt and the fireman would jump from the footplate and go forward to open the rustic wooden level-crossing gates which guarded the country lanes that the railway straddled. If the road was clear then with a plaintive whistle we would start off once more, accompanied by much jolting of the couplings, amidst the swirling steam and smoke of the accelerating locomotive.

In 1980 Olly and I took a rail trip of a very different kind. That year saw the 150th Anniversary of the world's first passenger carrying "inter city" railway, the line constructed between Liverpool and Manchester by that worthy engineer of early railways George Stephenson, in 1830. A special train to commemorate the occasion was organised for which Olly and I managed to secure seats. We drove up to Manchester where we boarded the train to Liverpool, some thirty five miles distant. It was a highly evocative experience travelling over that historic and symbolic route. One hundred and fifty years earlier tens of thousands of spectators lined the way, many cheering but equally as many booing, for the principal guest of honour in the procession of inaugral trains was none other than the Duke of Wellington, the villain of Peterloo, and highly unpopular in the North of England. The local M.P. William Huskisson, took the opportunity for a public show of reconciliation with the Duke when the procession paused at Parkside. As he stepped across the line to shake hands with Wellington through his carriage window he was struck down and fatally injured by the oncoming locomotive "Rocket". The locomotive "Northumbrian" was hurriedly detached from its train and on a futile mercy dash with the unfortunate Huskisson aboard reached a hitherto unknown average speed of 36 mph, the fastest man had ever before travelled. Poor Huskisson himself earned the unenviable distinction of becoming the world's first railway fatality.

All this was in my and Olly's minds as we were carried through the poignant

Tal-y-llyn Railway: the end of the line at Abergynolwyn.

Welshpool and Llanfair railway: "Countess" locomotive of 1902.

159

We watch the last scheduled service pass through Toddington, 23 March 1968.

Olly "underneath the arches," Toddington viaduct. January 1968.

landscape, crossing the Bridgewater Canal and heading over the infamous Chat Moss, that huge area of marsh which nearly defeated those early railway engineers. On through Rainhill, the scene of the pioneering locomotive trials of 1829 which set the standard of railway traction for the world to emulate. We rattled over the Sankey Brook viaduct, at seventy feet high it was the forerunner of all those mighty viaducts which are among the glories of our railway system. Our train soared loftily across the mile long Roby embankment before diving through the chasm that is the Mount Olive cutting. Liverpool was arrived at via a series of tunnels and cuttings to our final destination, Edgehill. Ahead lay a deep tunnel of over a mile which led the last stage of the railway under the City to the Merseyside Docks.

I feel privileged to have been a part of that re-enaction which celebrated the vision of those Georgian engineers, who in turn helped shape the destiny of Britain and ultimately the entire world.

Back in Gloucestershire, our "home" railway, the Honeybourne Great Western line, was one of the very last to have been constructed, opening in 1906. It became woven into the fabric of our daily lives, and as the poet Siegfried Sasson so eloquently expressed his own experience, "its habitual travelling somehow comforted me, making my world seem safer, homelier, sure to be the same tomorrow, and the same one hopes, next year".

Sadly, by the end of the 1970's we realised that there was going to be no "next year" for a serious derailment of a goods train and the subsequent damage to the track provided British Rail with a plausible reason for closure and one which they took up with indecent haste.

Previous to this incident, Olly had contrived invitations for us both to spend a couple of afternoons in the signal box at Toddington on two widely spaced occasions. The traffic had by that time been drastically cut back and what there was comprised exclusively of goods trains, passenger trains having ceased running in 1968. It was nevertheless a most interesting experience to observe at close quarters the detailed signalling procedures which enable the smooth and safe passage of trains on our lines.

Our second visit to the signal box was marked by the arrival of the Area Operations Manager who was making a surprise "spot check" and unfortunately, through a breakdown of communications, was unaware of our pre-arranged presence in the box, therefore we were forced to beat a discreet retreat. No facet of English law is so rigorously enforced as the rule book of railway operation on British metals, and for obvious safety reasons, the presence of non-authorised personnel there was strictly prohibited.

Some years earlier Olly and I had stood in the bitter cold of a January day to photograph the last Diesel Multiple Unit carrying passengers crossing the nearby Toddington viaduct during the final scheduled services of the railway. My memory of the "photo shoot" is of poor Olly, frozen to the bone, discovering that he had not cocked his camera shutter as the critical moment arrived, when the train was visible atop the viaduct before rapidly disappearing from view.

Fortunately I did not make a similar error so that we had one useable picture between us!

Olly's great interest in local history manifested itself in an occasional series of illustrated articles which he produced for the county magazine, Gloucestershire Life. Needless to say I was conscripted to help him with the photographs, either by printing up his own negatives or copying original material for its inclusion and sometimes going out with him to photograph various scenes or features relevant to his writings. Typical subjects of these submissions were "Cotswold Carriers", "Cleeve Hill Racecourse", "George Stevens, Champion Steeplechase Jockey" and "Cleeve Hill, a Cotswold Resort". From these articles one can presume that Olly was drawn time and again to the history and legend of Cleeve Hill, that twelve hundred acre mass of Cotswold upland rising so abruptly from the Severn Vale.

From those early days when he and I walked the hill Olly had frequently discussed the germ of a notion that one day he would consolidate all his knowledge and researches into a single book.

Thus it came about that in 1990 "Cleeve Hill - the History of the Common and its People" was published by that great champion of local history books, Alan Sutton. It was a masterpiece of documentation, covering in fascinating detail every facet of the Common from prehistoric days to the present era, and I considered that it represented the flowering of Olly's genius as an historian.

I was proud to not only have supplied many of the illustrations from my own archive of photographs but for the acknowledgment in the book of my own modest contribution via the encouragement and support I had offered Olly over many years. He has since conducted several interviews on local radio regarding the history of the area and is in great demand as a popular speaker with societies and institutions far and wide.

Olly retired from his full-time career in the teaching profession some years back, at the time of writing, and we both have met regularly about once a month over that time, usually to indulge in an interesting day's walk.

Canal towpaths present an obvious choice of route being well-defined rights of way with the added bonus of being on the level. Our strategy is to drive to a convenient village or town on the canal and take a local bus out to a pre-determined destination at around fifteen miles distance. We then make our way back, with a halt on some canalside bench or bridge to partake of the packed lunch we carry, and find our car waiting to transport two very weary and footsore walkers back home.

In this way we have walked the entire lengths of the Oxford, Brecon to Pontypool and the Stratford-upon-Avon Canals, each one entailing two or three day's separate day's walks.

One leg of the Oxford Canal was covered on an archetypal morning in May under cloudless blue skies. This particular stretch had as our starting point the town of Kidlington just to the North of Oxford and we aimed to finish at Lower Heyford around twelve miles further on.

Two local Cleeve Hill characters, stonewaller Pikey Gaskins and shepherd 'John' Denley c. 1920.

On the Stratford-upon-Avon canal: the Bearley aquaduct.

The Oxford canal at Shipton-on-Cherwell.

A characteristic barrel-shaped lock-keepers cottage on the Stratford-upon-Avon canal.

My favourite canal book is that pre-Great War classic, "The Flower of Gloster" in which Temple Thurston describes a journey, by a horse drawn narrow boat of the same name, which he undertook in the spring of 1911. He too had travelled this same way that Olly and I were walking and I was enchanted to stand and see Shipton-on-Cherwell church just as he had seen it and expressed his love of the spot nearly ninety five years before. "I only love the place as I saw it, with its elm trees and cow parsley, and all those wild flowers of the field which combine to make it the most restful spot I have ever seen".

Not all our walking of the Oxford Canal was so idyllic, for a second occasion some weeks later found us both bent double into a strong head wind and driving torrential rain like stair rods, as we forged southwards through Aynho and Somerton. I was not moved to wax so lyrically as previously!

One of the three days we spent tramping the Brecon Canal is particularly memorable.

We had parked at the Abergavenny train station and made our way to the nearest access to the canal at Llanfoist wharf where the navigation is cut into a shelf, following the contours around the lower shoulder of the Blorenge mountain. We set off westwards towards Brecon and by the end of the afternoon and some fifteen miles walking we reached our destination, the small hamlet of Llangynidr. Here we found the bus stop and waited patiently for the Abergavenny bus. It turned out to be a futile wait for we discovered a notice pasted up on a board proclaiming that on the very day that we wished to travel all services had been suspended due to a temporary road-bridge closure somewhere along the route. There followed a frantic attempt by us to secure a taxi from wherever we could manage. The local inn amazingly was actually open and we obtained the telephone number there, the only number listed, of a cab operator. After many futile attempts, including discovering that the mobile phone network coverage does not extend to places as far-flung as Llangynidr, to our utter relief contacted the one-man taxi firm. Rather incongruously the driver turned out to be a Scotsman with the broadest accent imaginable, as non-Welsh as could be, but to us he was an angel of mercy as he took us back to Abergavenny and the welcoming sight of our car.

Two prominent landmarks which lie round about Abergavenny are the Skirrid and quaintly named Sugar Loaf mountains. Their characteristic forms can be identified from afar, even from as far afield as the Cotswold edge of Gloucestershire. Olly and I planned to scale their respective summits, both on the same day, a total climb of around two thousand feet.

Unfortunately the weather on the day we made our ascents was extremely gloomy with poor visibility, particularly for the morning climb of the Sugar Loaf. Potentially the views from both peaks could have been spectacular, but it was not to be. Maybe one day we will repeat the occasion.

By far the most arduous and demanding walk of them all was that following the course of Offa's Dyke through the uplands of the Clun Forest. Offa's Dyke itself is an ancient earthwork running some 130 miles from the shores of the

River Dee near Prestatyn in North Wales to the banks of the Severn near Chepstow. For much of its length it is barely visible, if at all, but around Clun and Knighton it is at its most dramatic, consisting of a ditch some twelve feet deep and bounded by a rounded bank sixty feet broad. It must surely rank as Britain's most incredible historic edifice, for to walk it as we did, for mile after unrelenting mile and observe its course striding away ahead, up hill and down dale, a great gash through the rural landscape, beggared our contemplation of its construction. One cannot begin to calculate the untold man-hours required to dig and align the hundreds of thousands of tons, maybe even millions, of rocks and spoil by sheer human muscle power using primitive wooden shovels and picks. On our first walk, from the town of Clun in west Shropshire when we first encountered the Dyke, I was completely flabbergasted by its sheer scale, and the almost spiritual remoteness I experienced. I stood atop of its rampart, gazing over into the ancient principality of Wales, to the accompaniment of the eternal soughing of the west winds through the trees above our heads, like the soughing of the hapless armies of workers who laboured there in those wild empty spaces of thirteen hundred years before.

The second visit that Olly and I made to the Dyke was on a day in early Spring, and the incessant westerly wind that buffeted us bore a flesh numbing chill in its icy blast. We had taken the bus south from Knighton, lying in the meadows of the infant River Teme, down to Kington, a small market town on the River Arrow in the shadow of Hergest Ridge. Both Knighton and Kington lie on the Offa's Dyke and between them we faced the most severe and testing stretch of the entire long-distance path. By the time we descended down the hillside, almost stumbling our way, into Knighton once more, some seven hours later, we had climbed three levels representing the summit of the Dyke and totalling two thousand feet ascent in the course of some fifteen miles of hill-walking. Coming down that final descent I was forced to walk backwards as the cartilage in my right knee was causing me such excruciating and unbearable pain. Olly always comes with a pedometer strapped to his person and typically our day's walking measured around thirty two thousand paces. Little wonder that my cartilages protested so vehemently!

One of the walks of recent years which I found most pleasant was that Olly and I enjoyed following the course of the River Wye downstream from Monmouth to Tintern.

It was on a fine spring morning in April when the dew was wet underfoot as we crossed the meadows from Monmouth's old stone bridge and took the path along the bank. We were following in the footsteps of the Reverend William Gilpin who so popularised this stretch of the River Wye with his classic "Book of the Picturesque" which he had published over two hundred years before. In his wake followed countless trippers all eager to experience the "romantic tour", artists, writers, poets, including amongst the latter William Wordsworth, who expressed his sentiments in a long doggerel "Tintern Abbey" written during a tour of the area in the summer of 1798.

On the Offa's Dyke long-distance footpath, here in the Clun Forest, Shropshire.

The remains of the twin railway bridges which once spanned the River Wye at Monmouth.

A misty morning on the summit of the Sugar Loaf mountain.

*Olly and I perched on the last vestiges of the chapel which once crowned the summit
of the Skirrid mountain.*

The Wye was a commercial artery for quite large boats in those times and traces of weirs which assisted in raising the all important water levels can still be found. Brockweir, just upstream of Tintern, was an important centre for the building of ocean-going sized boats, incredible as it is to imagine today.

Similarly at Redbrook, just south of Monmouth, a thriving industrial complex of charcoal furnaces and a major tin plate works stood near the river banks. But on that April morning when we passed by the silence was broken only with the Spring birdsong and the gentle tinkle of the Wye, cascading past the arbour of fresh green overhang, under which we picked our way.

Olly has been a steadfast and dependable friend to me over so many years, and has by example inspired in me an active interest in the landscapes and of man's influence over his environment, of railways, canals, of our own local communities with their fascinating histories. He is indefatigable in his pursuit of knowledge and having found it is most generous in disbursing his largesse to any who care to listen. Little wonder I consider him such a stimulating companion, and long may he continue to be so.

When I was about nine years old the orchard at the rear of Nutbridge Cottages was purchased by a firm of builders for development. I sat on the roof of "Henry's house", our late departed cockerel, and watched with a heavy heart the diggers and bulldozers tearing down the ancient gnarled fruit trees where once our family hens had pecked and scratched and where I had scrogged the Autumn apples. Within the year there was instead a road named "Greenway" lined with modern white semi-detached houses. They were each priced at around two and a half thousand pounds, a fabulous amount to our way of thinking, and far beyond the scope of the average couple. However, they were all sold remarkably quickly, and we gained new neighbours and made acquaintance with one family in particular. Peter and Elizabeth Mills and their three children, Jane, Mary and youngest sibling Frank moved into a property whose rear garden just adjoined the corner of our own, and it was across this divide that my mother and Elizabeth used to pass the time of day and thereby became firm friends. I can recall them exchanging various offerings with outstretched arms, a packet of runner beans or maybe a pot of freshly made plum jam being passed across the fence from one to the other.

The children started to attend the afternoon Sunday School where I was also despatched every week with great reluctance. Thus came about one of my most enduring friendships.

Jane was nineteen months older than I was, a huge difference at my tender age of nine. She also seemed far more mature and sensible than my own contempories in the village. I remember my total admiration for her when she performed a solo rendition during one afternoon's Sunday School....such courage, such poise, such confidence!

Jane went to school at the Pate's Grammar School for girls at Pittville on the fringe of Cheltenham town, so when I too caught the same 8.25am Kearsey bus on starting at the Boy's Grammar School we both inevitably travelled together. I used to greet her with a shy "hello" and usually spent the rest of the journey feeling extremely ill at ease and with all the gauche of a typical young adolescent schoolboy.

I was quite taken aback to receive a letter from Jane, written to me whilst she was on a family visit to Coventry. It was a totally unexpected yet thrilling surprise. I could not comprehend why such a sophisticated and cultured young lady should wish to correspond with a gawky, socially ill-equipped village lad as me.

However, I did reply, what I wrote about I cannot recall, but it certainly could not have been easy. Letter writing to me was something one undertook very begrudgingly thanking elderly aunts for their birthday gifts, and most definitely not as an expression of ones deepest thoughts and sentiments. However, I persevered and as a result our correspondence now has continued, through good times and bad, for the past forty six years.

It was not until I had left school that Jane and I had our first "grown up" tryst. It was after the chapel's carol singing around the village, just before the Christmas of 1963, when she agreed to accompany me and my friend Michael Dewey into the Apple Tree Inn for a quick noggin. Such an unexpected financial outlay left me having to borrow five shillings and sixpence from Michael with which to buy my round of drinks!

It was to be another two months before Jane and I had what was to be our first proper date together. That Christmas of 1963 was to be the last one my father ever lived to celebrate, for a fortnight later he so tragically lost his life.His death left me alone and bewildered, a young teenager just turned seventeen, the last of the large family that had once been crammed into Nutbridge Cottage.

Jane's companionship lifted my spirits and helped fill the void in my life just when I needed it most. We were both attending evening chapel services by this time, and after we had shaken hands with the visiting preacher who stood in the little porch bidding farewell to the villagers, Jane suggested coming round to see me at home one evening, possibly Tuesday that week, the 25th February. My heart raced with anticipation, and the next two days seemed interminable. The evening finally arrived and when Jane turned up I suggested going out for a drink at one of the Cotswold pubs on my Vespa motor scooter. To my surprise she agreed! I came to appreciate later what a risk she took in displeasing her father. I am sure he meant well, but he did seem rather over-protective of his daughters, and did not approve of public houses, staying out late and, for all I knew, motor bikes as well, and here was I about to commit all three sins in one evening!

It was a memorable night, the full moon cast an ethereal luminescence over the misty Cotswold landscape. The roads were deserted, except for the young girl and her swain chugging quietly through the darkening lanes. I wanted it to go on forever. At this distance in time, the whole dreamlike occasion appears as some composite picture of memorable moments. We stopped at the Farmer's Arms in Guiting Power on the hills above Winchcombe. A juke box was blaring out the latest hit from the Transatlantic "wall of sound" era, all-girl group "The Crystals" chanting "And then he kissed me". The rear snug was full of noisy locals, but there was only one person that I saw, the girl by my side. I was truly, madly, and passionately head-over-heels in love!

That springtime and early summer I was walking on air. Jane enjoyed the theatre and classical music concerts to which I accompanied her. We used to catch the early evening bus to Cheltenham and be at the Everyman or Playhouse theatre in time for a pre-performance drink. The Everyman then maintained its own resident cast, with the occasional guest appearance of a nationally known name, so they all became very familiar faces to us in the course of the season.

The Playhouse was the venue for a number of amateur local groups, and as Jane knew one or two of the performers at certain shows we were able then to enjoy a drink in the private member's bar down a corridor alongside the stage.

Music was, and still remains Jane's enduring love. Cheltenham Town Hall hosted visits by the City of Birmingham and occasionally the Bournemouth Symphony Orchestras. I remember the former being conducted with great verve and panache by those eminent conductors Harold Gray and Hugo Rignold, with Felix Kok the lead violinist. Guest pianists in those days included Colin Horsley and John Ogden, putting their all into spirited renditions of such pieces as Rachmaninoff's Second and Beethoven's Fifth "Emperor" piano concertos. Jane herself is an extremely accomplished pianist and in our early days used to accompany the hymns at the Chapel on its wheezing ancient harmonium, the wooden pedals creaking loudly as she strove to maintain the air pressure which operated the music pipes. Her presence there on Sunday evenings was a great fillip in persuading me to become a regular worshipper!

Peter Mills used to complain at his daughter's piano practice in the family home, so Jane acquired the key to the chapel which enabled her to go up there of an evening and indulge in private practise without interference, using the old upright piano which was kept for Sunday School.

I went with Jane to hear a couple of these sessions and took with me my tape-recorder. I still possess the reel of magnetic tape holding the recordings I made on those summer evenings so long ago. To replay them, as faded now as they have become, is to evoke memories of that little chapel with its creaking harmonium and tinkling piano. Once again I am sat listening to the wonderful Chopin's Fantasie Impromptu Opus 66 reverberating within the quietness of those four walls or Handel's Largo swelling from the heart of the trembling harmonium and filling the chapel to its ceiling with the music written over two centuries earlier.

That May time Jane entered the spring Cheltenham Competitive Music festival to which I escorted her. On that glorious sunny morning she filled the Town hall with her rapturous playing, a Fugue for solo piano, and even I considered there to be only one result. To both our delights the judge awarded her the top marks and presented her with the magnificent silver Rosebowl trophy. To celebrate her success we lunched at the Black Tulip restaurant in the Promenade to the style which the occasion demanded!

Cheltenham boasted three cinemas during the mid-nineteen sixties, the Gaumont, the Coliseum and Regal, so we were able to enjoy many of the memorable classics of that period. Our very first film "The Running Man" starred a young Alan Bates alongside Lawrence Harvey, with other gems to follow such as Doris Day and Rock Hudson in "Move Over Darling" and an urbane Cary Grant with Leslie Carron in "Charade".

Unfortunately the last bus home to Woodmancote left the Royal Well terminus at 10.15pm so there was often a choice of either missing the bus or the end of the film. One ploy was to arrive at the cinema early in order to see the closing scenes of the film during the late afternoon showing and then leave "where you came in". This way you could even contrive a cup of frothy expresso coffee in Geraldine's Coffee Bar in the Promenade before catching the last bus back home. Courtship was never easy!

I was playing cricket for Woodmancote most spring and summer weekends, as well as regularly mowing the cricket field using the small grey Ferguson tractor with the clattering set of triple gand mowers in tow, so carrying on any sort of romance became a juggling act of one's free time. Needless to say, where Jane was concerned, the noble game of cricket came off the worse. I did however persuade her to help with the match teas on several occasions, which involved brewing up vast quantities of scalding hot tea in the W.I. tea urn and making mountains of sandwiches. These were demolished in minutes by twenty six players, umpires and scorers plus anybody else who ingratiated themselves into the tiny corrugated iron village hall which backed onto the cricket ground.

Away from the demands of village cricket we would take ourselves off for long country walks on the hills which lay about our hamlet.

On one hot summer's afternoon we pitched and bumped our way on my Vespa down the old coach road which leads to Postlip and the Wash Pool on Cleeve Hill. Here rises the River Isbourne, dammed to form an ancient sheep washing pool before trickling on its course through the grounds of Postlip Hall.

We lay at ease in the warm sunshine, occasionally refreshing ourselves with the icy water bubbling in abundance from the spring at our side, and listened to the soporific chirping of an army of invisible grasshoppers concealed about our bower. Such are the simple pleasures of young love.

Bushcombe Wood, sitting atop Nottingham Hill, was our other favourite destination. Here I took supreme pleasure introducing Jane to the secret hidden places I knew as a child. I remembered the shady glade whereon grew banks of Lily of the Valley and the marshy area where a myriad of Kingcups glittered every springtime. The most hallowed and cherished spot of all was the ancient beech tree, the elder statesman of the wood, which bore on its bowl the carved initials of other lovers who had whiled away their hours in this same place, maybe it was their special spot also.

Jane was far more adept at expressing her feelings and emotions than I was, and this was manifested by the neatly bound anthology of poetry which she had composed, and illustrated with charming pen and ink cameos. She presented it to me "with her fondest love". A Small Garden of Verses" remains on my bookshelf still, as one of my most esteemed possessions.

I should have realised that this blissful euphoria could not continue for ever but I little thought just how soon my happiness would end.

Later that same year Jane took up with somebody else, a man older than me, more mature and better educated. I felt utterly rejected and heartbroken. The fact I had undergone one of life's bitter experiences which goes hand in hand with growing up was little consolation. My teenage angst knew no bounds as my world collapsed in tatters about me.

Paradoxically we remained friends, which makes coming to terms with estrangement all the harder. In a desperate and futile effort to persuade Jane back I bought a second-hand television, for that was another indulgence denied in the Mill's household. I reasoned that maybe she would call around on occasional evenings to watch it, perhaps "Dr Finlay's Casebook", on a miniscule twelve inch fuzzy screen, but my outlay of four pounds was spent in vain!

Even more reckless was my purchasing of an old upright iron-framed piano from an emporium in Cheltenham. Again, Jane was discouraged from practising in her own home by her father, so she would be more than welcome to play to her heart's content at Nutbridge Cottage. The instrument was delivered by two decrepit old men from the shop in an equally decrepit ancient small lorry. They heaved and puffed their way up the front steps and through into the living room, with much shoving and bumping until the piano was finally in place. They might as well have left it in the shop. The only time it was ever played, by my friend Charles Smith after a late night's return from the local pub, merely succeeded in arousing my neighbour from his sleep and who then retaliated by tossing his empty milk bottles over the fence, smashing against my paving under the living room window!

Jane and I gradually drifted apart, for she left home and took rooms in Cheltenham. Her parents had sold up and left Greenway, thus severing the remaining family links with Woodmancote. As she still played for the chapel services Jane used to come out on the afternoon Sunday bus and visit me for a cup of tea and a chat before going on to the evening meeting, but then even these brief get togethers ceased.

I did go and hear Jane compete again at the next Music Festival, this time discreetly sitting aloft, and incognito, above the main auditorium. She had a new companion with her, a man I did not recognise, and within twelve months she had become his wife.

Nearly ten years were to pass before we met again, quite fortuitously at the funeral of an old mutual friend and neighbour. We sat together in the chapel behind the organ screen, but I sensed things could never be quite the same again. In those ten years her marriage had ended and I myself had been married to Loretta for seven years. We left the chapel together when the service was over and after a rather restrained exchange of social pleasantries we parted once more.

Just before Christmas in 1979 I spotted a notice in the local paper advertising the Bishop's Cleeve Choral Society's forthcoming concert. The secretary's name listed with the contact details was none other than my old soul mate, and actually living in Bishop's Cleeve. I had been passing her cottage for twelve months on my way to work without ever realising the fact. Needless to relate, I went along to the Choral Concert that night and during the interval Jane, who had spotted me in the audience, came over to greet me. It was wonderful to renew our friendship and continue to enjoy each other's company again so effortlessly after so long. It somehow rekindled the flame which had been smouldering away in us both for the past seventeen years. Jane herself was moved to pen a short poem celebrating our re-union, which expressed so perfectly how we both felt. I felt extremely flattered, for it was the only time verses had ever been composed in my honour!

I write these words some twenty eight years on from that re-meeting and in that time we have never been too far from each others thoughts. Jane has remarried, so we rarely ever actually meet except by chance, but we still remember our respective birthdays and Christmastide with a card, and of course that special anniversary, the February night in 1964 which remains so cherished between us both.

With Jane Mills on Bushcombe Hill, Woodmancote in November 1964.

Forty years on: Jane at her piano.

Teddington: as seen from 'Applegarth.'

Teddington: from church tower towards 'Applegarth.'

TEDDINGTON DAYS

The new decade in 1980 brought with it the onset of a degree of restlessness in both Loretta and myself. We had celebrated ten years of marriage and living at Nutbridge Cottage with the feeling of "what now?".

As the next few years passed the feeling grew stronger to the extent that Loretta became desperately unhappy, a state compounded by new extremely noisy neighbours who had moved into the house adjoining our own.

So it came to pass that after forty five years of sheltering the Curr family, Nutbridge Cottage was placed in the hands of a local estate agent. It was, of course, my first introduction to the world of buying and selling houses, and the prospect of leaving the one I was actually born in felt a daunting prospect. Ironically, the day Nutbridge Cottage went on the market, one of my many nephews rang me. He was on the estate agent's mailing list and had that morning received the particulars for our home, and straightaway agreed to the asking price, adding that he was committed to leaving his present bungalow fairly urgently. All this spurred us into the laborious process of searching for a new home. We mentally listed a number of diverse requirements such as distance from my work and Louise's school, a property with an open fire and completely detached (no more risking noisy neighbours!) and most crucially, within the limit of what we could afford. From the number of properties we viewed, only one fulfilled our expectations.

"Applegarth" stands in the small village of Teddington, in that area of "no man's land" betwixt the Vale of Evesham and the Cotswold edge, where the ancient Tibblestone stands guard at the crossing of the Tewkesbury to Stow-on-the-Wold old drover's route with the Cheltenham to Evesham turnpike coaching way. Although only some five miles from Woodmancote it was a village I had never actually set foot in until then.

The earliest recorded reference to Teddington was in AD780 when Offa, King of Mercia gave land there to the Monastery at Bredon. Over the following several hundred years Teddington was involved in a number of ownership wrangles between monarch, Church and noblemen. Its present status was shaped at the dissolution of the monastries when it passed to the Crown and was granted to the Dean and Chapter of Worcester in 1542.

The village along with our neighbour, the much smaller village of Alstone, now lies in the diocese of Worcestershire, although since 1932 it has been administered by the Gloucestershire authorities and falls within the present borough of Tewkesbury.

It is claimed that moving house and all it entails is almost as stressful and potentially traumatic as divorce and even bereavement. It is not an undertaking I should wish to repeat again these twenty two years on. The fifteenth of July, St Swithin's Day 1985 stands out as one of the landmark dates in my mind, representing as it does the starting point for what has proved to be a complete life-style change, albeit allied to various other factors. Possibly the day of our move has been the most gruelling and arduous I have ever experienced, due to the decision to move personally our "lares and penates" plus the myriad of other effects, large and small, which a family accumulates with the passing years.

My good friend Rob Dewey offered his services as the official driver of the 7½ tons lorry which I hired, the largest possible under the vehicle licensing law which then prevailed. Despite its cavernous capacity it took three separate journeys to and fro before all our cherished possessions were piled in every available space at "Applegarth", awaiting their assembly into some sort of domestic order. Never has a hot bath and a sustaining dinner felt so welcome as at the end of that day.

It was a very surreal experience to awaken under an unfamiliar roof, within those four strange walls, and yet be surrounded by all ones familiar furniture looking somewhat ill-placed in their new settings. Even returning back to Teddington after a day out of the village was akin to coming back to one's holiday accomodation instead of the security of a permanent home. It was to take a long time for me to lose my self-consciousness and relax in our new community.

One of "Applegarth's" greatest attributes was the panorama we enjoyed from the lounge picture window. We were high above the village street, and opposite the lane leading to the church, with cottages flanking the small embrasure formed by the junction of the two lanes. Beyond lay the church itself, against the backdrop of the orchards clothing the north facing slope of Teddington Hill which rises steeply to 350 feet above the village. Other deciduous trees add to the verdure of the hill including a large grove of mature limes, all providing a changing spectrum of colour throughout the seasons.

Soon after we settled into our new abode I lost no time in visiting the church, and even arranged with the churchwarden to ascend the tower. The nave and chancel date from the 13th and 14th centuries with the tower a somewhat later construction. Its ascent is made via a series of short wooden stairways and finally a ricketty ladder, from the uppermost rungs one has to reach up and lift the weighty lead-clad trap door leading to the square platform guarded by a low castellated wall on its four sides. The fine views across the village and to Bredon Hill beyond makes the effort worthwhile. Down below lie the graves of past village worthies including that of William Creese, founder and first secretary of the Y.M.C.A in 1844. Creese lived at Home farm on the village street and established a Y.M.C.A reading room and village institute at the top of the village in the building now called "Cotswold Cottage". He must have been only a young man of around 22 years old at the time of his involvement for he died in 1910 at the grand old age of 88 years.

Our first few months at "Applegarth" were ones fraught with unforeseen expense. Apart from the usual anticipated fees and outlay associated with a house move, I had to purchase an electric cooker, a large wooden shed in which to store the garden requisites, commission a sizeable built-in wardrobe for all our clothes, furnish the bungalow with curtains and carpeting and then, most inconveniently, the 600 gallon oil tank for the central heating system had starting weeping oil from its underside rather ominously and so needed replacing.

Overlaid with all this expense were the regular outgoings for Louise's school fees and, then to crown everything, the engine of "Dumpy", our, by this time, thirty years old Morris Minor car started clanking to the point of imminent disintegration. It had been rattling loudly for the previous year or so, to the extent that heads would turn in the street at the sound of our approach. But now the provision of a new engine was inevitable, so with Loretta in our second Morris as escort in case of disaster, I drove the ailing little car with the greatest difficulty to a specialist Morris Minor repair firm near Evesham. I nursed her those fourteen miles with my heart in my mouth, expecting a major breakdown to befall me at any moment. On our eventual safe arrival the proprieter was outside waiting to greet us. He had heard the commotion and guessed its source, making the comment "I do not know how you got here, but you would never have made it back home again!"

The result was an updated larger engine and matching gearbox in "Dumpy" and when I later supplemented this work by fitting a higher ratio crown hub in the rear axle, the gallant old car accelerated and bowled along at speeds hitherto unimagined.

Teddington is twinned with its neighbouring village of Alstone a mile and a quarter up the lane, both sharing a common Parish council which meets alternatively in each village. Alstone lacks a village hall, but does possess a playing field, a facility Teddington lacked when we first arrived in 1985. Seven years later a small field was released by a local builder in a planning deal and thereby we acquired our own village play area. By some device I found myself seconded onto the committee tasked with the setting up of the playing field and did suggest naming it "Orchard Park", a casual aside but one which was taken up.

The village hall in Teddington was the hub of what few social activities there were. It had been built with the support of local philantropist and banker Edward Martin long before the Second World War and thus lacks many of the refinements expected in a more modern building. A Women's Institute met there until its disbandment a number of years ago, indeed, Loretta was appointed as its last secretary, and later I was to become a regular hirer as I will explain in a future chapter. Teddington hosted a series of annual village 'open days' when many of its inhabitants welcomed the visiting public into their gardens and laid on refreshments and various displays. I cleared out the garage at "Applegarth" and Loretta sat gently spinning yarn on her two wheels, to the delight and curiosity of a number of people who stood in a semi-hypnotic trance gazing at the strands of raw wool being fed into the revolving maw of the spindles.

An even more popular stand was the 'Pimms Bar' set up on the grass verge in Church Lane. As a drinks licence would have been necessary for the sale of alcohol, they adopted the clever ploy of selling you the lemonade and threw in the Pimms 'gratis'! I doubt whether such a ruse would have successfully stood the scrutiny of the law, if it was so challenged.

In the week preceding Christmas the Church Elders organised a carol singing party to tour the village, usually the same handful of loyal supporters supplemented by "guest" singers from neighbouring churches in the Parish. There are many large detached dwellings with long driveways in Teddington so covering the entire village in one evening was an extremely arduous process. We would stand straining our lungs, by the light of flickering hand-held torches, with verse after familiar verse of the old classics, but we might just as well have sung to the stars which shone down on our little group. In this modern age of double-glazed insulated homes and quadraphonic television the witless residents responded to our knocking on their doors with an expression of utter bewilderment on their faces. They obviously had not heard a single note of our belaboured efforts! A much-anticipated feature of an evening's carolling was the invitation back to Bengrove Farm, the home of Alec and Libby Hopkins. Here our band of stalwarts enjoyed their welcome hospitality in the traditional style, surrounded by the old-time décor of their wonderful stone and timbered farmhouse. Alec was extremely generous in the dispensing of his Scotch whisky and after one particular evening when he had been especially liberal with the 'water of life' I recall one of our party paying the inevitable penalty. The poor chap in question had been sat unobtrusively all evening, quietly imbibing the warming amber spirit until he came to take his leave. He rose to his rather unsteady feet, lost his balance and reeled backwards, disappearing into the decorated Christmas tree behind him. My laughter at his misfortune was short-lived, for on returning to "Applegarth" at midnight I roused the entire household by getting myself entangled in the heavy velvet curtains which were drawn over the front door. My daughter left her bed to come out into the hallway and help extricate me from the shroud in which I had tightly wrapped myself, as a fly is caught in a spider's web!

The carol singing forays around the streets were abandoned a few years back in favour of a Christmas service with food and drinks in the village hall, and a collection taken at the end of the night amongst the participants. It makes for an infinitely more comfortable and civilised evening but nowhere near as much fun!

We were fortunate in enjoying the company of good neighbours in the immediate vicinity of "Applegarth".

Opposite us and across the lane lived Barry and Judith Luxford whom we had known from our Woodmancote days. Barry had been the one-time landlord of the Apple Tree Inn and Judith, his young wife, actually born and raised in the village to an old local family. She seemed quite homesick at living 'over the hill' in Teddington and longed to be back nearer her family and her roots. It was through Barry and Judith that we became acquainted with Jim Firkins from the Manor at the top of Church Lane. Jim owned the fruit farms, including the hundred acres on the slopes of Teddington Hill, but soon after we became friends

'Applegarth' 1985.

Village Open Day: Loretta displays her spinning skills.

The tombstone of William Creese.

Celebrating my fortieth birthday in 1986.

he planned to sell much of his businesses, and emigrate with his large family to Australia. He remained behind for a year or so in order to finalise his affairs and in that time was living alone in the Manor. We enjoyed many nights of parties there for Jim was a most generous host.

One summer's barbeque around the swimming pool was enlivened by me flinging myself into the water, no doubt spurred on by 'Dutch Courage', nearly losing my new yellow bathing trunks in the process, and floundering away like some startled aquatic mammal at a zoo! A hugh monkey puzzle tree grows on the lawn in front of Teddington Manor which I have an enduring memory of. As we were all leaving after a get-together late one gusty night, I happened to glance up and see, like some giant animated octopus as the wind caught its tentacles, the tree enacting a grotesque tarantella, silhouetted against the scudding moon-lit cloudscape. There are various superstitions associated with the monkey-puzzle tree and it is easy to understand why the Araucaria would 'puzzle a monkey to climb it'!

Louise had been very friendly with several of Jim's children and enjoyed the freedom of the hill, the pool of course, and the tennis courts. When the old farmyard, including these courts, was sold for housing, Louise was in high dudgeon, and to this day still rankles at what she viewed as an act of treachery in destroying "her" playground.

I celebrated my fortieth birthday at this time and was joined by my coterie of close friends at a party held in my honour at "Applegarth". To my utter surprise they had between them arranged a 'Kissogram' for me, which took me completely unawares, evidenced by the photographs taken, for I am sat still wearing my carpet slippers with the leggy young "provocateur" perched seductively on my knee. This was my first experience of such a prank and I felt extremely uncomfortable and self-conscious, and ill at ease regarding what was expected of me. I suppose one has simply to submit and sit there masquerading a look of enjoyment on your face!

Just around the time that I left my full-time employment with British Coal we welcomed new neighbours into the cottage opposite "Applegarth". John and Sharon Ash ran their own business of a photographic studio, specialising in advertising and publicity-style photography and based in central Cheltenham.

When John learnt that I had spare time on my hands he immediately started offering me a variety of interesting commissions on a casual basis, none too demanding or time-consuming. This arrangement suited me very well. Two of their major clients were the Chelsea Building Society and Bovis Homes, the building company, and these were the accounts that I became involved with.

Most of the former's work concerned photography of the Society's support for local causes, which was extremely generous. I suspect there was an element of competition with the Cheltenham and Gloucester Building Society, who too prided themselves on their public relations portfolio.

Examples of the diverse assignments for the Chelsea include the opening of an adventure playground for youngsters at the Churnside Centre near

Cirencester; covering a charity football match at Whaddon in Cheltenham; discretely recording a performance by the Abbey School choir during a rehearsal in the historic Norman Tewkesbury Abbey, and photographing a happy couple who had won the prize of dinner at the prestigious Greenway Hotel in Shurdington on the outskirts of Cheltenham. The latter commission was the cause of a ridiculous minor 'skirmish' with the hotel's manager and proprietor. As I swept up the imposing long driveway off the main road and parked "Dumpy", my archaic old Morris Minor,on the apron of tarmac flanking the grand entrance to the hotel, I was aware of a small party standing outside as if waiting to greet the arrival of expected guests. I was some time emerging from my car, having to sort out my equipment and so on, and the party, comprising the proprietor himself supported by his 'maitre d'hotel' and head waitress, was still hovering outside, looking slightly impatient by now. I was early for my 'dinner date' and consequently was mistaken by the management as the guest of honour! After that unfortunate start things deteriorated. As it was a hot summer's evening I had no jacket, just a shirt and tie. That did not please his nibs, and he requested that I don a dark tuxedo that was found for me. It simply did not match my brown flannel trousers and consequently I looked a right mess! Then, when my two subjects arrived for their luxury dinner, they were made to sit on the patio for the photographs - their fellow diners were not to be disturbed! It was altogether a totally embarrassing experience and so unnecessary to boot.

One very different commission I recall with amused pleasure, is that of picturing the Mayor of Cheltenham in his parlour making some presentation or other, I have long forgotten to whom, but meeting there his chauffeur and aide, Arthur. Some years earlier he had driven for British Coal, and had chauffeured me on countless occasions. Arthur seemed very 'well in' at the Municipal offices, and he invited me into his pantry to partake in a discreet drink to mark our reunion, proceeding to unlock His Worshipful's drinks cabinet and pouring two extremely generous measures of malt whisky. As we sat musing over past times together so the level in the spirit in the Mayor's decanter was going down like the Spring tide. I have no idea how Arthur eventually came to explain the deficit!

My assignments for the Bovis Homes Group were far more commercially orientated, and involved photographing various districts and communities where new housing developments were underway, with the intention of marketing such locations as desirable areas to reside in.

One typical task entailed a journey down to Devon to record sites at Colyford near Seaton, on to Chudleigh near Newton Abbot and finally to Torquay, taking in such places of interest and scenic beauty as Cockington Forge en route. Altogether a very strenuous and arduous day's work!

One great advantage of these commissions was that all the 'back up' effort was undertaken for me. The locations were researched beforehand, and all the camera equipment, top of the range Swedish Hasselblad kit, supplied. A studio car was assigned for my use, usually an extremely nippy fuel-injected sports saloon, ready filled with petrol. On my return the exposed films were taken off me for processing 'in-house', a cause of some disquiet on my part as I never actually got to see the results of my efforts, but in the absence of any adverse feedback from John Ash I assumed I had completed my brief to his satisfaction. There was only one occasion when the demands of the job overwhelmed me, and that was the photographing onto slides of seven major town centres in and around the Cotswolds and Vale of Evesham - Stroud, Cirencester, Gloucester, Cheltenham, Tewkesbury, Winchcombe and Evesham. The pictures were required urgently to make up a promotional slide/tape presentation and the expectation was that I could take all the shots in a single day! The logistics of merely visiting the towns and parking the car made the task impossible, adding to which it was mid-November and the useable light was limited to a few hours either side of midday. My reasoning prevailed and two days were allotted for the job!

It was through the offices of a mutual friend that I was introduced to the American author Alison R. Ridley a.k.a Alison Evans. She divided her time between the U.S.A, where her husband, publisher Curtis F.Garfield, lived, and England, renting a picturesque stone cottage in the centre of Snowshill village above Broadway. She had been commissioned by the Lygon Arms Hotel in Broadway to produce the definitive illustrated history and guide book for them. She certainly had a wealth of material to weave into her writings, for the Lygon is probably the most famous hotel in Britain outside of London, and boasts a history tracing back to around the thirteenth bentury.

Originally known as the White Hart, the royal emblem of King Richard the Lion Heart, it was visited by monks journeying to Winchcombe and Pershore Abbeys and being on the London road acted as a posting house for the merchants and drovers who travelled that way.

Alison had a very forceful personality which she brought to bear in order to gain one's co-operation and so it was that I was detailed to take photographs to accompany "The Story of the Lygon Arms". I even found myself picking her up from her cottage in Snowshill and transporting her down to Broadway on the morning of our assignation! She wanted some pictures of Lygon's sports and health club facilites which were the last word in luxury and design, being set out in the style of Romanesque baths.

The book on its completion was a masterpiece of meticulous research and literary expression, all painstakingly cross referenced and illustrated throughout with a series of brilliant bespoke pencilled sketches. The guide was launched with great ceremony and huge expense with a pageant produced and presented at an evening's reception in the hotel. I was privileged to be invited as a guest and witnessed the long history of thc Lygon Arms brought to vivid life by a procession of actors and actresses in period costume who trooped across the stage to a live commentary explaining who they were, and their role in the colourful past of the hotel as we know it today. The managing director, Kirk

Ritchie, was the most perfect host, and we enjoyed a repast that night from his kitchens which would have graced a King's table!

In this period of 'semi-retirement'. when life took on a somewhat easier pace, I was only too pleased to undertake odd jobs mainly as favours to help out certain friends. Two such friends were Nigel and Irene Fisher, who still live, as then, on their farm in our neighbouring village of Alstone. The business interests they enjoy are many and varied, and on several occasions, when asked, I did tasks for them which gave me a fascinating insight into some of these activities.

Irene and her late brother ran two immensely popular shire-horse centres, open to the public, with the added attractions of a cafeteria, wagon rides and so on. I visited the centre at Maidenhead in the Home Counties on an errand to deliver an urgent package, and was welcomed on my arrival with a personal guided tour of the site, with the opportunity of viewing those magnificent animals at close quarters. They are truly huge, their rippling muscles expressing the potential power bred into those vast bodies. Their ancestors supposedly came to Britain with the Norman invaders in the eleventh century, bearing the great weight of the armoured warriers astride their backs. This particular centre is deservedly a very popular destination for families living in the London area and represents a thoroughly entertaining yet informative day's outing.

Another journey eastwards turned out to be not so leisurely when Irene asked if I would assist in the delivery of a brand new Mercedes car over to her brother's Huntingdon office. The arrangement was that I should meet her there and we would travel back to Gloucestershire together. That January day in 1990 saw the worst storms to hit southern England since the devastating ones three years earlier. I set off quite early and before half a mile experienced the first delay at the Hobnail's Inn on the main Stow road, where the County fire brigade were battling to prevent the ingress of storm water from the adjacent farmland entering the building. With the still raging wind rocking the heavy Mercedes I bumped over the web of fire hoses which criss-crossed the highway and cautiously continued onwards. Ascending Stanway Hill was a nightmare, for the road was littered with debris from the bordering trees which themselves were being blown sideways by the force of the cross-winds. I just got through, and learnt later that the hill had been closed to all traffic shortly after. The remainder of the hair-raising journey was a catalogue of damage and destruction. One heroic driver of a large pantechnicon just in front of me was desperately trying to control his vehicle which was developing a series of ever-increasing alarming zig-zags all over the road's width until the inevitable happened, and the whole equipage disappeared off into the scenery. The good Lord was with me that day and I eventually arrived in Huntingdon unscathed. Before leaving for home, Irene had some business to transact in Cambridge. My two enduring memories of the time I had to while away whilst waiting for her, were the mass of bicycles being blown across the pavements from where their student riders had left them, and the double-decker buses parked on Drummer Square being buffeted and rocked by the incessant wind, like boats at anchor.

In complete contrast to this day were the two consecutive trips Nigel and I made on the long haul north to Ellesmere Port on Merseyside. He had two enormous four-axled dustcarts to deliver and our plan was for me to follow him, driving his luxury Saab saloon car, and he would thus have transport back home. We chose the two hottest days of that Summer for the exercise, and as we slowly trailed in convoy northwards on the motorways, I sensed that poor Nigel was flagging with the heat as the hours passed at our maximum speed of forty miles per hour. I was enjoying the bliss of the Saab's air-conditioning system, and when we both pulled off at a service area for a well earned break I emerged from my cool comfortable cocoon into a blanket of enveloping stifling humidity. Nigel meanwhile had probably lost a stone in weight since leaving home!

My turn at enduring the rigours of long-distance haulage awaited me for soon after the dustcart adventure I agreed to assist Nigel with the transporting of a batch of empty waste skips from Smethwick on the outskirts of Birmingham back to his farm. The steel skips were stacked one inside another, four or five per load, onto the truck and I proceeded back and forth all day, until the M5 motorway became as familiar as my village street. I did four round trips that day, totalling some three hundred miles of gruelling, laborious driving along one of Britain's busiest and over-crowded arterial routes. It proved a salutary appreciation by me, and respect regarding our nation's under-estimated long distance truck drivers, who supply the never-ending demands of society every day and night.

Nigel had taken on the managing of the historic carriage and coachwork company J Billinge Co. of Smethwick, which specialised then in the restoration and rebuilding of horse-drawn vehicles. In his challenge of promoting the company's services and reviving its flagging fortunes he planned the publication of an illustrated booklet setting out the activities of the firm, and asked me to take the series of photographs necessary. I readily agreed, and it proved to be a fascinating day's work, for I bore witness to a range of traditional crafts being enacted, still untouched by the modern technological age. In those unpretentious workshops man was still master of his craft, and not subservient to some impassive machine. In a humorous aside, I was flattered when the blacksmith played his age-old customary prank on me, the novice. When he wetted his anvil, on striking the iron work-piece a deafening bang like a firecracker resulted, showering the stone floor with white-hot clouds of tiny sparks, much to everyone's unrestrained amusement. The most spectacular of operations which I recorded was the shrinking on of an iron-tyre around the wooden rim of a large cart-wheel. A crude fire of shavings and cut-offs was lit around the circular iron-hoop laid flat outside in the factory yard. Alongside it lay the assembled wooden wheel with its elm nave and ash felloes attached in perfect symmetry by the array of oak spokes radiating from its core.

When the wheelwright judged the tyre to have reached correct temperature, the expanded hoop of iron was deftly gripped by him, aided by a fellow worker, using enormous long-handled steel tongs, and lifted quickly over the waiting wheel. The two items were perfectly matched, the tyre being tapped into place around the wheel and being immediately quenched with buckets of cold water, rapidly contracted, gripping the wheel in an immovable embrace. The whole process of fitting the tyre took no more than a couple of minutes, a display of dextrous agility and immaculate timing co-ordinated into one perfect successful operation.

I was to make one further visit to these premises, this time to take publicity photographs of a completed restoration project. It was a horse-drawn 'double-decker' omnibus with outside stairs, typical of those plying the streets of London in the late Victorian age, and on which the early motor buses were modelled. Nigel subsequently arranged its transport down to Gloucestershire where it was the centrepiece of a commemorative journey, marking the centenary of cricket between two old local rivals, Winchcombe and Dumbleton. The latter team, all dressed in period costume, boarded the omnibus in the pub yard of the village inn in Gretton, a few miles outside Winchcombe, and with much carousing and jollification clanked and clattered their noisy way to Winchcombe's secluded cricket field in Corndean Lane. Heads were turned in the town's narrow streets as this curious equipage passed on its merry way!

Throughout the nineteen nineties Loretta initially had a part time job, and later embarked upon an academic course which eventually led her to achieving a B.A. (Literature) degree. This consequently meant that I had time during the weekdays when I was free to indulge in days out or long walks alone. These excursions inevitably drew me westwards of Severn, a stretch of 'workaday' country I am particularly fond of. Once the river is crossed then the character of the landscape and its people changes, not altogether in the physical sense, but in a more intangible manner. It is as if life in those western reaches of the County has yet to 'catch up' with the pace and rapid development of the neighbouring communities to the east. The reason is that until relatively recent times the two adjacent areas were isolated from each other by the River Severn. Gloucester, of course, has been a bridging point since time immemorial for travellers heading into Wales and beyond, but upstream the river was not crossed at Tewkesbury until the Mythe Bridge, with its charming miniature toll house, was designed and constructed by Thomas Telford in 1826. Haw Bridge, a few miles to the south, was built some years later, and represents a monument to the abandoned Anglo-Irish route from London via Cheltenham and Milford Haven. It was Telford himself who ruled against the scheme, but oddly enough Haw Bridge was sanctioned and built, but not the proposed new road connections. So it remains to this day almost the only major road bridge, crossing an important river in Britain, which carries only local rural traffic with no apparent any other purpose.

Shrinking an iron cart tyre onto the wooden wheel at J. Billinge Co.

Travelling to the cricket match by horse-drawn omnibus – Dumbleton v. Winchcombe Centenary game.

Haw Bridge.

The Great House, Hasfield, under Woolridge Terrace.

190

The original Haw Bridge met an untimely and sudden end with tragic consequences, when in December 1958 John Harker's petroleum tanker "Darleydale" struck the bridge's ungainly structure whilst travelling empty downstream, with the unfortunate loss of life of her skipper. Harker tankers earned a reputation concerning accidents on the river for less than two years later two of their craft brought down the central spans of the imposing Severn railway bridge at Lydney, this time with the loss of five crew members.

Beyond Haw Bridge is Tirley Cross and the lane to the left follows the course of the Severn skirting the village of Hasfield. At this latter place has stood the magnificent Great House for the past five hundred years, its vast double-winged half-timbered structure sitting four-square against the rising backdrop of the Woolridge Terrace.

I came to know its current resident, farmer David Banwell and his wife Sally, very well over the course of my visits to the area. When Sally started a 'bed and breakfast' business Loretta and I decided to experience a night there for the joy of sleeping under those medieval roofs. As it happened, mine host and his wife were away on that particular night so Loretta and I were the sole guardians of "The Great House" during that time, having our breakfast attended to by the cowman's wife who lived in an adjacent cottage. The upper rooms were reached by a broad oak staircase wide enough to drive a horse and carriage up, and on the first floor there still existed a remarkable toilet where the waste was discharged down a vertical stone-built tunnel to ground level, a device not still in use, I am happy to report!

The domestic lawns of the property are divided from the adjacent farmland by a 'ha-ha', a clever solution in providing a stock-proof wall whilst still preserving an uninterrupted view of the surrounding landscape from the windows of the house. It was achieved by cutting a deep sill in the ground along the boundary with its face cut outwards from the house. Thus a "trompe l'oeil" was created and the casual observer saw only unbroken lawns merging into the fields beyond.

Leaving Hasfield the lane reaches the riverside village of Ashleworth, the object of my journey being a lunchtime sojourn at the historic "Boat Inn" on Ashleworth quay. Reputedly the most original and unaltered pub in England, the Boat occupies a classic setting. Its approach is made down a narrow lane lined with poplar trees, which leads past the 15c. Court farm with its Tithe Barn and past the Parish church adjacent, virtually in the farmyard. Around the next corner ahead lies only the river and the Quay, and built close by, on the river bank the red-brick "Boat Inn".

As the name suggests, it owes its origins to the once thriving river traffic which plied the Severn and it was here that the old river tow-path crossed from the east to the west bank by means of a ferry. The inn has been run by many succeeding generations of the Jelf family and it was they who were granted the original ferry rights by Royal assent. Popular belief has it that King Charles the Second crossed here after his defeat at the Battle of Worcester, the last major conflict of the English Civil War, in 1651. Others consider the rights were granted even earlier, by a grateful Prince Edward of March, later to be King Edward the Fourth, fleeing from enemies in the house of Lancaster around AD1460, and who was assisted by a Jelf in his escape.

It was in this historic spot that I used to find solace on fine summer's days, sitting at ease on the river bank quaffing my amber pint of foaming ale, drawn from the stone-flagged bar of the Boat. In this tiny bar five or six of us would sit on the wooden settles, facing each other across a small divide, and engage in humorous conversation of the most entertaining kind. Occasionally I and several friends would make this journey across the Severn and enjoy an evening of home-spun entertainment, singing and playing our guitars to which the locals would often add their voices, regaling us with their particular 'party pieces'. Through it all the aged landlady Miss Rene Jelfs, would stand beaming benignly across the bar and seeming to enjoy every minute. Rene had been born in the Boat over eighty years before, as had her father and grandfather, of course, and she had operated the last ferry before the final demise of the service some forty years earlier. These nocturnal visits tended to extend way beyond respectable opening times, and one memorable night we all emerged into a silent moonlit landscape. Standing on the river bank, with the mighty Severn quietly surging by as it had since time immemorial, someone started singing "Moon River" to which the rest of us softly joined in. Truly one of my life's more memorable moments.

A feature of the countryside hereabouts are the river terraces, laid down when the Severn was much wider and higher than now, the result of the melt-water of the ice-sheets and heavier rainfall during inter-glacial periods. The aforementioned Woolridge Terrace's distinctive shape stands a level two hundred and fifty feet high, as is Norton Hill on the opposite side of the river. Intercut on the sides of these great geomorphic structures are lower terraces of gravel, some fifty feet above the present Severn flood plain and now a convenient platform on which many settlements and farms have evolved.

One such farm, The Villa at Tirley, is home to one of the remaining traditional cider and perry makers in the area. I used to regularly visit here and enjoy clandestine tasting sessions in the barn, where was arranged the long line of hogshead barrels, each with a capacity of fifty four gallons of 'agricultural wine'. The old cider maker, the late Ray Hartland, could judge to a nicety the blend suitable to your requirements, and with a knowing look on his face pass deftly from one cask to another, and produce a sample for your tasting which he would hand to you with a meaningful wink of his eye. I generally bought a blend of perry, a cider made from pears, which could hold its own when matched against any commercially fermented concoctions, and would grace any dining table to compliment one's repast, like a fine Sauternes. The cider house at the "Villa" boasted an inner sanctum amusingly christened "Ray's Hilton" where on a Sunday lunchtime could be found a huddle of old local farmers and other characters, ensconced comfortably in various decrepit armchairs and sofas and participating in a pleasant afternoon of 'passing the jug around. At the back of the cider house was sited a traditional showman's caravan, all a-glitter with

The Boat Inn, Ashleworth Quay.

My weekend retreat at Hartland's Farm, Tirley.

Telford's Mythe Bridge, Tewkesbury.

The Greyhound Inn, Lime Street.

chrome in art-deco styling and fitted inside as a holiday home with cooking facilities, bunk beds, a refridgerator and even a small television. Much to my many friends' amusement I hired this accomodation for a long weekend one summer, managing to squeeze my bicycle into "Dumpy" by the expedient of removing the front wheel and a pedal, and enjoyed a relaxing few days exploring the lanes round about.

Just along the road from Hartland's farm there is a single track lane curiously signposted "Lime Street" and down it lies the other of my favourite destinations, the Greyhound Inn. From the front windows of the snug bar room you can look out over fields and hedgerows, enjoying your "Butcombe Bitter" whilst perhaps two old locals play the now rare game of quoits alongside the doorway, gently lobbing the rubber rings with a soft plop onto the spiked board laid out on the table. It is such a restful unhurried game that the term 'quoits hooligan' simply does not exist in the English language!

Through my regular visits to the Greyhound I was persuaded to turn out for their cricket team in an evening match against arch-rivals "The Boat" from Ashleworth. Each member of the fielding side had to bowl two overs apiece, with the exception of the wicket keeper, limiting each innings to twenty overs. I had not turned my arm over "in anger" during a match for many years, and my deliveries were more akin to throwing hand-grenades during battle. Amazingly I actually took a wicket, the poor batsman being taken completely by surprise as the ball came down out of the clouds and landed on the top of the stumps behind him.

There was a paddock behind the Greyhound and once a year, on the August Bank Holiday Sunday, a classic car show was held there, organised by an enthusiastic local regular. It was extremely well supported, boasting a wide ranging turn out of vehicle entries, from everyday cherished family saloons to quite rare and desirable luxury and sports cars. One year I optimistically entered "Dumpy" on the basis that it was all for a worthy charitable cause, and taking part mattered more than the winning. This was just as well for my part as poor "Dumpy" with her bedraggled home painted and battle scarred appearance, complete with roughly-putted window seals done in a vain attempt to cure her eternal leaking problems whenever it rained, looked so shabby against the rows of gleaming other prized limousines. As she had travelled the equivalent of some eight times round the world over the previous forty-five years then she was entitled to look a little travel-stained!

One morning of early summer in the May of 1993 Teddington village found itself rudely thrust into the national news spotlight for the worst and most tragic of reasons. A young children's nanny arrived as usual for her duties at "Orchard House", just around the bend from "Applegarth", and to her unimaginable horror discovered the two children lying dead in their beds, apparently smothered. Nearby lay their mother, the victim of a vicious attack, also dead. Of the husband of the house there was no sign, but several days later his body was pulled out of the sea at Gorleston on the East coast. The shock waves from this terrible event left the village reeling in utter disbelief. It was the first time I had witnessed at first hand the national media 'circus' in action. Within a couple of hours the village street was lined with 'hi-tech' vehicles of the newsmen, many with huge satellite dishes erected on their roofs. I received a visit from the chief reporter of the Daily Mail (?) who was desperate for photographs of the unfortunate family. I later learnt that his demand had been met by some unscrupulous villager receiving an alleged £100 for a tiny blurred snapshot, although that may only have been one of the many rumours which started to abound round about Teddington. That same evening a C.I.D Officer called at Applegarth on a fruitless mission to enquire if I could help at all with their investigations, unfortunately to no avail. A couple of weeks later I witnessed the extremely moving spectacle of the hearse passing "Applegarth's" gate on its sad way to the churchyard. In it lay the distressing burden of three coffins, the larger one flanked by two pitifully small caskets. It was a private and unpublished interment.

May that little family rest in eternal peace.

Less than two years after this unhappy episode my own family suffered losses of their own.

My sister Jean had been unwell for many months and from her condition it was evident to everyone that she was in need of urgent hospital treatment. Sadly she was of the 'mind set' which dismissed any suggestion that there could be something seriously wrong and any broaching of the subject by her own nearest family immediately triggered a hostile and indignant rebuttal from her. Eventually, of course, there was no option but to undergo an operation. By this time it had become too late and Jean passed away in the February of 1995. The little chapel in Woodmancote's Stockwell Lane was overflowing into its vestry and out into the street, so many were the mourners who wished to pay Jean their final respects. She was a much loved and popular lady in Woodmancote, and was grieved for deeply by all the people who were ever privileged to have known her.

At the funeral service I sat next to my sister-in-law Gillian, the widow of my late brother. Within four weeks she too was dead, taken suddenly without warning under conditions that caused considerable distress to my surviving sister, Sheila. The two had been out enjoying their habitual Sunday afternoon walk on the shoulder of Holder's Hill, around the bottom of the Coppice which lies above Woodmancote, when Gillian collapsed as she crossed a stile. They were some distance from any form of help and poor Sheila had no option other than to leave Gillian lying where she fell and run frantically for assistance. It was the scenario of which nightmares are composed.

The outcome of these two twin tragedies was that I started suffering with the old symptoms which had remained dormant and not surfaced since my brother Tony's death over twenty years earlier; My reasoning telling me it was a manifestation of nerves was of little comfort. By unhappy chance I had given myself a nasty jolt when I accidentally touched a live electrical mains connection in the course of my work, just around this same time, and I convinced myself that the shock had somehow strained my heart. A totally irrational fear but one which became exacerbated the more I brooded over it. Once again I was caught up in a vicious circle of worry which only begets further distress, and from which the only escape is strenuous self-discipline. It took time but eventually the stress subsided and my imbalance came back 'on an even keel' once more.

Of the many and varied ventures we undertake throughout our lives there is, of course a first time for each and every one. In the summer of 1995 I added to my list of "firsts" that of posing for a local artist.

I met Carolyn at a house-warming party held at a neighbour's cottage, the home of Mike Atkinson. Mike too was a very talented artist and professional cartoonist, perhaps best known for his creation of "Fat Cat", and it was a fairly Bohemian gathering of folk who were assembled at his home on that summer's evening. I had known Carolyn only on a casual basis previously but appreciated she was of an artistic 'bent' in quite wide ranging fields, especially that of bespoke dress design and tailoring. She had recently taken up watercolour painting with the intention of undertaking paid commissions. I do not think that she had ever received formal training in that discipline but appeared to be gifted with a natural aptitude as an artist.

Mellowed no doubt by the ambience of the evening, and the persuasions of an extremely attractive lady, I ended up volunteering my services as her model in order that she gain some informal practise before undertaking other work of a more lucrative nature. I sat for her in her beautifully furnished and appointed house over two consecutive evenings. She set some gentle unobtrusive music playing in the background and I found the whole experience a totally relaxing, almost soporific, few hours. When Carolyn presented me with the completed portrait I was immediately taken aback at the characteristic likeness to my elder brother. Up until that moment I had never considered there to be any similarity between the two of us, but seeing that picture recalled old photographs of Roland from thirty years earlier.

Carolyn was then a staunch member of the Winchcombe Art Club and the following year invited me to their Summer Exhibition private preview evening. It was the first time I had ever attended such an occasion and I thought it a very civilised affair, where one could view the displayed work at leisure whilst enjoying a glass of wine and nibbles. I chose a marvellous watercolour entitled "Sheep in the Lane" by Mary Wilkinson to purchase as a memory of the delightful evening. Unbeknown to me this picture had been voted 'Best in the Show' which was an unexpected added bonus and enhanced my appreciation of its appeal.

It was through my neighbour Mike Atkinson that I became involved on 'the sharp end' of the world of commercial art. Mike undertook regular work as a caricaturist and cartoonist for greetings card publishers including the well-known "Emotional Rescue" company whose speciality was the production of quality pictorial cards with incongruous humorous captions.

They planned a 'set-up' photo shoot in Mike's previous home, a rambling double-fronted three storey old red-brick farmhouse, involving a childrens tea party where the youngsters would be given a free rein to behave as they pleased. A complimentary bar was laid on for the accompanying parents, who proceeded to join in almost unrestrainedly as their offspring! In the meantime I and a fellow photographer had been detailed to discreetly take as many pictures of the ensuing mayhem as possible. We did actually pose some of our shots to a pre-arranged brief in order to guarantee at least a proportion of useable images, but overall it was a most unusual and uninhibited-style of commision. The exposed colour films were taken off us for subsequent processing, so I did not see the end results of our efforts, which was maybe just as well!

The December of 1996 heralded my fiftieth birthday and to celebrate the occasion I and my good friend Rob Dewey organised a party in Teddington Village Hall along the lines of the regular Summer Romps, which I intend to describe fully in the following chapter. This particular milestone in my life's journey was significant as, after some eight years on from ceasing my employment with British Coal, I now qualified to benefit from their excellent staff superannuation scheme to which I had contributed for a goodly number of years.

In addition to the regular pension payable I also received a handsome cash sum and decided to treat myself to a modern car. Loretta and I had muddled along with two old Morris Minors all our married life, which meant the last twenty six years. Those aged workhorses were fine for trundling around the locality but for any distance, especially motorway driving, a vehicle with longer legs was needed and one more in line with the safety demands and speeds of modern motoring.

I scanned the newspaper 'classifieds' hoping to spot a middle-range Ford saloon, but actually ended up with quite a 'beefy' Ford Sapphire two-litre Ghia model. It was somewhat larger and boasted more refinements than we needed, but it served its purpose and took us out and about so effortlessly over far greater distances than little Dumpy ever could. Now we could actually make it to Weston-Super-Mare and back in a single day!

One baptism of fire, which it had to undergo, was a full service and a couple of minor repairs at my regular local garage. A family firm, it is a traditional country business handling most aspects of vehicle repairs, servicing and testing with the usual forecourt fuel pumps and a small shop. It is run entirely by innumerable members of the family, all seeming to play a part in the everyday affairs of the business.

I have given them my work to do since moving to Teddington and our relationship has become something of a 'love-hate' one, straining my usually placid patience to breaking point on occasions. I suppose it is probably the same with any other small family business, but it is nigh on impossible to spur them into making a start on the proposed work. You deliver your car to them on the agreed booked date and after a decent interval has elapsed of maybe a week or two an enquiry to them elicits a long doggerel concerning how busy the work load has suddenly become and so on. In the meantime one's vehicle has disappeared to a 'dead park' out the back of the premises, in the case of my Morris Minor "Dumpy" entailing buckets having to be left under the dashboard to catch the rainwater which leaks through the windscreen seals whenever she is left outside in wet weather. The weeks roll into months until you have virtually forgotten you ever owned the car, when out of the blue it is delivered back to your house, work completed and the documentation, certificates and the dreaded bill neatly left on the front seat. Straightaway one's attitude changes from 'never again' to 'they are not so bad really'. And neither are they so bad, the work is always honestly well done by conscientious mechanics who are as friendly a team of men that you could wish for.

Only once has anything gone seriously wrong with my dealings with them and it was, in fairness, a totally unforeseen incident and one in which I can now see the humour. At the time it was a very different story. I had gone to the garage for our second Morris Minor which was ready for collection after some repair work and the statutory Ministry test. As I was reversing her out of the workshop clutching my M.O.T certificate of road-worthiness, there was an almighty crash and the front nearside of the stricken car seemed to collapse into a chasm which had opened under her. What had happened in fact was the threaded trunnion bar supporting the front nearside suspension had become detached from the corresponding threaded socket with the ensuing calamitous result. It is actually an inherent design fault in Morris Minors that with time the offending threads wear to such an extent that it is only the weight of the car holding the joint together, and as soon as that weight is removed, as it had been whilst on the repair ramp at the garage, then the two components are free to spring apart. The blessing was that the mishap occurred where it did, as this particular mechanical breakdown usually happens out on the road whilst taking a bend at speed. The consequences of that event are not to be contemplated.

Before the end of the prevailing decade, and also the last years of the dying century, Loretta and I were invited two years in succession to join my elder brother Patrick and his wife Barbara in sharing their rented holiday accommodation in West Wales. They are both keen naturalists, especially ornithology, and possess a natural affinity with the countryside which is reflected in their obvious enjoyment and active interest in 'all things natural'

when on holiday. We did not hesitate on either occasion to accept their kind offer, and consequently spent two very fulfilling visits to that most interesting area of the Principality. There were still disturbing nuances in my memory of those unhappy holidays to the area so many years before, in fact we even passed the tin hut at Brynberian, still standing and the scene for us of so much distress on that infamous 'holiday' of 1973. But all these troubles seemed far behind us as we enjoyed the stimulating company of Patrick and Barbara with my sister Sheila who made up the fifth member of our party.

It was fascinating to observe the huge grey seals sprawled across the rocks on the Cardigan Bay coast. They had the appearance of enormous boulders themselves until one would suddenly move, ponderously dragging its great body of blubber like a giant slug over the stoney platform and disappeared into the sea with a large splash. There is a good chance of spotting schools of dolphins off that Western coast, but despite keeping my field glasses trained seawards for long periods I was disappointed in my hope of observing them.

One spectacle of Welsh wildlife we were treated to in full measure was on the visit we made to the red kite feeding station at Gigrin Farm just outside the inland town of Rhayader. Here the farm's owner has stimulated the natural increase in the kite's population by establishing a regular feeding cycle for these hitherto rarest of British birds. At one time there must have been a real danger of them disappearing completely from our skies as they were relentlessly persecuted by gamekeepers and even by naturalists themselves in less enlightened generations. But now there is a daily manifestation of this success story in conservation when at two p.m. every afternoon the skies above Gigrin Farm come alive with those wondrous swooping birds as they fly in from far and wide, up to twenty miles distance, it has been calculated, to gorge on the huge chunks of meat bucketted in off the farm tractor. The kites are joined by numbers of ravens and common crows during these feeding forays, and the general public can observe the whole spectacle from an array of purpose-built wooden hides at the bottom of the field, later visiting the adjacent smart new information centre for further edification. It was altogether the most truly memorable experience of our enjoyable break in those western reaches of Wales.

Gigrin Farm red kite feeding station.

Loretta at Laugharne Castle, 1997.

Carolyn on a visit to the Bugatti Trust.

*My fiftieth birthday party with storyteller Worcester Jerry,
once declared the 'biggest liar in Shropshire.'*

MUSIC AND SONG

From the days of my earliest memories music and songs have never been far from my conscienciousness. I recall my eldest brother Roland returning from his travels abroad with the Royal Navy, bringing back collections of large twelve inch diameter 78 R.P.M records which were played on the old wind-up gramaphone at home. Two in particular that still evoke reminders of that time are Franz Liszt's "Etude in E" and a flowing orchestral piece, which I think Roland acquired in India, entitled "The Jewels of the Madonna".

Later on my brothers Patrick and David both took up the guitar, David actually constructing his from raw materials as part of his apprenticeship in carpentry and joinery. Whilst Patrick was somewhat more inhibited in his musical performances, preferring to quietly strum away in the privacy of our home, David went on to be a member of the renowned local skiffle group "The Isaac's Cavemen". They regularly played 'alfresco' on Summer's evenings at the village inn, The Apple Tree, and I would lie abed at nights listening with ears pricked to the sounds of "Don't You Rock Me Daddy-O!" wafting across the fields and in through my open window.

I'm sorry to relate that the music and song we were taught at school did very little for my sensibilities. The school's percussion band attempted by Bizet's Carmen to the accompaniment of the music master desperately endeavouring to preserve some sort of timing and rhythm on his piano whilst the rest of us created a crescendo of wild discordant bangs and crashes from the assortment of instruments which we had bagged. The dispensation of the various instruments had been a case of a mad rush to see who got to the drums first, with yours truly ending up with a tiny triangle which merely tinkled no matter how hard it was bashed. Our singing was little better. From this it may be judged that I was somewhat in contempt of my musical tuition and appreciation, until one day my attitude was changed in an epiphantic moment.

There was a gaggle of us boys congregating in the village bus shelter, as we did habitually most evenings, when a young woman came walking by. She had a guitar case on her back and as she came abreast of us she paused and asked how far it was to Tewkesbury. It was eight miles by road from Woodmancote but if it had been eighty we could not have held her in greater awe. I had never been to that foreign town up until then and she might as well have told us she was walking to Timbukto! As we chatted she took her guitar from out of its case, asking if we would like to hear her sing a song. I was utterly capivated by this wandering minstrel, so spellbound was I that to this day to hear "There was an Old Lady who swallowed a Fly" still evokes memories of that far-off summer's evening and that age of boyhood innocence.

I resolved that one day I too would have my own guitar and learn to play and sing like that free-spirited girl, who carried her music with her to charm anyone who cared to listen as she went on her way.

It was to be several more years before I eventually did get my guitar, bought second-hand off a friend who was in a financial hole. It cost just twelve pounds, money well spent for it continues still to give me pleasure forty years later. I am ashamed to admit that my ability to play does not extend beyond that of knowing perhaps a dozen chords, enough to strum out a handful of basic accompanying tunes to what rustic songs I know. Performing in public is a giant leap for which I have yet to gather the courage.

The Falklands War was in the headlines when Rob Dewey and I first visited the Gardener's Arms music night by happy chance in the April of 1982. These weekly get-togethers were enjoyed by us both regularly over the next ten years. The format of the night's entertainment followed the pattern of two or three paid individuals who took turns to each perform on a cycle of maybe once a fortnight. Others turned up with their instruments to help out with the effort of entertaining the often rowdy assembly of locals, needing to play and sing louder and louder songs as the night progressed and became more boisterous. Electric amplification was strictly against the house rules, which created a severe test of vocal chords towards the end of the sessions.

Music forms a common bond between people of all manner of backgrounds and persuasions and the friends that we made during those nights of over twenty years ago have remained close to us. Thus stimulated by these bacchanalian evenings Rob and I ventured further afield seeking out fresh pastures of musical pleasures, one favourite venue being the historic Fleece Inn at Bretforton hidden away in the Vale of Evesham.

This interesting old pub is unusual in that it had been bequeathed to the National Trust by its late owner and landlady Miss Lola Taplin. It had been in the possession of her family for generations and under the terms of Miss Taplin's will the Fleece was to continue virtually unchanged. Thus it remained, with its collection of pewter goblets and chargers, and the witches' circles engraved on the bar room stone flags, these being an attempt in a bygone age of superstition to prevent an ingress of evil spirits down the chimney. Under the windows by the back door can still be seen the chutes built through the wall for the charitable dole of corn to lepers, who had perforce to remain at a safe distance from their patrons. Across the dusty pub yard lay the half-timbered barn and this is where the larger gatherings of musicians and singers performed, joined in the summer months by energetic displays in the yard by visiting Morris sides, the Pebworth men or maybe the Ilmington dancers, each with their jealously guarded age-old tunes and traditional dance movements.

Encouraged no doubt by exposure to all this talent Rob and I developed our own small repertoire of songs which could be given the very occasional airing to an exclusive and unsuspecting audience. My nephew Terry had recently invested in a purpose-built recording studio at Stroud and suggested we went up and lay down some trial tracks of a few of our more successful songs. So it came about on a cold January day in 1989 that "Attic Studios" resounded to the strains of "Pleasant and Delightful" and "Willie McBride", to name just two of the six or seven numbers which we labouriously assembled as a multi-track montage.

It was an extremely demanding day, for the setting up of the sophisticated equipment involved balance and recording level tests throughout the session and by the time we actually did a 'live take' poor Rob and I were mentally drained and hoarse to boot. Terry was regularly plying us with cans of beer at intervals, which in my case tends to reduce the quality of my performance somewhat. Should I ever be in need of some cheer these days then I play that little cassette tape which Terry presented me with, and within seconds I am reduced to a paroxysm of mirth on hearing the two of us launching with great gusto into one embarassing rendition after another, indefatigable to the very end!

During those early years of music nights at the Gardener's Arms, Rob and I had built up firm friendships with so many like-minded people, and one in particular deserves a special mention. Peter Doggett used to come over from his house at Toddington, some four miles away, and stand quite unobtrusively by, although it was clear he appreciated the entertainment immensely. We made a point of befriending Peter and to our pleasant surprise learned that he had once played rythm guitar in a band but was reluctant to 'go solo'. Rob and I encouraged Peter to 'take the stool' one evening, on the basis that he couldn't possibly sound worse than the two of us when in full song, and since that day he has never looked back. He subsequently became the regular singer at the Gardener's Arms, and through meeting other fellow musicians there established his own band, "Pete Dee and the Occasionally Big Band". They have become extremely successful and are in great demand thoughout Gloucestershire and even as far afield as the Home Counties.

One rather galling feature of these otherwise enjoyable nights was that of everything abruptly coming to an end when the bar closed, which in those days was a ridiculous ten thirty p.m. The music would be at its glorious best with everyone, musicians and clientelle alike, in a state of blissful rapture, borne along by the sheer exhileration of emotion, when the landlord would loudly ring the large brass handbell hanging behind the bar with a shout of 'time please!' The magic of the moment had been shattered, silence gradually fell and we slowly wended our way homewards, the music still in our heads.

An idea suddenly hit me at the end of one particularly uplifting night. What if we all went and sang somewhere else, hiring a local hall, buy a barrel of beer and even lay on some food? No money changes hands, we give our time and hospitality and others their talent. Thus it was that the Teddington Midsummer Romp was born.

Our very first Midsummer Romp we planned for the Saturday evening of June the Twenty Fourth - actually midsummer's day - in 1989. I hired Teddington Village Hall, ordered a nine gallon barrel of real ale, Jouster Bitter, brewed by Marcus Goff and his small team on the banks of the Isbourne in Winchcombe, whilst Rob organised some simple food. We set the hall up 'a la cabaret' style with candlelit individual tables, soft coloured room lights and a pair of my old red velvet lounge window curtains pinned up as a stage backdrop. These latter embellishments have become a symbol of the Romp and have been ritually draped behind the stage ever since they graced that first night. The evening was an instant success. To their credit, all our musician friends turned up as promised, with Peter Doggett even flying in from a business trip in the U.S.A. Peter has remained an unstinting supporter of the Romp, and has been the mainstay of the twenty or so ones held over the intervening years. He has unfailingly supplied and set up his amplification equipment, and on the night he, and usually his band as well if available, entertain the assembled company with his ever popular set.

Inspired by our triumph Rob and I became involved in supporting other events held around the area, not only for the enjoyment they provided but as an opportunity to meet other performers, and introduce the Romp to them in the hope they would maybe support us with a turn on the night.

The Royal Oak in Gretton has for many years hosted Wednesday night live sessions under the auspices of those two stalwarts of the local music scene, Mike Finch and Martyn Weirret. Mike is the "impressario" on these nights and is an invaluable contact with any local act worth knowing. When he is not out performing himself he manages his family business, the world famous Winchcombe Pottery. Mike's father Ray Finch M.B.E worked there under that maestro Michael Cardew during the nineteen thirties and took over the business on Cardew's departure.

Martyn, the other half of the duo, enjoys youthful looks which belie his advancing years - he is actually my senior, as I delight in reminding him on occasions! He and Mike have been friends since being teenagers.

In the early nineteen seventies they drove an old Ford Transit van from England down across Africa via the Sahara Desert, even managing to climb Mount Kilimanjaro en route, and giving impromptu concerts to the local people as they went. Martyn still retains that spirit of adventure and is a seasoned globe trotter of many years experience. He unhesitatingly takes up with great enthusiasm any fresh challenge or activity offered to him. He and I have become firm friends through our mutual love of live music, and he too is a much-appreciated supporter of our Romps. Martyn usually undertakes that most difficult of roles, the "warmer-up spot" by opening the night with a display of his inimitable repertoire. He invariably appears again with Pete Dee and the Occasional Big Band at the close of the evening when by tradition the chairs are pushed back and those who can still manage to do so enjoy this final session with spirited dancing.

The Gardener's Arms, Alderton.

The Fleece Inn, Bretforton.

The very first Teddington Midsummer's Romp. June 1989.

144.   Musicians and singers at a later 'Romp' – the red velvet curtains became a regular feature!

Much of the talent which has fuelled our romps year after year is drawn from the Royal Oak line-up, and from this has flowered the highly popular live music and real ale festival which the pub organises in the late summer, held outside against the glorious backdrop of the hills, woods and meadows of the Evesham vale. Rob and I have regularly been invited onto the stage at the afternoon session to entertain the mercifully small gatherings of die-hards who linger on after lunchtime.

I consider music is enhanced when performed "alfresco". The audience does not feel so inhibited as they might if seated in some claustrophobic hall; they can move about and discourse amongst themselves whilst still enjoying the total ambience of the occasion.

Perhaps the ultimate expressions of this style of performance are the fringe events held concurrent with the International Folk Festival in the seaside resort town of Sidmouth on Devon's south coast. For one week a year this small gentile community is transformed by the influx of many thousands of like-minded devotees of traditional music and dance. The nucleus of the event is the 'ticket only' arena where the more formal displays are held, acts drawn from diverse cultures and races worldwide. Quite separate are the countless groups and individuals who perform 'impromptu' in the pubs, street corners, along the esplanade, even in bus shelters, representing every conceivable act, no matter how peripheral or obscure, in the traditional folk gamut.

I have been a regular and enthusiastic visitor to Sidmouth for this week in late summer over the past ten years, enjoying the opportunity to become acquainted at close quarters with such an entertaining and eclectic mix of characters.

My very first visit was in the company of my daughter Louise and unfortunately it was literally a baptism for us both, being the wettest week ever experienced in the forty or more years the festival had been running. Our general misery was compounded by the fact that circumstances dictated the necessity of having to camp under canvas. Regular bed and breakfast accommodation in Sidmouth during this week of mayhem is impossible to find, for one has virtually to step into dead men's shoes to secure any sort of roof over one's head. Once found, bookings are retained year after year by the same patrons 'ad infinitum'.

Thus it was that Louise and I had perforce to pitch our pitiful little nylon 'fun tent' on the only site available, a soggy field over two miles from the activities and reached via an excruciatingly steep narrow lane rising away from the town towards Salcombe Regis. We had 'staked out' our pitch on the camp site on arrival that morning, leaving our vehicle there still fully loaded before walking down into the town. It was a scene of desolation. The esplanade, usually animated with lines of noisy artistes, morris sides prancing their routines, buskers, face painters, ceilidh bands and the razzmatazz that proclaim the spirit of the Sidmouth Folk week, had been abandoned. There was one brave undaunted soul sat on the low wall right at the end, mournfully playing a didgeridoo, its booming fog-horn note sounding out its clarion call of despondency. Even the public houses and bars had lacked their usual gaiety on that rain-drenched day. People were coming in all po-faced, shaking out their plastic mackintoshes, all prognosticating about the weather. Louise and I stuck it out until nightfall and then of course had to walk back to our sodden field, trudging our weary way up that relentless hill in pitch darkness through the increasingly heavy rain. The campsite, that euphemism for a marshy plateau, was unlit. Louise and I had to set-to and erect her little tent virtually by feel and somehow managed to achieve a shelter of sorts in the blackness. We may as well have laid down in the open field to sleep, as water poured into our refuge and became trapped in the water-proof groundsheet, which in turn was transformed into a paddling-pool. I awoke from what little sleep had been granted to me in the early hours of morning to discover myself awash, my sleeping bag heavy with rain water and my polished brown leather brogues at the foot of my bed floating like miniature canoes. Louise had fared little better. Needless to relate, our initiation into the "Sidmouth Experience" was brought to an abrupt end, and that morning saw us returning whence we came, back up the M5 motorway, somewhat dampened in body and spirits.

I was determined to give the Festival another try and the following year wrote off for the official town guide. After several phone calls to accomodation addresses listed within its pages I was booked into the "Salty Monk" inn at Sidford on the main road leading eastwards to Lyme Regis. It was a very fortuitous choice, ideal in virtually every respect. The "Salty Monk" lay near the old pack horse bridge over the River Sid, and every morning I would follow a path down the Sid Valley, a walk of about one and a half miles, to emerge from a wooded park into the town barely a further two minutes walk onto the seafront.

I stayed at the "Salty Monk" for another two consecutive years running, and what hugely enjoyable and relaxing breaks they were. No more leaking tents!

My good friend Rob Dewey expressed a wish to join me one year and contrived an invitation to stay with an ex-colleague of his partner, Clancy Kitson, who lived in Newton Poppleford, some three miles out of Sidmouth on the busy Exeter road. Clancy made us so welcome in her home, seeming to enjoy our company as a change to her usual solitary lifestyle. The three of us celebrated our departure and her hospitality with dinner at the local Italian restaurant at the end of each of the three or four years that Rob and I visited her. It made a fitting end to a stimulating few days of music, song and dance.

As Rob and I continued to garner more and more performers to support our annual Teddington Midsummer's Romp so did the event become bigger by the year until it had hopelessly outgrown the tiny village hall in which it was held. I was acutely aware that under the terms of the hiring agreement we were

The Royal Oak Beer and Music Festival at Gretton with Pete Dee on the stage.

Sidmouth Folk Week with regular 'fringe' musicians providing the seafront entertainment.

The Midsummer Romp marquee at Red Barn Farm.

Ken Langsbury with his charismatic entourage "The Bubonic Wind Band."

permitted a maximum of only seventy people in the hall. This was very difficult to police as folk were continually coming and going all evening and many stood outside on the lawn enjoying the last of the summer's warmth. There were other considerations, such as noise levels and general disturbance, parking problems and the onerous task the following morning of restoring the hall to its pristine state, hoping anxiously that no serious damage would confront us as we drew back the curtains.

Fortunately the worst drama was the discovery of a red wine stain on the Women's Institute President's oak armchair which luckily a judicious application of warm soapy water eventually removed!

After the particularly well-attended Romp of 2001 our good friends Nigel and Irene Fisher of the Red Barn farm in our neighbouring village of Alstone offered to host the following year's Romp on their land in a marquee which they would organise for us. It was an incredibly generous gesture and one which Rob and I accepted with sincere appreciation. The potential for our Romp was now far less restrained. The following year Nigel, for whom the word 'small' does not exist, hired an enormous marquee, the largest the company could supply and one which could have contained the entire Bertram Mill's Circus show complete with elephants! Another of our loyal friends David Cramp of nearby Alderton village arranged the loan of the sectional wooden stage from their village hall. The transporting and re-erection of this stage has proved to be the most arduous feature of setting up the new-style Romp every Summer. It consists of a series of heavy cumbersome chipboard panels which when slotted together form a series of four feet square podiums, a maximum of sixteen altogether, each about fifteen inches high. These can be butted together into a purpose-built configuration to suit the layout of the space available, and the resulting stage provides the 'nerve centre' around which the Romp revolves.

There was an extra dimension added to the Romp's character when Nigel offered the field normally set aside for the Caravan Club rallies as an overnight campsite for dedicated 'Rompers' who wished to prolong their stay. When I return the morning after to assist with the stripping down of the stage and general clearing up, most of the ragbag collection of tents are still securely zipped up, with their bleary eyed occupants yet to emerge and face the new dawn!

In 2003 Rob and I decided by mutual accord to make that season's 15th Midsummer Romp our final one. Much to our surprise and mild embarrassment towards the end of the evening a presentation was made to us in recognition of our efforts by that stalwart and good friend Peter Doggett, first making one of his characteristic and thoughtfully composed humorous speeches. Rob and I then each received a marvellous framed watercolour caricature representing us both on the romp stage backed by those famous red velvet curtains. In addition, Peter handed us both two boxes containing pairs of zoom binoculars with the result that we were both rendered speechless. I deduced later on that our thanks for organising such a touching display of appreciation must go to Rob's partner

Patricia and David Cramp's dear wife Veronica. Both these super ladies lent their wholehearted support with assisting me and Rob over the years and really they too deserved their own presentations.

So overwhelmed were Rob and I on that night that it took very little effort to persuade us to continue running the Romp for a further five years!

But now, as I write the twentieth Romp is nigh and we are determined that shall be our very last one. Time will tell if anybody else takes on our mantle and carries on the Romp tradition in some form. It has been a totally rewarding experience and we have enjoyed the making of countless friends far too numerous to credit in the course of this account. But I take the opportunity here should any of them ever chance to read these words, of thanking them all for the supreme pleasure and memories that they have freely given us and so many others to savour during the last twenty years.

It has been a lot of fun!

PRESCOTT AND BUGATTIS

Many people, if asked about Bugattis, would probably reply along the lines "it is an old make of Italian racing car". They would be only fractionally correct, for there are indeed pre-war racing cars badged "Bugatti", but the story is far deeper and wide-ranging.

For a start, Ettore Bugatti the car maker, although Milanese by birth and spending his childhood in that Italian city, established his new factory in 1909 in the Alsace town of Molsheim near Strasburg.

Ettore sprang from an artistic family background, his father Carlo was a talented and successful artist and maker of a bizarre style of furniture, now highly collectable as examples of the 'Belle Epoch'.

His younger brother, christened with uncanny perspicuity Rembrandt, became a brilliant sculptor whose genius was tragically cut short when he took his own life at the young age of just thirty one years old in 1916.

The cars which Ettore designed and built were an instant success, both commercially and on the racing circuits of Europe. A clever ploy was to make available for sale the sports and racing cars concurrent with the saloon and touring models of the margue, many of the latter enjoying a similar cachet as their thoroughbred cousins.

Not for nothing was the phrase "Pur Sang" coined to describe the exotic products issuing from the factory in Molsheim.

During the 1920's Bugatti cars earned a deserved reputation for luxury , speed and glamour, and on the fashionable racetracks of Estoril, Miramas, San Sebastian and Monaco the cars in their livery of French Racing Blue carried all before them. Their drivers were accorded the adulation normally reserved for film stars, indeed many were extremely wealthy in their own right and raced cars as an indulgence.

It is not surprising therefore that to own and be seen driving a Bugatti became a desirable aim and in this respect England in the 1920's and 1930's was a profitable market for the company.

In 1929 a small group of these owners met with the intention of uniting to form a club and so the Bugatti Owners Club (B.O.C) was born.

Many of the models driven by these enthusiasts were of phenomenally high performance by the standards of the day as they were virtually modified Grand Prix racing cars.

For example the Bugatti Type 43 sports tourer was powered by a 2.3 litre supercharged engine similar to that in the archetypal classic Type 35 'blown' grand prix model, and boasted a top speed in excess of 110mph.

This was in that period before 1930 when the maximum permitted speed on Britain's roads was a paltry 20mph! Understandably, those London-based wealthy club members were frustrated and in order to use their limousines to full potential they started organising speed trials and hill climbs on private roads, such as those serving the bourgeoning housing estates of Chalfont and Amersham in the Home Counties. This was clearly an unsatisfactory and short-term solution to their problem, but in 1937 the ambition of owning their own track was finally realised.

A young man, Tom Rolt, later to earn fame as the successful author L.T.C Rolt, regularly visited his parents at their home in Stanley Pontlage near Winchcombe. He had in 1934 co-founded the Vintage Sports Car Club, then a keen but impoverished body who were also seeking a suitable course on which to campaign their cars. Tom became acquainted on these visits with Prescott House, barely a mile from Stanley Pontlage, and was struck by the suitability of its long, winding and steeply graded driveway up the hillside as a potential speed hill climb track. The whole estate comprising the big house and several cottages, all set in forty acres of woods and orchards, was available for purchase, and as Tom's own club had insufficient funds of its own, he arranged a meeting with the relatively affluent B.O.C. The rest is history. They bought the estate, rebuilt the driveway to a suitable standard and in the spring of 1938 ran the first of the many competitions to be held over the next seventy years on that now historic hill.

Woodmancote is less than two miles as the crow flies from Prescott and as a lad on Summer weekends I would hear the roar of the supercharged engines powering those Bugattis and other exotic machinery up that winding track.

Curiosity would overcome us village boys and we set out to walk up the steep lane to Bushcombe Wood, crossing the ancient green lane of the Grinnel track way and descend the muddy fields towards the ever increasing staccato of racing engines working at 'full chat'. We would finally sneak through into the spectator enclosures by means of the schoolboy's traditional 'hedgerow ticket' to be immediately thrilled by the sights and sounds of cars being driven at 'ten tenths' and of course that ever present evocative smell of castrol R oil pervading the air.

We could not have appreciated the finer aspects of the competition which we witnessed, but the aim of the drivers, their arms flailing wildly, was to beat the relentlessly ticking clock in their blast up the hill and thus achieve the coveted F.T.D - fastest time of the day.

I was not old enough to have seen a certain young eighteen year old make his first ever competitive drive on Prescott Hill in 1948, for by the early nineteen fifties Stirling Moss was already taking the International Motor racing world by storm and earning his well-deserved immortal fame.

As I grew older other interests began to occupy my time and these forays over Bushcombe Hill diminished. It was to be many years before I was once again drawn to Prescott and the start of a twelve year close association with the Bugatti Owners Club.

In the Autumn of 1989 I spotted a small advertisement in my local paper inviting applications from persons with photographic skills to undertake some occasional printing on a part time basis for the Bugatti Trust at Prescott Speed Hill Climb.

Although Prescott is only about three miles from my home, via country lanes, it had been many years since I had last visited the venue. I had passed by regularly, but was unaware of any Bugatti Trust, so I went up there that Saturday morning to investigate the post being advertised. To my surprise there stood a large prestigious-looking brand new building in dressed-reconstituted Cotswold stone, screened by tall trees and a hedgerow from the public highway, and cleverly designed to blend into its surroundings with a similar style to the two old Cotswold stone barns which have long characterised the vicinity of the main entrance to Prescott Hill.

Here I met the late Mrs Rosemary Burke who had been appointed to oversee and manage this innovative venture on behalf of its founder, the late Hugh Conway C.B.E. Hugh was a Bugatti owner and enthusiast of many years and acknowledged as a world authority on all things Bugatti, having several definitive and much revered books to his name.

At this time he was seventy six years of age and clearly concerned that nowhere was there established a repository to which he could bequeath his unique collection of drawings, photographs and much other Bugatti miscellany for preservation and to be made available for study 'in perpetuity'. Therefore he canvassed a number of his wealthy fellow club members, both at home and abroad, for financial backing in order to found the charitable trust at Prescott.

In the late 1980's the value at auction of artistic artefacts had reached record high levels, and vintage and classic cars were no exception. Hugh was able to fund the construction of the building in which to house the Trust from the proceeds of the sale of one of his several Bugattis, a Type 37a Grand Prix model.

A fellow founder, Alan Howarth, left his Type 35c Grand Prix car to be auctioned on his death on behalf of the Trust.

It was a well-known Bugatti, with a genuine provenance, which Alan had owned for many years and at auction fetched several hundred thousand pounds. This sum provided the necessary money for the day-to-day running of the venture, offset, it was anticipated, by proceeds from the sale of photographs and reproduction fees plus other sundry incomes. It was towards this aim that my proposed services would be utilised, all the work being done 'in house' using the purpose built darkroom.

I evidently 'passed muster' with Rosemary and with the proviso that she would confirm my appointment with Hugh Conway I could start that Monday.

Hugh was a very capable amateur photographer himself, amassing a large file of both Rolleiflex 2¹/₄" inch square and Pentax 35mm monochrome negatives and paid a photo-laboratory to enlarge them to professional-sized whole-plate glossy prints. In addition to these he had commissioned copy negatives and prints from photo-libraries and other agencies and individual sources worldwide of period historic records portraying the Bugatti story right back to the earliest days in the late 19th century.

My initial task was to sort and categorize this huge archive of photographic material and establish a library of prints mounted in twenty-four large heavy albums, all carefully cross-referenced with a readily accessible filing system.

Concurrent with this work I started sourcing additional material from other collections and individuals for copying and adding to Hugh's existing collection, at the same time fulfilling requests from customers for reprints for their own variety of purposes.

Such customers could be Bugatti owners seeking period photographs of their own cars, artists and model makers needing to authenticate details in their creations by reference to correct pictures, auction houses wanting illustrations suitable for sale catalogues, and of course the many authors of books and writers for the media, plus T.V and film production companies, all clamouring for examples from the Trust's collection. One massive tome for which we supplied well over two hundred period photographs for reproduction was the superbly researched "Bugatti - the Man and the Marque" by motoring journalist and author Jonathan Wood. I was proud on his behalf when it was awarded the coveted "Gold Star" by the American Guild of Writers on its eventual publication.

In the twelve years I spent amassing the collection it grew into what is claimed to be the biggest single collection of Bugatti-related photographs under one roof in the world.

In the course of all this effort I necessarily learnt a great deal about the Bugatti family and their many achievements. It was as if I had been handed a giant jig-saw puzzle of 20,000 pieces to put together, but finding 19,000 of them missing and having no picture on the box lid. But with time the more pieces I found and fitted into place then the easier the remaining ones were to find and slot in, and so the overall picture slowly emerged. And what a fabulous picture it was, a story of a family and of its triumphs and disasters, one which even after one hundred years seems to have no end.

Naturally, all this was still ahead of me when I joined that small team in those early days of the Trust's history. As well as myself and Rosemary Burke as curator, the administration and secretarial work was ably undertaken by Julie Bate who had previously assisted with the running of the Bugatti Owners Club.

The archiving and documentation of the priceless collection of original drawings and other similar material was in the hands of a charming American lady volunteer, the late Mrs Roselle Mary 'R.M' Eldridge. R.M was an experienced archaeologist and a long-standing friend of Hugh Conway, having originally worked for him at his London flat before moving down to Gloucestershire in order to continue the work at Prescott. Her regular home was in New Hampshire in the U.S.A and this necessitated regular and frequent trips across the Atlantic to visit her family. On these occasions I would accompany her up to Heathrow International Airport and drive her car back home, enjoying the use of it during her prolonged absences.

Hugh Conway used to make whirlwind visits to Prescott from London once a week to check on the progress of his project and liaise with us on any matters concerning the work.

I was sorry not to have come to know Hugh better, but it was not to be. Sadly he became ill that autumn and died in November 1989. My abiding memory of him during our brief acquaintance is one of a man with enormous energy and drive; great enthusiasm backed by a formidable knowledge; a man used to getting what he wanted, not by coercion but by gaining the respect of those around him. I sensed he didn't suffer fools gladly although he was magnanimous enough to admit that the other man could occasionally be right! In his younger days, at the height of his power, he had a brilliant career as an engineer, becoming the managing director of Rolls-Royce Ltd, and was responsible for the development of the Olympus engines that powered the supersonic jet airliner, Concorde.

It was apparent after his untimely death that for a short while the Trust was akin to a newly-launched ship that had lost its rudder.

Our little team were all of us on a pretty steep learning curve, everything was so novel and untried. Even the builders were still working on the premises, installing display lighting, doing various plumbing jobs and laying an attractive block paving apron in front of the Trust.

Over all this hung the spectre of the official opening of the Trust, scheduled for March 1990, and to be performed by none other than H.R.H Prince Phillip, Duke of Edinburgh. I understood that Hugh Conway had made his acquaintance whilst acting as the Technical Member on the British Metrication Board and was not a man to let the opportunity pass of asking the Royal favour. (as an aside, Hugh designed the fifty pence piece and claimed its characteristic seven-sided shape is based on pure engineering calculations!)

To compound our problems Rosemary Burke left in the New Year. She lived in a rambling period manor house near Cleobury Mortimer in Shropshire and the daily journey to and fro down to Gloucestershire had become rather onerous and time-consuming. She had plans for converting the home she shared with her partner into a high-class bed and breakfast which would have conflicted with her duties at Prescott. In her place David Sewell, a long-time club member, was appointed as curator whilst the vacancy of replacement Chairman was filled by Barrie Price, the specialist Rolls-Royce restorer and proprietor of the Lea-Francis Cars Co.

Those first three months of 1990 were all directed towards the grand opening of the Trust on the 30th March. My own efforts were mainly in providing monochrome copy negatives for which the public relations firm, commissioned to produce the elaborate display boards, could enlarge and manipulate to the best advantage.

The big day dawned bright and sunny and the Trust looked a real picture, inside and out. A large marquee had been erected to one side of the building and a local florists had lavished displays of blooms unstintingly to wonderful effect.

At eleven A.M. the red helicopter of the Queen's Flight, from R.A.F Benson in Oxfordshire, appeared in the skies and landed on the temporary pad constructed in the field opposite the Trust. The Squadron Leader piloting the aircraft later told me that His Highness frequently enjoys taking the controls himself on these short 'hops' and is a very capable pilot.

The Prince emerged, to be met by Barrie Price driving a 'James Young' bodied Type 57 Bugatti Convertible borrowed from one of the Trustees, and after a spin up the hill they returned to the Trust where the formalities of greetings from the Lord Lieutenant of the County and other V.I.P's was enacted. These niceties out of the way the visit proceeded with delightful informality, for it was a private occasion away from the intrusive lenses and microphones of the national media.

The only official photographer present was me, which made it actually quite difficult to achieve satisfactory coverage of the train of events as they occurred. For example, having pictured H.R.H arriving on our premises, protocol demanded that I stood back for Phillip to enter the building ahead of me. Consequently by the time I squeezed past the tight knot of guests following in his wake he had already signed his name on the frontispiece of the pristine leather-bound visitor's book, a gesture which I had hoped to record. Generally the Prince was very easy to photograph and actually suggested a couple of view points and poses to me which he considered suitable, literally pictures by Royal Command.

The assembled invited guests comprised a wide representation of the automotive industry and associated interests, albeit a somewhat disparate range of people, with names such as Lord Montague of Beaulieu sitting down to lunch with engineer Keith Duckworth, the one half of the world renowned Cosworth race engine name.

Altogether it was a supremely successful visit, and everybody, including our guest of honour, was totally relaxed. The one rather sad aspect to the day was that Hugh Conway had not lived to witness his vision, which he had striven so hard to turn into a reality, receive such a Royal approbation. However for our small team, the junkettings were over. It was now necessary to set-to and establish the Trust as an institution whose credibility would be respected worldwide.

Once I had settled into my new job I was struck by how fundamentally different the conditions were to any I had experienced elsewhere.

For one thing, the people I had to deal with, both the Board of Directors who were responsible for administering the Trust and also many of the 'customers' who used our services, were only doing what they were out of enjoyment. The Bugatti owners were in the main true enthusiasts and only too grateful for any help we could give them in order to perhaps enhance their knowledge of their

The Bugatti Trust building.

I appear to be stalking his Royal Highness in an attempt to catch an interesting pose!

The many invited guests at the official opening.

"Black Bess" – 5 litres of raw power.

cars, or maybe aid in the maintenance or restoration of them by supplying relevant crucial technical drawings. With regard to the directors I was conscious that we enjoyed a relationship based on trust, and one perhaps that could have been taken advantage of.

Looking back, my conditions of employment were simply a gentleman's agreement. I had the freedom to virtually come and go as I pleased and at the end of every month I wrote my 'hours worked' on a slip of paper which was sent to the Trust's accountants. Julie, our secretary, then raised a pay cheque based on the returns from the accountant which she presented to me attached to the pay slip. In return for such faith in me I was only too happy to undertake any jobs outside of my regular remit. I cut the Trust's lawns for several seasons, painted display panels, put shelves up and even installed an extension telephone in the loft area. Julie too frequently abandoned her desk and could be seen maybe emulsioning the internal plasterwork or teak-oiling the large oak exterior double-doors which admitted in the building's gable end.

We usually boasted three or four interesting Bugattis on display, all on loan from their respective owners, which we liked to change periodically. At these times we would all literally put our shoulders to the wheel and assist in the manoevering of these fairly unwieldy vehicles into place once they had been brought in off their trailers parked outside. They were usually driven into the display area up the concrete ramp from the gravel apron which served as a car park. The normally church-like silence of the Trust's interior would be rudely shattered by the 'ripping silk' crackle of a 2.3 litre supercharged racing engine, the din often exacerbated by the smoke alarms sounding as their sensors detected the blue clouds of exhaust smoke being belched out into the room. Perhaps the noisiest car of them all in the confines of the display area was "Black Bess", one of the most famous and charismatic Bugattis ever built. Dating from 1913 she boasted a huge 5 litre four-cylinder engine of agricultural proportions and was propelled via pairs of thick driving chains. She was reputed to be good for well over 100 mph although it would be a brave pilot who attempted to prove it. Her original owner had been the famous French aviator Roland Garros who was killed on active service in the latter stages of the First World War. "Black Bess" was sold to an English owner before the Second World War, was raced at the famous Brooklands track and later bought by the actor-to-be James Robertson Justice whilst he was at college. Altogether an interestingly varied and romantic provenance and one which typifies the history of many other similarly historic Bugattis.

During my work researching the many hundreds of period images, it occurred to me that often the characters appearing in them were as fascinating as the cars themselves, frequently representing the glitterati of society in the Continental Europe of the 1920's and 1930's. There were elegantly dressed ladies posing in their finery against the long sleek bonnets of exotically-bodied Bugatti coupe´s or cabriolets at the 'Concours d'elegance' held perhaps at the Parisian Longchamps racecourse. Well-known owners at this time of pre-war extravagence represented the cream of 'art-deco' society. There were the wealthy Rothschild family, French entertainer Maurice Chevalier, the King Leopold of Belgium, the Princes William and Bertil of Sweden, the latter becoming a renowned racing driver. This royal penchant for Bugattis was recognised by the French Government when in 1939 they presented a Vanvooren-bodied Bugatti as a wedding present to the Shah of Persia.

In England owners from the upper echelons of society included the Hon. Dorothy Paget, Lord Cholmondely of Houghton Hall, Norfolk and even Aldous Huxley. Cars were raced by the most unlikely amateur drivers, Adrian Conan Doyle son of Sir Arthur, Dan Leno the music hall artist, Bill 'wakey-wakey' Cotton and sadly several high profile names were to lose their lives in pursuit of speed. Prince George Lobkowitz died on the Avus track in Berlin, Count Craykowski at Monza and the Duke of Grafton during the Limerick Grand Prix. The car involved in this latter accident had a subsequent unlucky history for in 1948 English driver Kenneth Bear was killed driving it in a race on Jersey, taking with him a track marshall and a policeman as innocent victims.

One of the most famous fatalities in history must be the actress Isadora Duncan, whose scarf became entangled in the wheel of a "Bugatti". The irony of the story is that it was actually a French Amilcar, a very downmarket vehicle compared to a Bugatti, and presumably didn't make for such a gripping news story. A possible cause of genuine confusion may have been that her driver on that fateful evening was a well-known Bugatti racing driver in a borrowed car.

Today, Bugatti cars may still be found in the possession of the rich and famous but often for very different reasons. Their value as desirable items for investment has put them out of reach of the average person, and ownership has become the province of wealthy bankers, industrialists, film and pop stars and the like, although many of these owners still use and enjoy their Bugatti to the full, even racing the sports grand prix models and embarking on adventurous inter-continental rallies. "Viva la Marque"!

Being a member of such a small team at the Trust meant that I inevitably became involved with activities other than my specific role as photographer. This became especially the case when David Sewell left to become an Independent Bugatti consultant and soon afterwards Mrs 'R.M' Eldridge fell ill, eventually returning to her home in America where she sadly died, leaving Julie and me to 'run the show' which we did quite successfully for over a year. Any particularly difficult enquiries were 'fielded' by certain designated members of the board, whilst Julie became company secretary, formalising the work which she had been making her responsibility for some time.

We hosted visits from a number of film production companies, both from home and abroad. The BBC T.V programme 'Top Gear' were frequent visitors and even produced a whole special 30 minute feature on 'Black Bess', taking her out for a spectacular blast up the Prescott track.

I recall the morning when the whole 'Masterchef' team descended on us, including the participating competitor, to film an insert for their immensely popular series. Interestingly, they were a private T.V production company working on contract to the BBC and appeared to work unfettered from the constraints associated with that vast unwieldy corporation.

One day we were approached by I.T.V and asked if we could supply an open four seater tourer for some filming. It was to take a certain Paul Gadd on a tour of his home town of Banbury whilst he reminisced on his younger days in that Oxfordshire market town. Mr Gadd was far better known as Gary Glitter, the 1970's glam-rocker before his fall from grace in the eyes of the law.

I never ceased to be amazed at the variety of people who beat a path to our door from all quarters of the world, and many of these visitors left a lasting impression on me.

One was the renowned model maker Gerald Wingrove, who had earned a reputation for his series of meticulously detailed scale automobile models. His background knowledge gained from researching every model he undertook was phenomenal, and he was able to assist me with accurately annotating several pictures in the album collection of the fabulous 'Royale' Bugatti. When Gerald retired a few years ago his own collection of exquisitely crafted models was auctioned and the Trust bid successfully for his scale-recreation of the 'Royale' rolling chassis, a bid of five figures being necessary to secure such a desirable lot.

Another feted visitor through our door was the motoring journalist Bill Boddy, often accompanied by his wife and constant companion Winifred. Bill had justifiably earned the reputation as a living legend over the many decades that he had been reporting the events and personalities of the world of motor sport through the columns of the much respected journal 'Motor Sport. Indeed, he had virtually run that magazine throughout the bleak austere war years and helped keep alive the interest in motoring pursuits. He possesses an encyclopaedic knowledge of the great British pre-war motor track Brooklands, as his definitive series of volumes chronicling the fortunes and dramas over the thirty two year history of that venue testifies. Bill's stocky erect figure, topped with a mop of tousled white hair, has become a familiar sight to generations of competitors and spectators alike at the many racetracks and club rallies, where he still continues to amass the material which so enlivens his prodigious output of motoring correspondence.

Whilst researching the huge range of Bugatti-related historic images, which we were acquiring for our photo-library, one venue regularly kept coming to my attention, the Worcestershire Hill Climb of Shelsley Walsh. Nestling in a cleft of the hills which border the River Teme some ten miles to the north-west of the city of Worcester, Shelsley has been hosting events since 1905, making it the world's oldest motor sport track still in use. The reason for its apparent remoteness from any large centre of population was the desire in those early days of avoiding adverse and often extremely hostile criticism concerning such a noisy and polluting sport. Hence burying the new mile-long track in deep countryside has resulted today in a delightful rural destination with spectacular views across the hills of the Worcestershire countryside. One of Shelsley's enduring charms is the way its character has been preserved down the years and it is instantly recognisable in any of the photographs representing the last century of its existence. I made my first visit there soon after joining the Bugatti Trust and was immediately struck by the deep sense of history and tradition which haunts the venue. The ghosts of all those long-dead drivers are all about you; the start line in the farmyard reverberates with the engine exhausts and squealing tyres which would have assailed the ears of those giants of 'yesteryear', Raymond Mays, Whitney Straight, Malcolm Campbell, Hans Stuck, even Jean Bugatti, Ettore's ill-fated son.

I walked up the narrow track, before the runs of the morning commenced, and all was so recognisable, the "S" bends, the tiered rustic seating below the woodland pathway, even the famous iron drain cover which cars can clip on leaving the 'Esses'. Those many sepia photographs with which I had become so familiar were made animated and attenuated to full colour in my brain everywhere I looked. It was indeed a very surreal experience.

In the quest for hitherto unseen photographs with which to help swell our ever growing photo-library and fill gaps in the massive picture puzzle that was slowly being assembled, I visited several potential sources of such material. The late Dudley Gahagan was one such benefactor of the Trust. His bachelor home was virtually given over as a shrine to motor sport and every available shelf and wall area filled with memorabilia amassed over many years. Dudley had been a very active motorsport devotee and had campaigned at various times a Type 37 Grand Prix Bugatti, and a rare E.R.A, the latter one of only seventeen produced by that great champion of British racing car development Raymond Mays.

I set up my photo-copying stand and lights on the study table in Dudley's rambling Surrey mansion whilst he rummaged around finding boxes of original Bugatti photographs for me to duplicate, and between while brewing up a seemingly inexhaustible stream of hot tea, served in huge china cups. It was altogether a most memorable day.

A most fruitful source of interesting and rare photographs sprang out of the relationship which we kindled with the National Motor Museum archive department. The N.M.M enjoys a long history, stretching back many years when the late John Scott-Montagu of Beaulieu developed a passion for the early cars which were then beginning to splutter their way along Britain's highways.

He had an extremely perceptive vision of the motor car's eventual evolution into what it represents today and sketches by him illustrating motorway junctions and fly-overs, even the road we now know as the M25 London Orbital motorway, would be instantly recognisable by modern highway engineers, sketches made all the more incredible by being dated 1911.

Scott-Montagu introduced the Royal Family to the motor car, giving the Prince of Wales, later crowned Kind Edward VII, his first ever ride in a Daimler around the New Forest roads of the Beaulieu Estate in 1899. This sold the idea of motorised transport to the Royal Family and incidentally established Daimler as their preferred choice, a preference which is continued to this day.

The car collection at Beaulieu started very modestly, the first models being exhibited in the drawing room of the Palace itself! The present Lord Montagu inherited his father's passion for motoring, and the museum in the form we know today was opened by him in 1962. Now the Beaulieu Estate is a major destination, not just for motor buffs, but for families who enjoy the multitude of fringe activities in the extensive Palace grounds.

The Bugatti Trust's Mrs. 'R.M' Eldridge met the Museum's curator Michael Ware at a major conference in America, where he was the guest speaker, and he kindly invited us down to Beaulieu on a 'goodwill' visit, as guests of Lord Montagu.

So it was that 'R.M', Julie Bate and myself made the first of our journeys down to Hampshire. Travelling through the Savernake Forest I was struck by the masses of fallen trees, their serried ranks bearing testament to the great gale which had devastated so much of Southern England a couple of years earlier.

On arrival we were treated royally, for after a guided tour of the museum, given personally by Michael Ware, we were taken out by him for a splendid lunch at the 'Master Builder' Hotel at Buckler's Hard on the Beaulieu River. This fascinating wharf, including the Hotel building itself, had a long history as a boat-building centre stretching back to Medieval times. The great oaken sea-going warships of the English Navy had their keels laid down in this famous yard, using timber taken from the adjacent New Forest.

Today the complex is still part of the Beaulieu Estate including the modern lucrative moorings bounding the riverside.

We returned after lunch to the museum for a more detailed inspection, focusing on their archives. The amount of material held there is staggering. For example, they have copies of virtually every motoring journal and magazine ever published, including all those of the multitude of different car clubs which once existed.

My interest, of course, centred on the photo-collection which was administered on an informal but effective system. The many thousands of prints were all classified into car or motorcycle types and simply stored as categories in large manilla thick paper wallets which themselves were kept in standard steel office filing cabinets.

On a second visit to the museum later that year, this time with David Sewell, the photo-librarian invited us to borrow the Bugatti photographs en-masse to take back to Prescott where I could research and copy them at my leisure. It was an incredibly trusting and generous gesture, and as a way of returning our gratitude I researched and annotated what pictures I could, or corrected mistitled ones, writing with a soft pencil on the reverse sides.

The N.M.M has one of the first Bugatti 1924 Type 35 Grand Prix cars on display, one of the team of six which appeared at that classic Bugatti type's famous launch on the occasion of the 1924 French G.P at Lyon.

It had pride of place near the centre of the main exhibition hall and presented an unrepeatable opportunity to photograph its chassis and engine numbers which are found stamped in highly inaccessible locations about its construction.

Hence I was spreadeagled on my back, firmly grasping my camera and attached flashgun, attempting to record what identifying numbers were still visible after seventy years.

I must have resembled the hapless victim of a road traffic accident to the bemused general public who were virtually stepping over my protruding legs as they passed by!

When Hugh Conway died so unexpectedly in the Autumn of 1989 his place as Chairman of the Trust was filled at short notice by one of the Trustees, Barrie Price. Barrie had been a Bugatti aficionado of many years, perhaps best known for owning at some time one of the rare Jean Bugatti-designed Type 57s exotically-bodied sports 'Atlantic' saloons. He had been involved in the car business all of his working life and as A.B. Price Ltd was renowned as a specialist Rolls-Royce and Bentley restorer. Barrie was also the proprietor of Lea Francis Cars Ltd, a name revered during the 1920's and 1930's world of motor sport but by the late 1950's it was a struggling concern and Barrie acquired the company in 1962 when it was really little more than a name and he thus preserved the badge if not a lot else.

I undertook several private jobs for Barrie, quite separate from my work with the Bugatti Trust, but never the less giving me a first hand insight into the world of classic vehicle restoration and also the development of new designs concurrent with the ethos and tradition of the historic badge from which those new designs sprang.

My first "field trip" was a visit to A.B.Price Ltd to record on film the range of services offered by that company for use in promotional material. Barrie owned two large premises in quite separate locations. The first, Hardwicke House near Studley in Warwickshire, is a huge red brick Victorian-style mansion set in several acres of its own grounds with a large stable yard and associated buildings. I understood the house had once been Barrie's former home but now was entirely turned over to the purpose of offices and workshops. The grounds themselves were completely overgrown and a veritable graveyard for a multitude of rusting old vehicles poking out from the brambles and nettles.

The second suite of workshops were at his private country residence in 'beggarly' Broom, south of the town of Alcester (Shakesperean scholars will recognise the sobrequet attached to the village's name!). This was where the specialist bodywork and prototype development work was undertaken.

I visited here first, turning off the public road down the private driveway to park on the courtyard where peacocks were strutting about the side entrance to the Hall. In a complex of outbuildings I photographed skilled craftsmen fabricating delicate cradles of ash frames onto which the shaped aluminium or light fabric body panels would eventually be attached, the completed structure being secured to the steel chassis frame of the vehicle.

Altogether the range of traditional skills which contribute to an entire restoration project is remarkable; joiners, panel beaters, tinsmiths, forgers, blacksmiths, upholsterers, leather workers, coachbuilders and painters all play a major role in addition to the more obvious skills of the engineers.

Such painstaking work does not come cheaply, nor quickly, and on a major project the total cost could effortlessly well exceed the final maximum value of the completed vehicle. But the accepted philosophy is that it is still money well spent and worth all the effort if only to preserve for one's future enjoyment the particular vehicle being saved.

Barrie asked me again to visit his works, this time to photograph for publicity purposes the result of a project to launch a new Lea Francis model, the Ace of Spades. The unusual name derived from the end configuration of the car's engine and twin-cam blocks, giving the appearance of that playing card motif.

The car's body was very distinctive, low and wide with a rather sinister 'crouching' posture. Barrie's son Hugh and I took it out through the Warwickshire leafy lanes to photograph it in a rural setting and also in front of the obligatory lunchtime rustic pub in the neighbouring village. Judged by modern standards it was none too comfortable and quite noisy, but probably when compared with, for example, the Mark 2 Jaguar of the 1950's it would stand up quite favourably.

I considered a subsequent 'Lea F' that Barrie developed, this one a collaborative effort with Coventry University and a well-known body stylist, a far better prospect and I suspect so did Barrie. He booked exceedingly expensive stand space for it at the National Motor Show in Birmingham's N.E.C. (to which he kindly invited me) and the BBC TV motoring programme 'Top Gear' later gave it a valuable spot on prime time television including an interview with Barrie.

The car was powered by a modern Vauxhall Omega 3 litre engine and sported looks to match. It deservedly attracted much interest and a large number of provisional orders were taken at the motor show, but I understood the big stumbling block was chronic under-investment for such a major project and production plans had necessarily to be delayed.

One final task I did for Barrie was to record a project of outstanding quality, the recreation of a Bugatti Type 64 rolling chassis. The original car represented Jean Bugatti's attempt at Molsheim in the late 1930's to develop the earlier successful 3.3 litre Type 57, enabling the firm to better meet the prevailing competition of the time. Sadly the Type 64 existed only as a single prototype, for with the untimely and tragic death of Jean Bugatti in a road accident in 1939 the project was shelved.

The gleaming rolling chassis produced by A.B.Price Ltd and which the workers pushed out onto the courtyard for me to photograph was simply stunning; aesthetically and technically it was a credit to the original designer and the team who, two generations later, recreated his vision with such perfection as a shining example of the best of British specialist engineering skills and in the true tradition of the Bugatti marque.

The Bugatti Trust enjoyed close ties with the B.O.C, its neighbour and landlord on Prescott Hill. Most, if not all the Trustees were also long-time Club members, the Trust building occupied land owned by the Club for which it paid a peppercorn rent, and the two respective premises faced one another across the wide entrance to the estate just off the public road. Therefore I found much of my work was inevitably involved in some way with the Club's activities.

The competitive events, with public admission, consisted of five weekends a year spanning British Championship runs through to grass-roots Clubmen competitions with a sixth weekend devoted to the traditional V.S.C.C occupation of the hill in August and by far the busiest with huge 'gates' of spectators, some years thought to exceed 10,000 people gathered on Prescott's famous slopes.

We always opened the Trust to the public on the Sundays for the five club weekends and on Saturday also for the prestigious V.S.C.C event. Our little team supplemented by several of our directors volunteering their services, provided continuous 'cover' to entertain our many visitors, assist with enquiries, sell books, posters, postcards and other memorabilia from our small shop counter and generally 'police' the premises. The latter was really just a gesture as in my experience people associated with motor sport are usually honest and trustworthy and I cannot recall any untoward incidents involving theft or vandalism. Our main concern was the safety of unescorted youngsters, who may have trapped their small fingers in our working 'hands on' displays of gearboxes if unsupervised.

The other main danger was the over-enthusiastic cranking of our sectional full-scale Type 30 two litre engine, with its open display of whirling gears and flailing pistons. This latter exhibit was the jewel in the crown of our displays, being originally built by the Molsheim factory for display at the 1922 Paris salon

The Lea-Francis prototype posed for publicity pictures in early 1992.

The Vintage Sports Car Club's Annual meeting at Prescott. It is nine a.m. and the cars are prepared for their timed runs on the hill. August 1997.

I enjoy a ride up Prescott Hill in a rare Bugatti Type 39 during the annual garden party.

On the startline in somewhat less decorous transport – note my full race harness! July 1997.

and later presented to King Leopold of Belgium. It is a masterpiece of top-class precision engineering - the whole cycle can be observed, pistons, valves, crankshaft, water and oil impellors all working in perfect synchronisation and providing a graphic visual demonstration of the Bugatti internal combustion engine.

It was on my very first weekend event, the opening meeting of the season in April 1990, that sadly a rare fatality occurred on the Hill. It was during the early Saturday morning practice session and made all the more tragic by involving a young man who was sharing his Westfield Sportscar with his father in the competition. Understandably the incident made for a wretched start to the new season. On a positive level, speed hill climbing is generally remarkably safe and this accident represented only the third fatality in the fifty two year history of Prescott.

That it was three too many is undisputable but in contrast I could name a dozen local road junctions which between them claimed scores of innocent lives before any official positive action was taken, and indeed many other accident black spots continue to reap their grim toll year after year.

I have ascended Prescott Hill many times, both privately as a driver and as a passenger, and hold a huge respect for the skill and judgement exhibited by the exponents of the sport.

The track is over 1132 yards of narrow tarmac, probably not wider than ten feet at any point, which snakes up the hill in a series of hairpins and 's' bends, culminating in the famous semi-circle bend at the summit, where its unguarded offside appears as a sheer drop down the hillside. This is really an illusion of the topography and in reality any drivers unlucky enough to leave the track at this point within sight of the 'Finish' banner, find themselves on a gently graded grassy slope down which they are able to bump their way to the return road and the safety of the paddock again.

There are optical timing beams at certain points on the track and at Prescott the fastest speeds are recorded under the pedestrian bridge, barely 100 yards from the start line. Here the Formula One engined cars, geared for hill climbing and putting down around a thousand brake-horse-power onto the tarmac, have been timed at over 110 miles per hour.

Only a fraction of the total membership of the B.O.C ever actively participate in the competitions on the hill, but once a year they have the opportunity of taking their cars spiritedly up the track should they so wish.

On a Sunday in high summer the Club hold the private "Garden Party" for their members on the hill. The morning is spent judging to "Concours" standard the assemblage of Bugattis in their own dedicated area of the paddock. It is by far the largest gathering of the marque seen at Prescott and the only time many of the cars are ever seen there, a number being brought from abroad especially for the weekend Bugatti 'social rally' which precedes the garden party. It is a very popular occasion with a huge range of other cars represented, with members disporting themselves around the orchard and paddock enjoying 'al fresco' their picnic hampers or maybe a booked luncheon in the restaurant.

The hill is opened for individuals to make ascents one at a time under a skeleton marshalling system and a long queue of vehicles rapidly forms, each awaiting his or her turn for a run up the track. There is always the chance of a ride in an interesting car by merely waiting for a spare seat to materialise in the line-up. Here for the first time ever I experienced the thrill of a blast in a genuine performance-tuned hill-climb car. It was in the 4.2 litre Dutton modified sports car of Chris Rutherford, a leading contender in his class on the hill at the time. We took off from the line in a display of raw power - it was as if the ribbon of tarmac was whipped out from under us. I felt my internal organs pressed against my backbone with the sheer force of massive accelleration, a truly amazing sensation, despite Chris 'taking it easy', as he told me afterwards.

Relatively far more gentle ascents were made in the Bugattis themselves and particularly impressive was the ascent with Hugh Conway Jnr, in his Type 44 3 litre tourer using only top gear from the start to the finish line, such was the torque generated by its straight-eight cylinder engine. A similar effortless climb I enjoyed in the Type 46 Bugatti saloon owned and driven by Lord Fitzroy Raglan. Its huge 5.3 litre engine seemed to be barely ticking over as we glided majestically around the steeply-graded Pardon hairpin. This particular car had been prepared in the 1930s for a crossing of the Sahara Desert, being fitted with a lofty 'shooting brake' style body for the purpose, but in the event did not make the attempt.

The second eagerly anticipated social event was the B.O.C staff Christmas dinner party to which our small group, comprising the Bugatti Trust staff, was always cordially invited. Over several occasions the twenty or so of us revellers, including partners, descended onto the comfortable home of those two club stalwarts, Geoff and Sue Ward. They were the most perfect hosts and unfailingly made us feel so welcome with a sumptuous dinner accompanied by delicious wines, rounding off the meal with the obligatory passing of the port - in the right direction! All in all, a superb evening spent in entertaining company and one which inevitably called for a late taxi home in deference to the law!

Life at Prescott did sometimes involve some serious work on my part, for example when the Club asked me to help illustrate their famous 'Spares Catalogue'. This service was administered from Prescott by a full-time spares controller who maintained a vast 'in-house' stock of every conceivable part needed by the members to keep their cars running. The range of intricate components, many commissioned from specialist manufacturers, was staggering. I was convinced that one could virtually replicate a complete car from the ground upwards 'in situ' so comprehensive a range of parts was held there.

I set up a temporary studio in the storeroom and painstakingly laid out the complete arrays of related pieces on a four feet square white melamine coated board. Slowly I worked my way through the stock of nuts and bolts, gaskets, castings, engine covers, flanges, brake parts, even bespoke special tools, all clearly identified and with no two items overlapping. Where possible I made 'exploded' views of composite items so as to clearly indicate their structure and the relationship of one component to another.

So large was the task that it took several days before the photography was accomplished.

On finally seeing the completed bulky catalogue, bound into an easy accessible form and destined for world-wide distribution, I was inwardly reassured that all the effort was well spent, but definitely not an exercise that I should ever wish to repeat, given the choice!

Prescott has frequently attracted the type of people whom one could define as 'interesting' and my years spent there highlighted this. For example Peter Candy, who managed the B.O.C spares, was a brilliant engineer, as the replica 1927 supercharged Type 35 Bugatti that he spent many years creating testifies. I discovered that Peter was also the engineer on the team responsible for the British attempt upon the World Land speed record for a steam-driven vehicle. This is no typically English eccentric and bizarre stunt, but a project undertaken in deadly earnest. It must be remembered that in 1907 the Land Speed Record was held by a Stanley Steam car achieved on Daytona beach, U.S.A at 127.66 m.p.h, a record it held for three years and not broken by more than 30m.p.h for another eighteen years. In fact, a second attempt that same year ended in near disaster for driver Fred Marriott when the Stanley crashed at a reputed 200m.p.h!

The honorary archivist working for the Club at this time was the late Chris Tooley. I learnt that prior to his retirement he had worked on the British 'Blue Streak' aerospace project, but his past concealed an even more thrilling activity. Chris had been a member of the British Motor Corporation's World Rally Team in the 1950s, managed by the legendary Marcus Chambers who entered his team for most of the glamorous Continental and European events. Chris's regular co-driver was John Gott, a decorated wartime hero and destined to be appointed Chief Constable of Northamptonshire. Between them they led the battle for supremacy against top International opposition on rallies such as the Tulip, the Liege-Rome, various Alpine rallies and of course the famous Monte Carlo.

Their regular competition cars were the MGA and Healey 3000 sports models, but I was fascinated to learn that Chris had also driven the Morris Minor 'NMO 933' to be later campaigned with phenomenal success by Pat Moss, sister to Stirling, and which she affectionately christened 'Granny'.

He readily agreed to an interview by me with the intention of producing an illustrated article for the Morris Minor Owners Club magazine and even loaned me his set of cherished photographs. Chris was more than happy with the published result and insisted on sending a copy to Marcus Chambers who apparently was still very much alive and in touch with his old protégé.

I became firm friends with Chris through this mutual interest and he invited me as his guest to a couple of meetings with the Gloucestershire Aeronautical Society of which he was a member. On these occasions he would pick me up in his own car and I straightway sensed the presence of a maestro at the wheel. Even as an elderly man Chris had lost little of that skill which had piloted him safely over the snow-clad Alps of fifty years before.

Of the lectures we enjoyed, the first was given by the chief display pilot from the Vintage Aircraft Shuttleworth Collection at Old Warden in Bedfordshire. He was an ex-test pilot and told his audience that only pilots with that background were deemed to have the skills necessary to handle the tempermental 'paper and string' machines which comprise his collection.

My second visit with Chris was to a talk given by the Professor in charge of the British project concerned with the Hubble Space Telescope. I was held spell bound by the extraordinary colour photographs captured by the telescope of distant galaxies and astronomical phenomena which he projected onto a huge screen. He went on to explain the incredible rescue mission which was mounted to repair the orbiting telescope 'in situ' and correct the manufacturing error which would otherwise have rendered the whole multi-billion pound project inoperable.

I was sorry when Chris suddenly became ill and sadly died in 1997 so soon after we had become acquainted, for I found in him an interesting and stimulating companion.

His role as Club archivist was taken on by Bob Light, the Club's regular photographer of the track events for many years. Bob's big interest lay in motorcycles, he had at one time commentated for races at such national venues as Brand's Hatch in Kent and one occasion was invited by I.T.V to the 'This is Your Life' studio recording and join in celebrating the life of centenarian Len Vale Onslow, the motor cycle pioneer and manufacurer, reckoned to be Britain's oldest working man and then still riding his own machines into his second century!

Bob is a very talented writer and has had published a marvellous picture album entitled 'Rich Mixture' which tells the previously un-recounted history of motor-cycle trials in the South Midlands. He ferreted out a wealth of unpublished original print material which I assisted him to copy prior to scanning, including the complete Leica negative file of the local motor-cycle sports photographer the late Bill Cole, to which Bob had been given privileged access.

A character who used to call in for mainly technical information to assist him with various Bugatti projects was Wolf Zeuner from Hereford. I believe he had at one time been a biology master at a well-known private school and had

L. to R.: John Gott, Pat Moss, Chris Tooley and Ann "Bill" Wisdom
with one of their team M.G. Sportscars. 1956.

Julie Bate and I receive a floral tribute from Michel Bugatti, son of Ettore, to commemorate
the 7th anniversary of Hugh Conway's death. November 1996.

Ninian Hyslop rounds Prescott's famous semi-circle in July 1938 with his Type 37 Bugatti.

*In July 1939 the Bugatti factory entered their 4.7 litre type 50B/59 single-seater
in Prescott's International event piloted by French ace J. P. Wimille.*

developed a passion for elephants, of all things. Wolf must have been a respected authority on those proboscidian mammals for I understood he was adviser to the ex-cricketer Ian Botham when the latter undertook his re-enaction of Hannibal's legendary crossing of the Alps in 217B.C with a team of elephants.

A local story which captivated Wolf was that concerning a travelling circus, one of whose elephants died whilst in rural Herefordshire maybe a century ago. The corpse of the huge beast had been buried in the field somewhere in the vicinity of the circus venue and Wolf tried to no avail in locating and exhuming the body as a curiosity and sadly died with his quest left unaccomplished.

A reconstructed elephantine skeleton displayed in the hallway of one's home to confront unsuspecting visitors would certainly have made a unique conversation piece!

Late one dreary day Julie and I had our afternoon enlivened by the visit of an elderly yet still sprightly gentleman who came marching briskly up our drive, his youthful gait belying his years. Thus came our first meeting with Ninian Hyslop, one of the remaining active pre-war club members and the best example of that 'old school' order whom it has been my pleasure to know.

Ninian had competed at Prescott in 1938 it's very first year of opening, driving his Type 37 Grand Prix Bugatti in road-equipped trim. He was proud to relate how as a volunteer marshall at the International July meeting the following year he had witnessed the Bugatti racing team ace Jean-Pierre Wimille take the factory-entered 4.7 litre Type 50B on its now famous outing up the track under the auspices of Jean Bugatti, the latter who had accompanied the equipage over from Molsheim.

Ninian became the first paid secretary of the Club, based in their London Mayfair office, and of course knew well all the original prime movers of the B.O.C. Concurrent with this involvement he played an active role in the formation of the fledgling Inland Waterways Association by assisting the two main founders of the astonishingly effective lobby group, L.T.C 'Tom' Rolt and Robert Aikeman with their crusade.

Ninian had converted a working narrow boat into a comfortable home and had 'The Don' berthed on an arm of the Grand Union in Northamptonshire where he had lived for the past twenty seven years. This idyllic lifestyle had been curtailed somewhat when he married the young lady whom he euphemistically referred to as 'his steerer' and the two newly-weds settled 'on the bank' as it is termed in canal parlance.

Ninian was then in his early-eighties and celebrated his forthcoming 90th birthday with the purchase of a Mazda MX5 silver sports car as a present to himself. His new bride told me she was rather apprehensive about travelling in it with him although I can testify that Ninian handled his new machine with great panache and style, so maybe her fears were unfounded.

Ninian became a good friend of the Trust, helping unstintingly on his regular weekly visits with the archiving and drawings collection and bestowing the benefit of his unique knowledge in enhancing the Trust's pool of information.

He enjoyed nothing better than being treated to a thrash up the hill as a passenger, preferably in a Bugatti of course, and displayed an almost childlike enthusiasm on making his fastest ascent in nearly seventy years.

It has been a genuine pleasure to have known Ninian and cement a firm friendship with him over the years and I mourned his passing in the early Spring of 2008.

During my years spent associating with so many people directly involved in the activity of motorsport I made a point of following the progress of the Formula One Grand Prix circus, the series of seventeen international races which attract such incredible interest worldwide. The man for many years most connected with the sport by the general public in Britain is T.V. commentator Murray Walker, considered by many to be the voice of Formula One. Murray had his own roots deep in motorsport, his father had been well known as a motorcyclist in his day and Murray himself had competed likewise with some success. But his greatest talent lay in commentating upon others efforts, which had begun when still a young man at the Worcestershire venue of Shelsley Walsh.

I was thrilled when one summer's weekend Murray came to Prescott as a guest of one of the sponsors and spent an hour with us in the Trust, taking a lively and intelligent interest in all aspects of our work. He was a delight to entertain as a visitor, so easy and natural to converse with and a prime example of a person whom you could truly describe 'What you see is what you get', he is totally modest and unpretentious and yet a personality who is recognised and respected literally the world over. He was in his mid-seventies when we met but still incredibly active, attending and commentating on the whole cycle of F1 races throughout the season across the face of the globe, from Canada, across Europe, South Africa, Japan, the Middle East and even Australia. It would be a most demanding schedule for a person of any age, all the more so for somebody who had qualified for their state pension for the ten years previously!

For several consecutive years during the mid 1990s the B.O.C hosted a leg of the Norwich Union Classic Car Rally. This enormously popular and well-supported rally regularly attracted entries numbering several hundred, which were sub-divided geographically into blocks of perhaps around two hundred with each block starting out from a regional centre. The plan was for each contingent to follow a prescribed route taking in places of interest along the way and the whole total entry eventually converging on a common venue, usually the Northamptonshire racing circuit of Silverstone.

The range of vehicles participating was extremely eclectic, from humble yet cherished Minis to highly desirable and important makes, Alfa Romeos, Delages and the like.

One regular entrant year after year was H.R.H Prince Michael of Kent, with his entourage of security men trailing in his wake, who always managed to be seen competing in one rare model of car after another, a Bentley Speed-Six followed by an Alvis Silver Eagle the next year and so on.

One particularly cold weekend he unexpectedly came across to see us at the Trust, casually walking through the door with his son, Lord Frederick Windsor. They probably needed to find some warmth after their fifty mile blast in an open sports car. 'Freddie' was a most pleasant young chap, then in his second year at Oxford, and was clearly enjoying immensely the weekend out in the company of his father. So it was with disbelief when a few days later I read a lurid report in the national tabloid press how he had been photographed collapsed senseless on the stairs at some drugs and alcohol fuelled party - journalistic licence at work, or what!?

From the foregoing it may be imagined that our days consisted of entertaining one celebrity after another as they all beat a path to our door, which is far from being the case.

The most pleasure was derived from the regular general public, the diverse stream of characters whom we enjoyed talking to and assisting with their enquiries. These individuals all had their own stories to regale us with and took an obvious and genuine delight in their visit.

One elderly American couple came cycling up the driveway, leaning their two machines with great care against the fence and proceeded to spend the best part of an hour with us. It transpired that they were on a five year bicycling journey around the world, a trip they had planned throughout their working lives and were now actually underway with that fabulous ambition. We were proud to learn that the Trust featured on their itinery for the trip. When they eventually took their leave of us I watched them go, two little wheeled figures disappearing round the bend in the lane. I often pondered as to their fate and whether they arrived safely back in their homeland.

"There's nowt as queer as folk" as the old saying goes and we were to discover the truth in that quip many times. Every person's character and their expectations vary enormously. Some of our visitors passively and quietly absorbed the displays, others had a burning desire to unburden their own knowledge to us or revel in maybe picking up a minor error on a caption board - "The Mannin Moar was won by the Hon. Brian Lewis in 1935 not '34" or "Louis Chiron drove a Type 35C not a Type 35B in the 1930 Monaco Grand Prix". I suppose such interest is better than showing no interest at all.

No visitor ever bettered the middle-aged lady who went about the exhibition waxing lyrically, gushing over every item from a Carlo Bugatti Art Nouveau table to a Rembrandt bronze animal study or the Jean Bugatti designed exquisite razor-edged Lidia Fiacre Coupe, which sent her into paroxysms of rapture. When she departed Julie and I collapsed with helpless mirth, for she had written in our leather-bound visitor's book "Thank you - I have just been sent to Heaven and back!"

I dare not imagine what our directors would think went on at the Trust were they ever to chance upon those comments!

By the 1950's the fortunes of the Bugatti company had dwindled dramatically. Ettore Bugatti had died in 1947, his son and natural-successor Jean already dead, the victim of a tragic accident in 1939, which left nobody in a company ravaged by the rigours of war capable of developing products necessary to meet the challenges which the new technological revolution was making.

In the summer of 1963 the business was wound up and the works handed to Hispano-Suiza. It was to be over a quarter of a century later that the Bugatti badge would once again adorn the famous horse-shoe radiator on a new car.

In 1991 the Bugatti EB110 super-sports car was launched. An enterprise had been established at Modena in Italy by a consortium of wealthy businessmen chaired by charismatic Italian Romano Artioli, and registered as Bugatti Automobili S.p.A.

The new car represented the culmination of huge investment by the Italians involving the construction of a 'hi-tech' factory supported by a fabulous promotional programme funded with virtually an 'expense no object' policy. The EB110 was a masterpiece of latest auto-technology, at its heart a 3.5 litre 12 cylinder engine boosted by no less than four turbochargers putting out 550 brake horse power through the permanent four-wheel drive transmission. Its top speed was around 240 mph making it the world's fastest legal road-going sportscar.

In 1992 the factory brought its demonstrator model from Italy to Prescott for a weekend of display and exhibition runs on the hill.

The Trust was appointed guardian of this amazing car and a small marquee was erected on the front lawn to host the reception of the invited motoring media and other V.I.P's. Our Italian visitors even produced several cases of quality champagne with which to toast the occasion, each individual bottle bearing the EB badge and contained in its own glossy blue signed box.

The EB110 made several demonstration runs up the hill, at a fraction of its potential performance, of course, but was later out 'around the block' on the public roads adjacent to Prescott.

An apocryphal story did the rounds as to how an effortless 140 mph was achieved in only third gear along the 'Poplar Row' straight on the Evesham road!

At the Prescott June 'Classic' in 1998 the Trust entertained the commentator Murray Walker pictured here with myself and Trust chairman Hugh Conway Jnr.

H.R.H. Prince Michael of Kent competed in the Norwich Union Rally of May 1991 with this 'blower' Bentley.

The world's fastest road-legal car: the Trust were the appointed guardians of the Italian Bugatti EB110 in June 1993.

One of the six fabulous Bugatti Royales: "Coupé Napoleon Sedanca de Ville."

In all some sixty EB110 sportscars were sold but the overall investment had overcome the new company and production was discontinued.

There was a subsequent 'marriage' between Bugatti Automobili and Lotus Sportscars with Romano Artioli overseeing the development and production of the Lotus Elise, apparently naming this commercially successful car after his granddaughter.

We at the Trust all received a personal invitation to the launch and demonstration at the Lotus testing ground at Hethel in Norfolk but I was unable to attend unfortunately.

The Bugatti name was destined to be resurrected yet again when the marque was taken over by the German Volkeswagen company who also acquired the revered Bentley name at around the same time.

The resulting car was again a formidable machine, badged the Veyron in recognition of Pierre Veyron the successful pre-war Bugatti racing driver, but with a price tag of some £880,000 was clearly aimed at an exclusive niche in the luxury exotic car market. With a 6.3 litre 'W18' engine producing 987 brake horse power and a claimed top speed of around 253mph it was even more potent then the Italian EB110, and its unveiling at Prescott on a wet weekend in the summer of 2007 attracted enormous world-wide interest.

The V.W company were keen on establishing a public awareness of the links with the original Bugatti cars and to this end they purchased the ultimate promotional prize, one of the only six Type 41 cars produced by the company, better known as the Bugatti Royale.

No car in history has ever been invested with such romance and legend. The six cars were produced between 1926 and 1931, being the flowering of Ettore's vision of a grand conveyance appropriate for the crowned heads of Europe. It was certainly an awesome car, with a chassis the size of a London bus powered by a straight-eight 12.7 litre engine enabling it to accelerate from walking pace to over 120mph in top gear only. Sadly Ettore's dream of a succession of Kings enjoying such luxury was destined never to materialise. For various reasons not one of the Royales was ever sold into Royalty - King Carol of Rumania suffered from what we now call 'cash-flow' problems, King Zog of Albania offended Ettore's sense of propriety with his appalling table manners and King Alfonso of Spain, actually a good friend of Ettore, who did express a genuine interest, was deposed before signing the cheque but in any case had already bought a Hispano-Suiza for himself.

All six cars survive to this day, and when I joined the Trust in 1989 the Kellner-bodied Royale had just been auctioned with great aplomb at the Royal Albert Hall in London. It had fetched the then record sum of £5.5 million and incredibly was sold on shortly afterwards to a purchaser in the Far East for a reputed £10 million!

With such a colourful history little wonder I so anticipated the visit to Prescott of the V.W car, the Binder-bodied Royale, in the Summer of 2006. Words fail to adequately describe the sight as it slowly emerged out of the massive closed transporter pantechnicon which delivered this monster car just outside the Trust's gateway. The bonnet alone, surmounted by the Rembrandt silver elephant radiator mascot, is about ten feet in length. The kerb weight of the car is nearly three tons and when we later exhibited it on the suspended floor in the Trust's annex it was decided prudent to keep the crowds of admirers at bay in case the total burden should strain the girders supporting the floor with possible catastrophic results!

Although my full time employment with the Bugattii Trust ceased in 2001 I am proud to be still considered a friend by the management team and look forward to receiving the quarterly club magazine 'Bugantics' and the Trust's own newsletter as well as the complimentary lapel guest pass for entry into the year's hill climb events. In addition it is with great pleasure that I continue to be asked back for special occasions for invited guests held at the Trust. These have been extremely interesting and unusual gatherings. For example there was a summer's evening wine and nibbles reception for the private viewing of the restored Bugatti Type 35B which won the first ever Monaco Grand Prix in 1929 and was being offered up for auction at that year's Goodwood Revival meeting with a reserve of some £3 million. It presented a fantastic opportunity to inspect at close quarters such a famous car and actually to hold the very same steering wheel that war-hero Grover-Williams had wrestled around the tortuous streets of Monte Carlo so long ago. The trophy which Williams was awarded on that victory was generously donated to the Owner's Club by his widow and was displayed on the night alongside his winning car, giving it an added poignancy.

In the Autumn of 2004 an evening talk was arranged to be given by Miranda Seymour, author of the acclaimed biography "The Bugatti Queen" concerning the life and tragic demise of Helle Nice, exotic dancer and Bugatti racing driver, the darling of the pre-war Continental racing circuits. The book was selected to be read as BBC Radio Four's 'Book of the Week' and I regret not asking Miss Seymour by what process it had been chosen for such a sought-after slot on prime-time national radio.

One the Trust's remits had always been to offer a consultancy service to any individual or organisation who needed specific information to aid any Bugatti-related projects. This help was extended in a private capacity by the curator when the long-established German company 'De Dietrich' decided to recreate their racing car of 1903. This huge veteran had been designed by Ettore Bugatti whilst engaged by De Dietrich and originally produced for the infamous Paris-Madrid road race of that year when Ettore was a young emerging designer still in his early twenties.

The Williams Trophy was won by Grover-Williams at the first Monaco Grand Prix in April 1929.

Hellé Nice: Héléne Delangle took the French 'she is nice' as her racing alias.

The monster thirteen litre Bugatti Type 5.

The Bugatti Trust Team c. 1990 (left to right): Julie Bate, 'R. M. Eldridge, David Sewell, T.C.

A replica engine, a massive four cylinder thirteen litre affair rated at 50 horsepower, was commissioned by De Dietrich and arrangements made to trans-ship it to their German works where it was to be installed on a corresponding giant replica chassis, replete with its enormous wooden artillery wheels of the period, and the completed car forming the centrepiece of an important exhibition in Strasburg.

Just prior to export, the great engine was erected on a crude frame in the Trust annex and special invitations sent out to interested parties for an evening demonstration when it was planned to fire-up the huge motor.

It was truly a spectacular event, three men were required for the procedure, one to trigger a large 5 horsepower mains electric starter motor whilst the other two held long decompression wires attached to the valve-lifters. On a given signal the starter groaned into life, turning over the heavy crankshaft and its enormous pistons and as the first deafening detonation of the combustion cycle shook the building, our two intrepid assistants dropped the valves and the whole engine burst into a staccato of explosions, filling the room with dense smoke belching from its exhaust manifold. After less than a minutes running, despite the operator desperately nursing the primitive controls, the giant beast gave out a last spluttering gasp and died, probably from chronic fuel starvation or massive advance/retard ignition failure or a combination of the two.

The demonstration enhanced respect for those early racing pioneers who hand-cranked their unyielding engines into life and then coaxed the huge jolting machines over several hundreds of miles of unmade roads at breakneck speeds of 90mph or more, with little or no braking power to cope with the certain emergencies which regularly befell them.

Hearing and observing that Leviathan recreation had a profound effect on the assembled guests that evening, so much that as the last reverberations faded we all burst into a round of spontaneous applause at experiencing history brought so vividly to life after one hundred years silence.

❧

It was with a real sense of sadness that due to completely unforeseen personal events at home I eventually had no option than to resign from the Trust in the Autumn of 2001. The day that I introduced my successor to his new role is an easy date to remember, for on arrival back home I learnt the news of the terrorists attacks in the U.S.A - it was Tuesday the 11th September.

To conclude this account of the twelve happy years spent in such a congenial job I can do no better than to quote the thoughts I expressed in a short article written for the Trust's newsletter published the following Spring:

"During my time with the Trust I have met and been helped by countless super and interesting people. The breadth and depth of knowledge held by enthusiasts of the Bugatti marque astounds me. Through our association I have made friends with so many people - Prescott and all things Bugatti forge a common bond which rises above all else. Such friendships appear destined to endure for a lifetime".

At the Trust A.G.M luncheon in December Barrie Price, on behalf of his fellow directors and several other well-wishers, presented me with a totally unexpected gift of an engraved cut-glass whisky decanter and set of tumblers. I was moved by such an unannounced gesture of kindness and appreciation and wish to thank all who contributed to that marvellous gift.

I am proud to have helped form the original team from those very early days. It has given me great satisfaction in assisting all the many 'customers'- engineers, historians, journalists, artists, model makers, owners or just ordinary day-to-day visitors, and along the way learning so much of the Bugatti story.

But above all else, its been great fun!!

THE WORLD OF BOOKS

I can never recall a time when as a child there were not books of one sort or another lying around the house. My mother was an avid reader, as was my elder brother Patrick, and between them amassed a most eclectic collection of novels which was swelled by membership of a mail order book club.

I started dipping into what for a young lad now seems a most esoteric list of titles. I worked my way through Ernest Hemingway's 'Old Man and the Sea', Paul Brick hill's 'Reach for the Sky' and was spellbound by Gerald Durrell's exploits in 'The Bafut Beagles'. These tomes were supplemented by the somewhat lighter adventures of the 'Biggles' books by Captain W.E.Johns. One battered old volume, 'Vanity Fair' by the old Harrovian and Oxford scholar Dornford Yates captivated my senses and set me off on a quest for that author's other books written in their characteristic style of 'derring-do'.

His series of 'Chandos' novels capture perfectly the genre of that period of the 1920's and early 1930's, stirring tales of grateful damsels in distress, Rolls Royces chauffeured by loyal servants who like faithful dogs showed total subservient deference to their masters and betters, and that 'noblesse oblige' which infected the upper classes when men would willingly die to perserve their family's honour. All this quaint scenario now reads very anachronistically to we who inhabit the twenty first century but nevertheless makes for a gripping narrative which is almost impossible to put down, in modern parlance a real 'page-turner'.

As my interests developed towards railway and canal topics and related industrial archaeology it was by happy chance that I discovered the excellent series of titles published by the "David and Charles" company. David St. John Thomas and Charles Hadfield were two men who enjoyed a deep passion for railways and canals respectively, and by expressing their knowledge in print came to found the publishing house bearing their names. The portfolio of titles by well-respected authors represents a cherished shelf in my bookcase containing books I have acquired over many years, most now sadly out of print and thus virtually unobtainable.

The undemanding reading usually indulged in by me as bedtime fare consists of lightweight detective novels of the Dick Francis or Agatha Christie variety. The former books chronicling the seedy unsavoury side of the horse race industry I found rather too confrontational and therefore stressful. The Queen of Crime, on the other hand, writes in a far gentler style, with little direct aggressiveness and what violence there is very much behind the scenes.

As my tastes in literature became more sophisticated I tended to settle on a handful of favourite authors whom I delighted to hunt for in second-hand shops, book-fairs and even charity shop bookshelves. As a last resort, if desperate to locate an elusive title, a number of book dealers offer a search service which comprises a computerised trawl through the inventory of other participating dealers nationwide. For me this strategy has usually produced results but lacks the excitement and satisfaction of discovering one's own obscure wish-list by dint of painstaking browsing and personal effort.

Two of the authors whose almost complete output fill several of my bookshelves both lived and worked a mere few miles from my home, albeit in opposite directions, and both men produced readable and nowadays highly collectable editions.

John Moore was raised and lived much of his life in and around the market town of Tewkesbury, and the love he harboured for his native soil finds expression in the country side and its characters that figure prominently throughout his writing. His very first literary effort to be published, the novel 'Dixon's Cubs' was penned when he was just twenty two years of age and represents an extremely mature style for one so young. Many critics have considered it to be one of his finest books.

John's middle period of work is almost Arcadian in form, portraying country life in the classic idyllic genre so beloved of sentimentalists and romantic searchers questing for that long vanished era of the pre-war days.

In contrast his very last novel 'The Waters Under the Earth' is almost visionary in content, describing a sinister changing world and the erosion and eventual disappearance of the old traditional order. The squire becomes superceded by the modern industrialist and the gentry displaced by the newly-educated proletariat. In all it is a most thought-provoking account and a fitting memorial for such a fine author whose premature death at the early age of fifty nine left the world of literature the poorer for his passing.

I met John Moore only on one occasion when I was privileged to stand alongside him and enjoy a drink in his company in the old Long Bar at the Everyman Theatre in Cheltenham, although I did make a subsequent closer acquaintance with his widow Lucille. I chatted with her at the John Moore Countryside Museum in Tewkesbury as I was dropping off a bundle of spare copies of John's books as a potential contribution to their funds. Lucille had then recently remarried, her new husband being my old headmaster from the Grammar School, Dr. Arthur Bell, and frustratingly for me she would not be drawn into talking about John but instead insisted on me meeting Dr. Bell, who would not have remembered me from Adam!

We were to meet again at a talk about John Moore's life and work held as part of the Cheltenham Literary Festival, an event which quite frankly was marred for me by one of the top table speakers, the T.V 'countryman' Robin Page, high jacking the rostrum in order to propound his own brand of political doctrine and by the chairman, Ludovic Kennedy, who was either too weak or too much of a gentleman to control him.

The second local writer whom I read and re-read with undiminished enthusiasm was the engineering historian, philosopher and pioneer of the railway and canals preservation movements, L.T.C 'Tom' Rolt. I had bought the first part of his eventual three part autobiography 'Landscape with Machines' way back in 1971 and was immediately captivated by both its content and Tom's highly readable and original style.

I regret never to have come to know him for sadly he too died relatively young in 1974. I did attend what must have been one of Tom's last public talks, at the Cheltenham Art Gallery, and the impression I came away with was that of an extremely knowledgeable and well-read man but also very sensitive and inherently maybe even a little shy.

Nearly twenty years later I was thrilled to become closely acquainted with his widow, Sonia Rolt, through my work at the Prescott Speed Hill-climb, which of course had become established before the war via her late husband's connections. Sonia still lived at Stanley Pontlarge in the old Cotswold stone house which featured so strongly in Tom's life and so when she asked me if I would take some photographs of various repairs and improvements just completed on the house I immediately accepted.

It was poignant to stand alongside the desk at which Tom had worked, turning out his series of classic biographies and engineering histories, and to look through the window in his small study at his beloved hills from which he drew so much of his inspiration.

Sonia herself had enjoyed a chequered background, having trained as an actress in the 1930's but when war broke out she volunteered for service on the English canals, joining that elite band of independent women who worked commercial-carrying narrow boats between London and the industrial Midlands. Many of these ladies were well-educated from interesting backgrounds and rather unfairly earned the sobriquet 'Idle Women' from the Inland Waterway's 'I.W' badge which was displayed on their overalls.

One of Sonia's compatriots, Emma Smith, wrote an entertaining account of their experiences entitled 'Maiden's Trip' which became a best seller when published in 1948. These two ladies gave a highly amusing talk which I attended at Postlip Hall near Winchcombe in about 2004, some sixty years after their immortal exploits in assisting with Britain's successful war effort.

Several other of this band of 'Idle Women' went on to record their adventures in print, most notably Susan Woolfit, estranged wife of that eccentric actor/manager Sir Donald Woolfit, but all of them with somewhat lesser degrees of public acclaim.

A year or so earlier Sonia had shared the rostrum at a Cheltenham Literary Festival event celebrating the writings of L.T.C Rolt in a question and answer session with novelist Susan Hill. Poor Sonia appeared somewhat ill at ease and I sensed she would have been far more forthcoming in a more relaxed and intimate setting than that of finding herself fronting an audience of several hundred people.

Books en masse are a heavy and space taking presence in one's home. Certain copies on my overflowing shelves I was unlikely to ever wish to read twice and my interest in their particular content had waned. I decided to shed that proportion of my collection which had become superfluous, and so it was that I found myself on the 'other side of the table' at several book fairs which were held from time to time in Cheltenham.

The first fair I did gave a fascinating insight into the world of book dealing. I contacted the organiser who booked me a pitch on the appointed day in the redundant church used as a venue, and I arrived in due course on the morning, Dumpy my Morris Minor packed to the gunwales with my stock, in good time long before the doors opened to the general public.

I had previously constructed a couple of quickly knocked together bookcases consisting of several open shelves, which could stand on a trestle table supplied. As I was placing my boxes of books carefully on the floor prior to sorting them out for display so my fellow stallholders descended on them, rummaging through my wares for volumes with which to boost their own stock. Amazingly I did more business that way before the doors officially opened than the rest of the day.

I was quite content to sell to the trade despite the convention which exists amongst dealers to offer a ten percent discount on such transactions.

My good friend Rob Dewey had agreed to share with me the modest cost of renting a table and thus we were able to split the duty of manning our joint stall, which gave each of us a decent break to relieve the long hours of sitting watching the endless sea of faces trailing past our table.

The afternoon became deathly quiet regarding trade and many dealers packed up their displays and left early, obviously satisfied with the busy morning's takings.

Participating in book fairs was an interesting experience but not one I should wish to repeat too often, for it was a tiring day's work bordering on tedium, all for relatively little return.

In a very peripheral way I too had become involved in writing, albeit of a minor and personal nature. For many years I had aided other authors with illustrations for articles and books and had even had published a few of my own modest efforts in magazines and the 'letters to the editor' section of the local press.

All this activity and interest conspired to lead almost subconsciously towards my own launch as an author in my own right, self-promoted and on a very small scale indeed.

The moment when the decision to write is triggered is akin to when a couple in a relationship decide to marry. The gestation of ideas and emotions builds up and which needs but a slight stimulus to explode onto the printed page.

Most first books are reputed to be semi-autobiographical. In my case I was idly sitting one day and trying to recall for my own amusement who lived where in Woodmancote village, the place of my birth and first forty years of my life. These casual jottings suddenly brought to life characters who had been dead, both in the wordly sense and also in my memory for nearly fifty years. And what a fascinating story emerged. I there and then decided to set down a formal account of these recollections, expressed in as literary style as possible, not with any intention of publication but merely to preserve such tales and details which until then had existed only in my mind.

I sat penning these thoughts and memories throughout that summer of 2002 in the splendid isolation of my summer house, undisturbed and undistracted by domestic matters. I shared my preferred seclusion with several far more illustrious writers in literary history, for Edvard Grieg penned his finest works in his writing chalet, writers Daphne du Maurier and Roald Dahl enjoying the privacy of their garden rooms, and I myself had just previously visited a nondescript 1930s style wooden garage up a narrow lane in the Carmarthenshire village of Laugharne. Here I stood and gazed at the desk where Dylan Thomas had sat agonizing with his tortured soul, producing his masterpiece 'Under Milk Wood' in the solitude of that little cabin overlooking his beloved estuary.

Thus, laboriously did my account gradually take shape, painstakingly written in long hand in a lined exercise book with its many crossings out and crudely added corrections, and being unable to type or use a word processor became a definite disadvantage.

As described earlier in this book I had assembled a huge collection of local photographs over many years previously and frequent use had been made in the past of these pictures to illustrate books and magazine articles by other authors. My natural thoughts were to incorporate a suitable selection of photographs drawn from my collection to accompany my own writings and these same thoughts led to the idea "Why not publish?"

Once that decision had been made I had to face the logistics of such a project, the first hurdle being to get my scribbles transferred into a readable form.

My daughter Louise advised me to borrow her mini-cassette dictaphone recorder and recite onto it my entire written effort which could then be professionally typed via a word processor onto a disc. I went ahead and located a young lady willing to undertake my task who worked from her home and not far from Teddington.

Then started the arduous process of slowly dictating each page, word for word, spelling out all the proper names or more obscure and technical words plus punctuations and other instructions. By the end of the session I had exhausted both my brain cells and vocal chords, and was convinced my unsuspecting transcripter would become heartily tired of the sound of my monotonous voice droning on in her earphone.

However she performed her task heroically and I drove over to collect the first set of typed proofs for checking and correcting. It was hilarious, the American spell-check system on her apparatus had either failed to recognise certain words or else conferred a totally different meaning to them, several being printed out as downright obscene! I will leave to the reader's imagination how the innocent noun 'chagrin' ended up on the typed page.

Despite carefully 'proof' reading the completed manuscript it was uncanny how mistakes still came to be overlooked and even checking through to the final completed book, errors which now glare out at me from the page.

A more pleasurable aspect of my book project was the selection from my large archive of photographs to accompany the text. Having chosen around one hundred such pictures my garden darkroom was pressed into service and the resulting prints incorporated in a paste-up of the entire book.

Concurrent with this work a title had to be decided upon and after much consideration I came down in favour of 'Under a Cotswold Height', partially reflecting Woodmancote's position, nestling on the lower slopes of Cleeve Hill, Gloucestershire's only mountain, and also echoing the title of the well-known gazetteer of 1919 by Dr. J. Henry Garrett, 'From a Cotswold Height'.

I also thought it expedient to use a 'nom de plume' to avoid the hassle of having the general public contacting me to point out errors, ordering reprints from the illustrations or generally having a moan about some personal bone of contention. In the event such people who wished to contact me merely did so through the printers. However, the name that eventually appeared on the jacket was Noel Septimus, my middle name as a Christmas baby being Noel, and as a seventh child Septimus seemed appropriate.

I did not approach a publisher, partly out of modesty but mainly the desire for independent full control over my creation, but instead invited quotes from a couple of printing firms. The prices staggered me to the point of nearly abandoning the project altogether. The first reply I received worked out at around £15 each for 200 copies and I knew that to ask even the magic £9.99 as a retail sale price was too much for such an unpretentious little volume. The big stumbling block was the initial cost of setting up a print run with subsequent copies over perhaps the first 100 books temptingly low, about £1.30 per copy in my case.

I decided to grasp the nettle and accepted a second quote where each individual copy came out at £7, still too much to expect any sort of profit on as I considered £6.99 a realistic cover price that people would be willing to pay. A retailer would expect to retain about 35% of this selling price leaving me with a loss of around £3 on every book sold, not the most canny of business deals!

The day dawned when a phone call from the printer informed me that the 400 copies I had ordered were ready for collection, and I recall now arriving back home with the four heavy cardboard boxes in my car and feeling a deep sense of anti-climax. I had accomplished what I had set out to do and sensed interest in the project waning in my heart. But of course the real work, that of actually selling the book was ahead of me. I realised that I had not thought the whole project through properly.

A publisher has the infrastructure to market his products on a national and even international scale. I was a complete novice, lacking expertise and the where withal to begin distributing those four hundred volumes sitting in my hallway at home. I remember optimistically visiting the newsagents in Woodmancote hoping to unload a sizeable chunk of the stock and feeling so crestfallen when told they would take six copies to see how they went, on a sale or return basis. On reflection I could not have expected anything more, for there was I , a complete stranger coming in cold literally off the street, attempting to peddle my wares. My saviour in this disheartening business was my old friend David Aldred, 'Olly'. He was an experienced author and restored my flagging spirits by straightway sending out several copies to professional reviewers that he knew with an accompanying covering letter in which he generously bestowed praise on my work. He also wisely submitted copies to the British Library and other national libraries for registration as necessary under the 1912 Copyright Act.

This was my first intimation that I ought to have applied for an I.S.B number which is an essential tool in the computerised stock control of bookstocks and their sales. The International Standard Book Number is advised even on the most modest of publications with low print runs.

Olly's other action for which I am grateful was introducing me to a small bookshop in Bishop's Cleeve, Courtyard Books. They accepted my book with a real enthusiasm, putting it up on their internet site and also offering copies to the Gloucestershire County Libraries who arranged hardbound versions on the local interest shelves of the twenty plus libraries which they administered countrywide.

Courtyard Books have for several years organised a bookfair in Bishop's Cleeve's historic tithe barn as a fringe event held concurrent with the Cheltenham Literary Festival. On two consecutive years I was invited to man a table featuring 'Under a Cotswold height' and offer to sign books for any purchasers.

It was rather an unnerving experience sat in the public gaze in company with twenty or thirty other far better known and seasoned writers. I was not even sure how to sign my name - should it be my real name or my adopted pseudonym 'Noel Septimus'?

In retrospect the whole exercise of writing and publishing a book was a learning curve of pretty mixed emotions. I learnt much concerning the workings of the world of books, the important practical considerations such as pegging the cover price to a realistic level, the optimum size and weight for postage purposes, the ISBN numbering, even putting the title on the spine so it is visible on a bookshelf (which I omitted to do).

There became evident a more subtle intangible aspect to becoming an author. Previously private thoughts appear in the public domain overnight and when writing down such thoughts this is often overlooked, as I found when ensconced in the isolation of my summer writing shed. However I received several letters of appreciation from a diverse range of readers who had enjoyed my book and had maybe happy recollections rekindled of times gone by.

Such approbation justified all the effort and agonising which the general public never sees.

SCOTTISH INTERLUDES

Before 1979 I had made only a couple of whistle-stop visits to Scotland and those in the course of my work, then in that year I had the opportunity of a holiday north of the border. My eldest nephew Terry invited me to make up a crew of six for a week's cruise on the Caledonian Ship Canal.

This historic waterway was originally constructed as a secure route from coast to coast across the Scottish Highlands, following the line of the Great Glen from Fort William to Inverness. The intention in its building was to avoid the treacherous and tedious traditional passage via the Pentland Firth around the north coast. The initiative was also part of a package of measures providing employment and to stimulate the economy of the ailing Scottish Highlands suffering from severe depopulation during the latter years of the eighteenth century.

The engineer appointed to overall responsibility of the project was a Scotsman, the acclaimed Thomas Telford who had about that time reconstructed the principle roads and bridge networks in that bleak inhospitable region of Northern Britain.

It was destined to be a triumph of innovative skills and determination, the largest undertaking of its kind in the world at the time.

Its route follows the geological fault line of the Great Glen for a grand total of 113 miles. 53 miles of this distance consists of sea loch whilst the freshwater lochs of Ness, Oich and Lochy account for a further 38 leaving only 23 miles of actual canal to be cut. Nevertheless the work took a gruelling 18 years toil with the first shipping passing through on its opening in 1822.

We had arranged to join our boat at Foyers on the south shore of Loch Ness at two p.m on the day of embarkation so it was decided to break our long journey from Gloucestershire northwards at an hotel in Edinburgh. This only left the final quarter of the trip to be made at a leisurely pace the following morning. As it turned out we kept our appointment at Foyers with only minutes to spare, having hopelessly underestimated 'Scottish Miles' as they exist through the Highlands, with their single carriageway main roads and relatively heavy traffic being funnelled onto them through the mountain passes and narrow bridging points.

None of the six of us possessed a jot of nautical knowledge or experience of handling boats of any size and yet just after ten minutes of briefing from the boat yard manager it was left to our initiative and commonsense to navigate Loch Ness and beyond.

We set off gamely across the choppy surface of that inland sea which actually constitutes the largest body of freshwater in Britain. Loch Lomond is superficially larger but Ness is far deeper, as our echo sounder testified, with several hundred feet of forbidding icy black depths swirling beneath our fragile glass-fibre hull. The suspension of peat particles in the water makes visibility virtually zero and its temperature of a constant 43° F. all year around means any person who has the misfortune to fall overboard loses consciousness within minutes with death ensuing shortly afterwards. Perversely, this constant temperature of such a vast reservoir of water makes frosty conditions along its shores extremely rare.

For our maiden voyage we headed westwards along the Loch towards the village of Fort Augustus, which lies approximately half way along the length of the Great Glen.

Loch Ness is a mystical stretch of water, surrounded by mountains to the north and south, and not much more than a mile or so wide. Its most prominent landmark is that of Urquart Castle standing proud on its outcrop of rock jutting from the north shore. We slowly but steadily forged our way across the wave-flecked water, breasting the white horses being whipped up by the constant fresh westerly wind. This wind is funnelled through the narrow configeration of the Great Glen and was to be a familiar characteristic of our voyaging.

There came faintly into view the clock-tower adjoining the monastery at Fort Augustus, forming a landmark on which to fix our general direction, although the distance was very deceptive. It was to be a further couple of hours before we came to make fast alongside a moored dredger lying in the canal basin. Ahead of us lay the flight of five huge locks rising up through the village. It made a most convenient berth for the night, with shops and hotels just yards from the canalside. It was to be very different at subsequent moorings on the lochs themselves as there we secured our line to floating buoys anchored someway off-shore. This meant us all clambering into the large rubber inflatable dinghy which we towed in our wake and rowing to the nearest likely looking landing place on the shore.

This was an adventurous enough procedure in broad daylight, but returning of an evening from the local hotel and crossing the inky depths in utter blackness of the Highland night, back to our boat bobbing on her mooring line, was an entirely different experience, ranging from exciting to a downright hazardous escapade.

The one slight disadvantage of nights spent in the shadow of the Fort Augustus monastery was the regular relentless clanking of the clock tower bell throughout the night which the thin walls of our cruiser did little to deaden.

The morning light revealed just how much condensation is generated in the confines of a cruiser's cabin with its six sleeping bodies. All cold surfaces were literally streaming with water, with sizeable pools forming at the base of the windows and the cabin walls aglisten with droplets. It was a feature of our home that proved to be inescapable for the entire week.

At eight A.M. the lock keeper appeared for duty and opened up the flight of locks for traffic. As built the chambers can pass craft measuring 150ft x 35ft with a draught of 13ft 6in or longer craft of 160ft on a shallower draught. By modern ship canal standards these figures are puny but in 1804 they were unprecedented. Today, with small cruisers and yachts typical of the craft which ply the canal, up to twenty boats can be squeezed into the chamber and be taken up or down the flight 'en-masse'.

The morning we made our ascent we had a fishing trawler as a fellow occupant, and as the hydraulically-operated paddles were opened and water came swirling up into the chamber the bulk of the far larger vessel began swaying about alarmingly. We amateur boatmen had secured our own cruiser by looping lines fore and aft around the lockside bollards in order to steady ourselves against this turbulence but our trawler men friends had no time for such niceties. They had probably just endured several days of the awesome waves of the North Sea breaking over their bows, pitching and tossing their boat like some child's plaything.

Later that same morning we entered Loch Oich, the smallest of the three freshwater lochs that straddle the Great Glen. Here we moored for lunch in the shadow of Invergarry Castle, now a ruin having been razed and fired during the Duke of Cumberland's vicious campaign over two hundred years earlier. Not for nothing did the notorious Duke earn the sobriquet of 'Butcher' Cumberland.

We had as a companion moored alongside us one of the last surviving 'Puffer' Victualling Inshore Craft, VIC 32. These game little steamers once plied the seas around the islands and isolated coastal villages supplying essential stores and ferrying islanders to and fro. Their flat bottoms meant they could be beached on any convenient sandy foreshore and merely floated off again at the next high tide. They earned the endearing name of 'Puffer' from the "bark" produced by the single-cylinder steam engine which propelled them, and the class has been immortalised in the charming Ealing Studios comedy 'The Maggie', the eponymous central character of the film.

No account of a visit to the Great Glen and Loch Ness would be complete without mention of the fabulous monster. One cannot help but be confronted with its promotion at every turn as it has become the basis for the local tourist industry. One evening in the Foyers Bay Hotel I experienced first hand the tales from the mouths of old locals which help to perpetuate the legend and keep it alive in people's consciousness down the years.

There was the local coach driver Ken Brown who had his vehicle frantically flagged down by the local police sergeant. The latter was on routine patrol when he saw this commotion out on the Loch and a great head rise from the surface. He stopped Ken's coach in the vain hope that some passenger may have had a camera, but to no avail. It was an old folk's outing, most of them were asleep and in any case they didn't have a camera between them!

An even more outrageous story was told by old Jock Forbes, a wily bent figure of a local, I would guess as being well into his eighties and with a penchant for spinning his yarn to innocents such as we, hearing the tale for the first time. It concerned Jock as a young man accompanying his father on a 'wild and moonlit night' along the loch side road driving in their horse and trap. Without warning the horse skidded to a halt and reared up in the shafts as a great black shape emerged from the bushes in front of them and crossing the road with a series of heaves on its flapping tentacles it disappeared with a splosh into the depths of the black water. It was the 'beastie'!

A cynic would look askance at such colourful evidence but one man we met

Menacing weather brewing over Loch Ness.

Ascending the flight of locks through Fort Augustus village, summer 1979.

Puffer Vic 32 at anchor below Invergarry Castle.

Frank Searle's Loch Ness Investigation HQ 1979.

with no such reservations was Frank Searle. Frank had left his career in the Army and devoted himself ever since on a lifetime's crusade to prove the existence of 'Nessie'. For the past twenty years he had lived in a small caravan on the shore of Loch Ness, going out every single day in his boat armed with a camera in the hope of securing that 'Holy Grail' of photographs, the legendary ichthyosaur reptile. Talking to Frank Searle one sensed his utter conviction and dismissal of any counter-arguments to his beliefs, although viewing the display of 'evidence' which he had set-up adjacent to his home, I thought it a case of seeing what you wished to see, with any convictions being in the eye of the beholder.

Over twenty years later a strange sequel to the story of Frank Searle caught my attention in the Radio Times. A T.V drama-documentary about him was listed and described how Frank had disappeared under mysterious and unexplained circumstances. Perhaps he finally obtained the evidence he had spent half a lifetime seeking, but not quite as he had anticipated!

I was destined to return to the Great Glen two years later with Loretta accompanied by my friend Rob Dewey and his girlfriend.

Rob had been inspired by the account of my previous visit and wanted to experience for himself the challenges offered by the navigation just as I had. He was not to be disappointed. We duly booked a similar cruiser, the 'Ness Naiad' from the Highland Charter Company at Foyers on Loch Ness, embarking in the September of 1981.

The four of us travelled together and as before the journey north was made in two stages. We broke the long haul only some fifty miles from our final destination at the small village of Killiecrankie on the main A9 road running through the Glen Garry pass.

It turned out to be the highlight of our week's holiday, for there we discovered a bed and breakfast in the farmhouse home of the redoubtable Mrs Wallace. This good lady was a bastion of the local Women's Institute and the perfect hostess.

We certainly did not suffer any pangs of hunger whilst in her care. That evening as we left to sample the local nightlife down in the valley her parting words to us were "You will be having your tea when you get back?" We were unsure just what this 'tea' consisted of, so as a precaution enjoyed a modest supper at an inn before returning back to the farm around eleven P.M. To our dismay Mrs. Wallace greeted us with plates of bread and jam, cakes and scones, accompanied by the largest pot of tea we had ever seen, and all laid out in the sitting room. We really had no option but to set to and tuck into this splendid repast under the watchful gaze of our hostess and her husband James.

This was not to be the end of our marathon eating trial for a few hours later we were sat down awaiting our early breakfast and looked on in utter disbelief as Mrs. Wallace wheeled in trays piled high with haggis, oatmeal cakes and black pudding for our delectation. Rob's girlfriend who had a rather delicate constitution, sat with an expression of resigned martyrdom on her face at the prospect of eating such a rich array of Highland fare. It was to be some time before any one of us had the stomach to face a plate of food again!

We arrived at Foyers under lowering ominous grey skies, the clouds hanging threateningly about the mountain tops. It was the harbinger of a week ahead for us of unrelenting rain and high winds of truly Biblical proportions. We had installed our personal belongings and general stores on board just as the raindrops began to beat on the cabin roof like drumsticks, but we nevertheless gamely cast off and headed out onto the Loch.

Once clear of the welcome shelter of our moorings 'Ness Naiad' began to pitch and roll alarmingly. In fact to turn across the prevailing current was to court disaster as the boat keeled over sideways to such a degree that the cabin table went crashing onto its side and all the pots and pans slid off the cooker in common with all the other items on board that were not secured.

We were later to learn that the Loch surface was running nine feet waves and it was considered by the locals as the worst week experienced on Loch Ness for at least ten years. Not for nothing was Foyers the site of the world's first hydro-electric power station, the squat four-square stone building still existing nearby although long since replaced by a more modern and up to date plant.

That afternoon we decided that caution was the better part of valour and made for a convenient sheltered inlet where we proposed mooring for the night on one of the yellow buoys marked on our chart. They were nowhere to be seen and it was then we discovered that the loch's water level rises dramatically under such conditions of high intense rainfall. The buoys were under the water, straining on their securing ropes and in order to make fast our mooring line we had to lean over the side of our craft and grope for the ring through which to pass our line. I ended up holding Rob by his ankles as a precaution against him tipping into the heaving black depths of the loch as he desperately plunged his arms up to their elbows into the water whilst endeavouring to grasp the errant buoy. His girlfriend passed the comment that it would be more profitable diving for pearls!

By dusk the wind had diminished and we decided to go ashore and find a bar where we could calm our frayed nerves with a dram or two. This was when we discovered that our inflatable rubber dinghy had a leak and was shrunken to half its normal size. By sheer chance we were carrying in the boat's 'service kit' a decrepit looking bicycle pump obviously included for just such a contingency. Pumping up that wretched dinghy became a feature of our voyaging for the week, even taking the pump out with us on an evening for fear of returning to our tender later that night and finding instead a giant wrinkled black rubber glove to ferry us all back to our moored cruiser.

We used to leave a small light aglow on board as an aid to help guide us back through the impenetrable darkness of the Highland night, not an altogether infallible strategy as on one occasion after rowing out into the bay towards the small beacon of the cabin lamp we discovered we were boarding the wrong boat - our own vessel lay some four hundred yards to starboard!

Nights spent in one's narrow bunk on such a storm-tossed inland sea are akin to attempting to sleep on a rocking fairground 'cakewalk' with the attendant danger of being pitched straight out onto the cabin floor. I was glad when we made the relative calm of the canal and the less aggressive smaller lochs of Oich and Lochy. Our eventual destination was the top of the famous staircase of eight locks, "Neptune's Staircase" at Banavie where the canal entered the seawater loch of Linnhe and as such beyond the permit of our licence. The town of Fort William lay ahead in the shadow of Ben Nevis, at 4406 feet Britain's highest peak. Trailing aslant down the slopes of those lofty heights could be made out the great flumes carrying water to power the aluminium smelting plant far below. There was certainly no shortage of energy available during our brief stay at that western extremity of the Great Glen, for my abiding memory of the place is one of seeing it out of our rain-besmirched cabin windows and through the torrential curtain of the incessant downpour, a monochrome landscape of utter desolation.

It was to be several years before the magic of those northern climes drew me once again. In 1987 Loretta and I decided to embark on a 'Grand Tour' of Scotland, with no definite plan, merely exploring wherever our fancy and intuition pointed us. For such a long and arduous journey using a Morris Minor was out of the question, therefore I hired a vehicle from a local company, giving us reliability and peace of mind in the event of mechanical breakdown or accidents.

So it came about that we set off up the M5 motorway one fine July morning in our canary-yellow Vauxhall Astra hatchback, clearing the Birmingham conurbation and taking the M6 on northwards, with the traffic density reducing by the mile as the open country of North Lancashire was reached. We had planned to break our long journey with an overnight stay in the Lake District and thought Keswick a suitable destination. By sheer bad luck we arrived in that picturesque little town on the shores of Derwentwater in the thick of the famous 'Keswick Bible Convention' week, and predictably all available accomodation was taken. Lady Luck chanced to smile on us that afternoon for the second guest house we enquired at had a cancellation which had just come through that very moment. We were charmed by Keswick and its attractions, with its bustling narrow streets and stone buildings spread around the central focal point of the town, the ancient Moot Hall tower. A short walk takes you past the quaint "Theatre on the Lake" to Friar's Crag on the northern shore of Derwentwater, a spot so beloved of that 19th century writer, artist and great visionary John Ruskin who drew much of his inspiration in the area. A glance back from Friar's Crag reveals the lakeside town with its glorious backcloth of Skiddaw peak. I was sorry on the morrow to bid farewell to such a captivating area and vowed to return one day for a longer stay.

However, Scotland was beckoning and by late lunchtime we found ourselves on the 'bonny banks' of Loch Lomond with the aim of making the west coast Scottish port of Oban by teatime.

We were later arriving there than anticipated for we lingered en route in the charming village of Inverary on Loch Fyne, but the lateness of the hour seemed to enhance the 'genius loci' of the town. We sat at ease on the harbour wall where behind us the 'Circus' gazed down, a noted landmark surmounting its lofty perch and burnished as a beacon in the dying rays of the westering sun, its empty shell a symbol of a failed hotel enterprise from an earlier age.

Across the harbour a David MacBrayne ferry was setting out for the Western isles, the setting sun gilding the vessel against the darkness of the far shore. In the morning we too were taking the 'road to the Isles', the iron road, for we planned to board the special steam-hauled train at Fort William and make the spectacular journey on the West Highland line northwards to the fishing village of Mallaig, and an embarkation harbour for the Isle of Skye. This railway was constructed as an extension of the West Highland route north from Glasgow and had the one basic motivation for its costly creation - fish. Vast quantities of herring were landed at Mallaig and presented enormous problems of transporting such a perishable harvest to the lucrative markets in the South. It was built by Robert MacAlpine and eventually opened to traffic in 1901. MacAlpine was an enthusiastic exploiter of the relatively new material, concrete, and utilised it so much in his work that he earned himself the sobriquet 'Concrete Bob'.

The 'piece de resistance' on the forty miles of heavily engineered route is undoubtedly the concrete Glenfinnan viaduct, its twenty one spans, each of 50 feet, striding defiantly across the glen at the head of Loch Sheil.

Our train left Fort William at eleven A.M and I estimated an hour would allow us ample time for the leisurely potter northwards, for a glance at my road atlas showed we had only about thirty miles to drive from Oban. It was not to be. For one thing the final mileage was nearer forty, taking all the many twists and turns into account and to average forty m.p.h for an hour demands speeds at times of reckless proportions. My anticipated leisurely potter became a desperate white knuckle drive as we sped around Loch Creran and along the shores of Loch Linnhe, arriving on the station concourse at Fort William with literally seconds to spare, hoping against hope that the train had not already departed. Luck was on our side for there had been such a queue at the ticket office that the departure time had been put back slightly to allow for the delay, and we joined the last two passengers waiting for their tickets, stepping into our carriage just as the guard was blowing his whistle.

It was a truly memorable journey and a welcome antidote to the earlier stress.

The mountains about us were still wreathed with the morning mists as we crossed the swing bridge over the Caledonian Canal, the scene of our traumatic voyage from six years ago. The weather could not have been more different today, Loch Eil was like a millpond, reflecting perfectly the symmetry of the hills in its mirror-like surface as we steamed along its shores.

The infamous dinghy, our only link to "Ness Naiad."

At secure moorings on the western end of Loch Ness.

The approach to the Glenfinnan viaduct.

The end of the line: Mallaig harbour.

The railway follows closely the route taken over one hundred years previously by Thomas Telford when he surveyed his historic road to the Isles, for there is no better way. It is only in recent memory that the roads have been upgraded suitable for the demands of modern traffic and thus the railway is no longer the only practicable link to the south for communities such as Mallaig.

Our train writhed its way through the glens and around the hillsides and with a sharp whistle disappeared regularly into the many tunnels cut through the granite prominences.

At Glenfinnan the approach is on a steep curve and I was able to photograph our locomotive and leading carriages as they passed onto the viaduct merely by leaning out of the window. When we passed Loch Morar, with its own legendary 'monster' it was but a few more miles to our destination, Mallaig. It is the terminus of the line although one could take the ferry across to the Isle of Skye, travel overland to Kyleakin some twenty miles north and across the new road bridge back to the mainland and the harbour town and railhead of the Kyle of Lochalsh. From the Kyle another railway, the Highland line, takes you on yet another spectacular journey across the Central Highlands from the west to east coasts and Inverness. That particular rail trip was an experience which would have to wait another twelve months for us to enjoy.

I regret not going on further north to see the wilder and more desolate areas of Sutherland but for one thing time was against us as the hire car had to be delivered back to Gloucestershire, and for another both Loretta and I secretly were yearning softer pastoral landscapes with which we were more at our familiar ease. By way of recompense we decided to explore the border country around the Cheviot Hills en route south and then take the rural ways across England and home. So it was back down General Wade's great military road, the modern A9, and across the mighty Forth bridge where we then turned east and followed the coast to the fishing port of Dunbar, with its ruined castle overlooking the harbour, the decaying curtain walls taken over by colonies of nesting seabirds.

Skirting the Lammermuir Hills we took a lunch stop at Eyemouth, a community with a sad history. It was from here in the October of 1881 that the entire fleet of local fishing vessels, forty five in all, was caught up whilst out at sea in the Great Storm of that month with the loss of 129 of that little town's men folk. Only 25 boats made it safely back to the shelter of Eyemouth's harbour.

Crossing the River Tweed at Berwick we left Scotland behind us and headed inland, our destination being the historic Border's town of Kelso. By incredible good fortune as we arrived, and left our car on the charming cobbled town square, a large company of mounted riders came sweeping around the corner and along the street right in front of where we were standing. It was the day of the famous 'Beating of the Bounds', an ancient ceremony enacted once a year by many of the local horsemen and women. It made for a memorable welcome and we lost no time in exploring the broad cobbled streets of the picturesque town. Through a gap in a wall we were treated to a view across the Tweed to Floors castle, the seat of the Duke of Roxburgh. Such an interesting area deserved a longer stay, therefore we found ourselves accomodation in the village of Town Yetholm, some five miles to the south east. We spent the following day discovering the ruined abbeys of Jedburgh, Melrose and Dryburgh (the latter the final resting place of Earl Douglas Haig and Melrose with its associations with Mary Queen of Scots) and visiting the grey stone towns of Selkirk, Hawick and Galashiels where Sir Walter Scott once resided nearby at his home 'Abbotsford'.

We continued our move southwards, down through Northumberland, crossing Emperor Hadrian's Wall and entering Teesdale at Alston, England's highest town, amidst hills patterned with remains of the long defunct lead mining industry. We chose not to linger at the famous High Force waterfalls on the Tees as car parking charges were payable due to the attraction being regarded as a tourist honey pot. Instead we went on to Barnard Castle where we joined the Great North road, the modern A1, at Scotch Corner and headed south, passing Boroughbridge with its sinister Devil's Arrows, huge prehistoric standing stones aligned in an uncanny north-south orientation. Our destination was York where I wished to visit the National Railway Museum. As a National museum, entry was free, and what a fascinating array of famous locomotives and unique artefacts are displayed under its roof. We wandered around, viewing at close quarters such diverse exhibits as Patrick Stirling's magnificent express locomotive with its eight feet diameter single-driving wheels, and opulent passenger coaches including the one enjoyed by Queen Victoria herself. It was all well worth the diversion from our prescribed route, the Great North road, on which we continued to travel southwards as far as Rutland. At an inn in the village of Greetham near Stamford we spent our remaining night. I wanted to show Loretta some of the area with which I had become familiar during my working visits several years earlier although in Oakham, the county town, the castle great hall held a surprise for me. Its walls inside are covered in emblematic giant horseshoes, many several feet in height, which have been presented to the town by long custom by all of its visiting monarchs. It was indeed an awe-inspiring sight to suddenly come across.

That same evening after supper we drove out on a foray around the local lanes and quite by chance arrived at an astonishing vista of bizarre topiary stretching across open parkland, long rows of huge yews sculpted into fantastic forms and lining a long grassy drive for as far as the eye could see. This we discovered was Clipsham Park, with its long-disused approach to the hall decorated and still maintained in such a striking fashion. Seen in the fading light of the lengthening shadows, the trees appeared as some living aboreal sentinels of a long-gone age. A few miles on is Little Bytham where the main railway line to the North is carried across the village street. In the shadow of the bridge a hanging sign on the local public house proclaims the occasion when on the 3rd July 1938 the L.N.E.R classic A4 steam locomotive "Mallard" streaked across this same bridge at 126 m.p.h and thus established the world record for steam traction, a record which will now stand for all time.

The following day we had one final call to make on the last leg of our journey homewards. Loretta wished to visit her paternal home town of Rothwell, confusingly pronounced 'Roel' by the locals. We crossed the Welland valley near Rockingham Castle, skirting the steel town of Corby and located Rothwell just west of Kettering. Loretta was thrilled to discover several large disused red-brick factory buildings lining Rothwell's main high street with the name of the works still plainly displayed "W. Ball and Son"- Royal Implement Works, an empty bracket over the doorway identified by the cast-iron lettering below it - Prize Plough where an example of W. Ball's patent plough was once proudly displayed for all who cared to glance up to admire.

In the churchyard we found the long rows of tombstones lying near the perimeter wall, all carved out with the names of previous generations of the Ball family, and Loretta posed standing amongst them for the obligatory photograph.

Rothwell church is famous for the ossuary in its vaults where the mortal remains of many thousands of souls moulder in their eternal sleep, but neither of us had the inclination to view such a macabre sight.

And so back to Gloucestershire and home. I swung up the driveway to 'Applegarth' later that afternoon and turned off the engine of our trusty little yellow Vauxhall. Since leaving, seven days earlier, we had travelled just on two thousand miles.

We decided to pay a repeat visit with a second tour in 1988 as our thirst for the Scottish Highlands had not yet been assuaged. At this distance of time the two holidays tend to merge in my mind, compounded by the fact that we were assigned the same yellow Vauxhall Astra for our second hiring. This year however we took a very different route north, opting for the east coast with the aim of making our first overnight halt in the Cheviots at Town Yetholm again where we had received such warm hospitality the previous year.

On the appointed day we set off from home in the bright sunshine of a May morning. We took an elevenses break in the small Lincolnshire market town of Brigg, known throughout the classical music world for Frederick Delius' "Brigg Fair", and soon after crossed the River Humber by its mighty bridge. When the latter was opened for traffic by H.M.Queen Elizabeth in June 1981 its single span of over one mile represented the longest of its kind anywhere in the world, a distinction it held for the next seventeen years.

Thus onwards through Hornsea alongside the Mere, Bridlington, Scarborough, Whitby with its cliff-top Abbey and Draculean associations, Middlesborough and its celebrated giant transporter bridge and then a steep dive under the River Tyne at Newcastle via the fume-ridden tunnel.

We were relieved to attain open countryside once more and enjoy the fresh green fields of the Border country. Soon after Coldstream we pulled up outside the 'Borders Hotel' in Kirk Yetholm right at the end of the Pennine Way long distance footpath, 270 miles of hard slog north over the backbone of England. We sat in the comfort of our car watching little knots of weary walkers coming down the final few yards of track and making a beeline for the bar of the hotel, hoping no doubt to claim their half pint of best bitter which that great walker and guide Alfred Wainwright had bequeathed to any who accomplished the gruelling walk in full.

Town Yetholm was but a half mile distant and we were soon being welcomed by the good Mrs Beverage, our landlady. Apart from the assurance of comfortable accomodation, I had another reason for visiting the Cheviot hills. I had noticed marked on the one inch ordnance survey map, a prominent peak rising to 1850 feet called 'The Curr' only 3_ miles from Yetholm and took up the challenge in my mind of attaining its summit on the morrow when 'Curr would conquer Curr'.

It turned out to be of difficult access involving a walk of two miles through rough terrain and forest before the climb itself was reached. I lessened the burden by driving the car off the metalled public road and bumping our way along unmade tracks until a gate barred our progress. Then it was a steady climb on foot over hillocky ground, keeping wary of treading on adders which appeared to have colonised the slopes and had a disconcerting knack of merging with the knotted mountain grasses which we were kicking our way through. Everytime we breasted a rise my hopes rose with expectation that we had finally made the summit but alas, there stretched out before us yet another sweep of 'dead ground' up to a further rise. But eventually we gained what I judged to be our goal atop 'The Curr' crowned with its cairn of rocks placed there by whose agency I knew not. I cast a glance westwards and realised with dismay that the tiny yellow speck in the distance of the darkening grey landscape far below was in fact our faithful Vauxhall to which we now had to stumble our weary way back. The pot of tea that Mrs Beverage greeted us with on our return was received with our undisguised appreciation.

The following day we made Inverness our target for we had promised ourselves the experience of a journey on the Highland Railway which follows that wild and desolate route across the neck of Scotland to the Kyle of Lochalsh on its west coast.

We found excellent accomodation in a quiet residential street on the south bank of the River Ness, facing the famed Eden Theatre on the opposite bank. It was from there but a couple of minutes drive to the station and catch the regular morning service to the Kyle, the train hauled by a diesel locomotive over the eighty two miles of extremely remote rural line.

Atop the Curr's 1850 feet summit.

The hotel which serves as a railway station: Achnasheen on the Highland line.

275

Kyle of Lochalsh station against the backdrop of the Isle of Skye.

Tarbert from our bedroom window.

The line was completed to Strome Ferry by 1870 but it was to be a further twenty seven years in the building before its terminus was reached, for those Victorian engineers had to battle their way the final miles through unyielding granite with a series of cuttings blasted through the solid rocky outcrops which obstructed the route.

Strome Ferry became the scene of the infamous fish riots when early one Sunday in June 1883 a fishing boat attempted to unload its catch there onto a waiting goods train and therebye reach the lucrative London wholesale markets by Monday.

By their actions the fishermen incurred the wrath of the strict Sabbatarians of that area of Wester Ross with the result that nearly two hundred local men obstructed the unloading and thus prevented such sacrilege on the Lord's Day. As the church clock chimed midnight the crowd melted away into the dark night and the load of fish was finally transhipped, somewhat less fresh by then!

We settled into our seats as the train set off from Inverness, rattling across the steel swing bridge which spans the Caledonian Ship Canal and heading around the Beauly Firth to Dingwall eight miles away. Here we turned off the main line and began the lonely journey westwards following a veritable succession of lochs; Garve, Luichart and Achanalt, coming to a halt at Achnasheen station near Loch Gowan. Here a royal mail van was awaiting our coming to exchange what mails there were. I noticed the station buildings also incorporated an hotel where guests could sit dining with a view directly overlooking the station platform. More lochs, Sgamhain, Dughaill and then along the shores of the sea loch of Carron, through Strome Ferry, the scene of such hostile confrontation over a hundred years earlier. Still hugging the coast and gradually swinging south our locomotive finally drew up at the buffer stop marking the end of Kyle of Lochalsh station platform and terminus of the line.

Ahead, across the neck of Loch Alsh, lay the Isle of Skye, maybe half a mile of water separating it from the mainland at this point.

A vehicle ferry was busily plying to and fro across the tiny divide and we availed ourselves of a free voyage as foot passengers to Kyleakin. We tarried there less than an hour before returning, but at least we could claim a visit to the Isle so associated with Bonnie Prince Charlie and his romantic legend.

Our journey back to Inverness was by the same train which proceeded to trundle the eighty two miles eastwards along the line where we found our car awaiting us. It had been a most memorable day's outing on one of Britain's classic "Great Railways".

I cannot recall what decided us to visit the Mull of Kintyre or by what route we arrived there from Inverness. I remember marking Campbeltown as a possible destination but long before arriving there we breasted a rise and came upon the most perfect small harbour town of Tarbert on the western shore of Loch Fyne. It was love at first sight for us both and by mutual consent we made it our base for the duration of the stay and were not to be disappointed. We booked into "The Manse" as paying guests of the young pastor's wife and discovered our room had an outstanding view overlooking the harbour with a seagull's eye across the grey roofs of the town and from where we were able to observe all the many comings and goings of sea traffic from the Sound of Bute and Loch Fyne.

Early the next day, before breakfast, I was thrilled to see entering the harbour our old friend the Puffer boat VIC 32, paintwork agleam in the morning sunshine and billowing huge clouds of black smoke from her funnel as she drew alongside the quay wall. I had last seen her at anchor under the walls of Invergarry Castle nine years earlier during my first voyage on the Caledonian Canal.

After breakfast we set out to explore the area about Tarbert towards Kintyre and were attracted down a minor road which led to the Kilbrannan Sound with views to the Island of Arran four miles across the water. We paused at a spot called Claonaig where there was a small shingle beach with a concrete slipway dipping into the sea, and there we witnessed a most surreal event. The freshening wind was whipping the surface of the Sound up into fairly high waves and as we stood gazing out to Arran there appeared a tiny speck bobbing up from behind the choppy seas and getting gradually larger as we watched. A few minutes later a MacBrayne ferry was butting onto the slipway and discharging its burden of passengers from Arran, including a N.H.S blood donor team aboard their motor coach. This animated scene dissolved just as suddenly as it had appeared and silence once more reigned, broken only by the shrieks of the gulls and the rushing tide. We were left wondering whether we had not dreamt the entire episode.

Whilst in this beautiful region of Argyll and Bute I was keen on seeing the Crinan Canal. This picturesque waterway was built as long ago as 1809 from Ardrishaig on Loch Gilp the nine miles to the tiny harbour of Crinan on the Sound of Jura, thereby saving an incredible 132 miles voyage around the Mull of Kintyre. On that bright May morning we left our car near Lochgilphead, a couple of miles from the canal's eastern reach, and set off along the towpath towards Crinan. There are 15 locks along the course of the canal, many of them with charming Keeper's cottages.

The traffic appeared to be extremely light on the day of our walk for we met only one sailing yacht and a single fishing trawler whose helmsmen shouted us a cheery greeting as he chugged past.

At Crinan harbour itself, time appeared to have passed it by. The silence was golden as we stood atop the harbour wall gazing out onto the blue waters of the Sound of Jura with its pattern of islands stretching across that glorious panorama.

There is a magic which pervades this enchanting region of Western Scotland as we discovered that same evening when we set out to investigate the coast of the area of the peninsula known as South Knapdale. On the deserted road we came to the hamlet of Kilberry where, at the Kilberry Inn we partook of supper.

The Crinan Canal.

A loch-side halt in the remote highlands.

Kelso: "Beating the Bounds."

Dusk over the Sound of Jura.

We were the only customers of the entire evening and the landlord came around and sat talking to us by the peat fire, glad of our company and the chance of somebody, with whom to chat and help ease the quietude of the night. We eventually bade him our farewells and in the light of the rapidly fading westering sun drove out onto Kilberry Head to watch its magnificent setting over the Sound. In the distance were the Isles of Islay and Jura and far beyond them to the north the Straits of Corryvreckan with its legendary whirlpool. The silence was sublime, the only sound the munching of cattle grazing about where we stood. We left this evocative spot in a state of sheer entrancement, but more was to follow as I pulled up a stony track in the half light of approaching nightfall to where an isolated ramshackle open-sided barn held its secret. Here were sheltered the famous Kilberry Standing Stones and Celtic crosses. As we moved about amongst them in the gathering gloom they took on fantastic forms, as if the spirits of the long dead ancient race whose hands had created them had been petrified into those granite monoliths.

The 'genius loci' was overpowering and we both were relieved to emerge from that hypnotic spot and gain reassuring surroundings of the twentieth century in the shape of our Vauxhall car.

We were due home on the morrow so embarked with an early start. Distances are utterly deceptive on those twisting loch side roads and it was to be over one hundred miles of driving before even Glasgow was reached, a city measured on the map as a straight line less than forty miles from Tarbert.

We crossed the border at Gretna Green and headed off the M6 motorway down through the southern fringes of the Yorkshire Dales to Skipton where we enjoyed an enormous helping of fish and chips for lunch. Then it was on to Haworth to stretch our legs with a walk along the Keighley and Worth Valley Steam railway and to see the locations immortalised in that much-loved classic film of Edith Nesbit's book ""The Railway Children".

A final break was taken in the country town of Holmfirth near Huddersfield with a much appreciated cup of tea in "Ivy's Café" of television's "Last of the Summer Wine" fame, then it was Gloucestershire and home by eventide. We had managed to add yet another two thousand miles to the odometer of our steadfast little yellow Vauxhall, but in doing so had enriched our lives with a wealth of unique Scottish memories to sustain us in the years ahead.

IRISH INTERLUDES

Ireland had long held a strong fascination for me over many years although it was not to be until 1997 that I finally got to cross the Irish Sea and visit the Emerald Isle.

In retrospect it may have been the logistics of actually getting there that deterred me, but those problems were resolved when our good friends Rob Dewey and his partner Patricia invited me and Loretta to make up a foursome at their rented holiday cottage on the Dingle Peninsula in West Kerry. The plan was for the four of us to travel together, taking Rob's car on the ferry from the north Welsh port of Holyhead to Dun Laoghaire, the port for Dublin.

Accordingly we all made the long journey northwards that September, through Snowdonia and crossing the Menai Straits onto Anglesey. We were booked from Holyhead on the latest high-speed ferry which the Stena Line were operating. Its performance was stunning and made all the shipping which we effortlessly overhauled appear to be stationary. Our vessel had a small outside observation platform at its stern and I stood there in awe watching the sea boiling and churning in our wake as the massive twin turbine-driven screws propelled us like a gigantic projectile across the Irish Sea.

In less than two hours we were disembarking at Dun Laoghaire and making our way into Dublin where we had arranged hotel accomodation in the anticipation of a night on the town.

My impression of Dublin was that of a vibrant and flourishing cosmopolitan city, and evidently benefiting from the huge investment programme underpinned by the support from the European Union.

We visited one of the many large bars where "Irish" entertainment was featured which I personally thought to be very much orientated around the tourist trade. It seemed that virtually every race except the local Irish themselves was represented there in the heaving mass of customers.

Our hotel was on the city's outskirts beside the main Belfast road out of town and consequently was extremely busy all night long. It was pleasant to get underway after a most convivial breakfast and head westwards and gain the verdant countryside around Kildare with its many horse-racing establishments and open gallops. Over ninety years previously the roads hereabouts had hosted the famed Gordon Bennett motor race of 1903 which hailed the birth of the British Racing Green livery. Racing on public roads on the British mainland has always been prohibited so when the race was due to be run on British soil the Irish authorities came to the rescue, allowing Irish roads to be used for this important International event. In recognition of such a magnanimous gesture, the Irish national colour was adopted by the British entry, as it still is to this very day.

The roads today are very different from when those Edwardian monsters were throwing up great clouds of dust in their wake and we made good progress westwards, crossing the mighty River Shannon at Limerick and arriving at the pleasant Georgian town of Tralee, the gateway to the Dingle Peninsula.

In 1891 a spectacular railway of the Irish "narrow gauge" of three feet was constructed from Tralee the thirty one miles to the town of Dingle, catering mainly for the monthly cattle fairs held in the latter place, the regular fish trade and local passenger traffic. It was one of the most severely graded lines in the British Isles, crossing as it did the Slieve Mish mountain via the Glenagalt Pass at 680ft above sea level in a series of hair-raising switchbacks resembling an enormous fairground big-dipper ride. As may be imagined, runaways and derailments were frequent occurrences though mercifully with remarkably few fatalities.

The first mile or so of track from Tralee to the harbour of Blennerville with its windmill landmark has been preserved and runs as a steam heritage line. The last surviving locomotive from the railway was found languishing in America and returned here to its original home, pulling the little rake of antiquated carriages crowded with happy holidaymakers. It was very different over a century ago for Blennerville has a poignant history as the embarkation port for the many thousands of Irish emigrees who set sail from there in the mid-nineteenth century, often whole families, escaping the poverty and hunger of their native land to head for a new life in the Americas. Sadly many passengers never survived the squalor, disease and deprivation of the long sea voyage to the extent that the vessels were dubbed "Coffin Ships".

A museum has been established at Blennerville in memory of those tragic times and a visit there is an extremely moving and thought-provoking experience.

Our way to Dingle closely followed the bed of the long-defunct railway, indeed long sections of the track originally ran along the public highway causing confusion and mayhem amongst the regular road users, as may well be imagined.

The cottage Rob had taken was situated on the road out of Dingle which headed north east to climb the Connor Pass. At its summit of 1354ft one can stand and literally look back over Dingle Bay and ahead the other side of the height, across miles of level swampy land pock-marked with loughs towards Mount Brandon and Brandon Creek. Brandon mountain at 3127ft is Ireland's second highest peak and its summit is crowned with the much-restored oratory of St. Brendan. Legend has it that around A.D 525 Brendan the navigator, as he was later known, set out from Brandon in his frail hide-covered curragh seeking the fabled 'isle of the blest', Hy Brasil, and reputedly reached the Canaries and some claim even as far as Florida's Everglades.

For much of our week's visit we were tormented by mist and continuous heavy drizzle which made any sightseeing trips unproductive so it was a welcome surprise during a particularly wet day's outing to discover Paddy Murphy's Inn right on the harbour side at Brandon Creek.

A great wrack of cloud was hanging over the Brandon mountain whilst a strong onshore breeze was whipping up the grey seas of the Bay causing breakers to scatter against the harbour wall and wash across the quayside almost into the stone-flagged bar of the inn itself.

I noticed an intrepid oil-skinned lone fisherman gamely casting his line from the end of the granite jetty, hoping to hook I knew not what creatures there were lurking in those churning waters.

We all trooped into the small bar and were greeted by Paddy's daughter from behind the counter. Our host was upstairs in bed, catching up on his sleep after a night's fishing the previous evening. There were only two other customers, a young girl and a much older woman, a neighbour from an adjacent cottage. The four of us immediately felt totally at ease and unanimously decided there was no better place to be ensconced on such a miserable afternoon as in Paddy Murphy's.

Well lubricated by the several slugs of Jameson's Irish Whiskey, Rob and I did not take much persuasion to burst into unrestrained spontaneous song, encouraged by our new-found companions. Joan, the neighbour, went next door and prepared plates of delicious toasted sandwiches which she bore back for us all to enjoy, a totally generous gesture and typical of the spirit of hospitality which we came across during our travels. A hilarious diversion was created during all this merrymaking by the arrival into the bar of the fisherman with a large wet mackerel which he had just caught. He came sploshing towards us, leaving rivulets of salt water across the floor, and proudly presented his trophy with great aplomb to Patricia. She grasped it so tightly that it flew from her hands like a bar of slippery soap and it went skidding sideways along the bar top, taking all our drinks with it to smash on the solid floor. We all collapsed into hysterical laughter, the mackerel was retrieved from where it had come to rest and was subsequently taken back to our cottage to be baked for our supper.

The unforgettable finale to our afternoon's sojourn in that oasis of convivial comfort was when one of the girls produced a whistle and accompanied her friend with a round of traditional Irish dance. We were bedazzled by the intimacy of the moment and I was later to set down my memories in a short poem expressing the profound wonder at how fate had led us that wet afternoon to Paddy Murphy's door.

The following morning bade fair, the sea was sparkling under blue skies and we made our way down to Dingle harbour, the natural focus of activity in the little town.

By sheer chance we discovered it was the day of the "Blessing of the Boats", the ceremony enacted every year by the Bishop and his senior churchmen walking the quayside and dashing holy water onto the bows of the moored fishing vessels. After this anointment the priests, accompanied by a huge entourage of the local population, board a flotilla of boats and sail out of Dingle Bay where they hold a service of thanksgiving far from shore. The whole procedure was to a background of stirring music relayed over loadspeakers erected on the harbour side, I especially remember that lovely folk song "Down by the Salley Gardens" with words taken from the poem of the same title by William Butler Yeats.

It is but a dozen miles eastwards along the southern coast of the Dingle Peninsula to the village of Inch with its wide sweep of open beach marking the bar of Castlemaine Harbour. I was quite taken aback on our first visit there to be

The Tralee to Dingle railway: No. 5 locomotive at Blennerville, 1997.

Blennerville windmill.

285

Dingle harbour and the annual "Blessing of the Boats" 1997.

Dingle's main street.

confronted with the miles of white sands and the vista across the bay to the distant range of the omnipresent Macgillycuddy's Reeks. Little wonder that the film producers were drawn here when recording John Millington Synges's classic story "The Playboy of the Western World" and more recently in 1970 the great movie director David Lean set that stirring romance "Ryan's Daughter" on Inch's picturesque backdrop.

From Inch we ascended inland over the shoulder of Slieve Mish mountain and down its northern slopes into the tiny village of Camp. As we rounded the corner in the lane a scene befell our eyes so timeless in character that for a moment we were transported back to a previous century. We had by happy chance arrived upon the day of Camp Sheep Fair when it seemed every country farmer and his dog in County Kerry had gathered there to buy and sell their stock.

The roadway was full of sheep, some loose, others in rustic pens with knots of shepherds, dealers or folk just there for socialising, standing bargaining or merely gossiping about the door of the ancient village inn. Thomas Hardy himself could barely have described a scene more colourful that the one that we witnessed at Camp.

Much of our 'sightseeing' during our stay on that peninsula thrust into the Atlantic Ocean was under conditions of constant mist and heavy drizzle when visibility could be measured in yards. It certainly added a piquancy to the atmosphere of the rugged Irish landscape thereabouts.

We negotiated several of the famous mountain passes in the interminable all-pervading fog, two that come to mind being the Gap of Dunloe near Killarney and the Healy Pass over the Berehaven promitory. The latter was constructed in 1931 and named after its promotor Tim Healy, 1st Govenor General of the Irish Free State. The crucifix which adorns the pass hails from that time although many of the shrines we came across on remote rural byways were erected in the Marian Year of 1954.

One obligatory tour which visitors to the region are urged to make is the "Ring of Kerry", 100 miles of coastal route taking in a string of interesting places and breathtaking views. One is advised to traverse the 'Ring' in a clockwise direction, the same flow as taken by the many tourist coaches and so avoid meeting these Leviathans head-on in the narrow roads.

Although it had been barely seven days since landing on Ireland's shore the spirit and culture of that unique country had endeared themselves to me. I had already adjusted my pace of life to that of the indigenous population and another week spent there in the local company would probably have seen my conversation peppered with the little witticisms and sayings, so infectious as they are, that characterise the Irish speech.

It was nearly seven years before I made a return to Ireland and once again experience the magic of that enchanting place.

Brandon Bay

Tis a soft day, hereabouts so they say
as the grey clouds lower round Brandon Peak,
and rain sweeps relentlessly o'er the bay
wetting oil-skinned fishermen, here for the week.

Waves raised by the ceaseless flow
continue their passage across the quay,
kissing the threshold of the Brandon Inn
wherein are sheltered such folk as we.

Paddy Murphy, mine host, is aloft at rest,
his daughter works the bar alone.
A coy young lass, how does she view us?
But we gain her trust and she our own.

More rain is lashing the windows
and more Jameson's finds a home,
there is talk of songs, of music
with a lady standing by named Joan.

Her daughter, it seems, does the dancing
and happens to also be here
Paddy's daughter produces a whistle
and leaves off from pulling the beer.

The daughter moves with an inborn grace
to a tune of timeless calling,
the Spirit of Ireland is borne up on her steps
under the Brandon Mountain

Rich folk pay the price to be moved
when in London such dances they see,
but none more so that day than we,
when a young girl danced by Brandon Quay.

As a lad I acquired a modest little book "Salute to Cycling" written by the veteran pioneer cyclist Frank Urry in which is described a touring holiday by bicycle through the wild terrain of rural Ireland in the company of his daughter, introducing her to those quiet pleasures discovered by journeying on two wheels.

Camp sheepfair.

The open sweep of Inch's vast beach.

Paddy Murphy's Bar, Brandon Quay.

Louise on the summit of the Connor Pass.

I little dreamt then that one day I would likewise share the joys of cycling the Irish byways with my own daughter, but in the springtime of 2004 she and I spent a day doing just that during the course of a week's holiday we shared in that fascinating country.

Louise lived and worked in London at that time therefore it was planned that I would travel up to Town by train and we could then both fly out from Stanstead Airport in Essex directly to Cork in Southern Ireland. I travelled up to Paddington on that May morning via the "Cotswold Line", once part of the Great Western's Oxford, Worcester and Wolverhampton route and unkindly dubbed "Old Worse and Worse".

Louise met the train and surprised me with a superb luncheon at the television chef Gary Rhodes's restaurant high up in the old National Westminster Tower where we both enjoyed the delicious food and impeccable service from ever-attentive waiters. As we sat eating an electrical storm was playing over the city below us and from our lofty vantage point we were able to track its course as tongues of forked lightning licked eerily around the forest of high-rise office blocks which comprise modern-day London.

After lunch we took the lift to the very top floor, some forty seven stories in total, and gazed down from the "Vertigo Bar" observation window on the teeming streets nearly five hundred feet below.

We had time to spare before entraining for Stanstead so spent an hour at the "Museum of Childhood" in Bethnal Green which is housed in one of the original pavilions built for the Great Exhibition in 1851 and later removed to its present site. I should have liked to have lingered there longer but the Emerald Isle was beckoning. By nine P.M. that evening we were collecting our shiny new Peugeot 307 hire car from Cork Airport, to drive into the City where we booked into the Hotel Grand Metropole. The first leg of our journey was successfully accomplished.

The following morning we took an all-too brief stroll around Cork which we found to be a bright colourful city straddling the delightful River Lee. However time was pressing and I knew only too well how long apparently simple journeys can take on the Irish byways, therefore we wasted little time in setting off north-westwards, crossing the gently sloping Mullaghareirk Mountains and reaching Listowel in time for lunch. This latter place has gone down in the annals of Irish railway history as the hub of the most extraordinary conveyance ever constructed to run on rails in the British Isles. The Listowel to Ballybunnion Railway was opened in 1888 as the world's first commercial monorail powered by locomotives that beggared belief. The single rail was raised some height above ground level and a double-engine steam locomotive was hung pannier-fashion across it, like some fantastic creation from the imagination of William Heath Robinson himself. Amazingly this bizarre nine miles long mechanical anachronism ran for thirty six years until its eventual closure in 1924.

We spent the night in the small coastal village of Ballyheige on the Shannon estuary where we breakfasted whilst looking out over Tralee bay with Dingle peninsular in the distance with Brandon Peak aglow in the morning sunshine. By late lunchtime that same day we found ourselves booking into a comfortable guest house just a stone's throw from Dingle Harbour. I wanted to introduce Louise to Dingle, not merely on account of it being such an attractive and interesting destination but I thought it a suitable area for the long-awaited cycle ride of my boyhood memory. There is no finer way to appreciate the landscape through which one is travelling than from the saddle of a bicycle (or even a horse!)

You enjoy a far higher vantage point than in a modern car, can see over the roadside hedges, and whilst ambling along at little more than walking pace you can concentrate on the scenery far better than when controlling a mechanically-propelled conveyance. The sounds and smells of the surroundings are sharply defined, as is one's consciousness of the elements, the latter especially so when battling a head wind!

The route we decided to take was the popular circular one around Slea Head and on to Dunmore Head, the most westerly point in mainland Europe. For most of its seaward side the road is cut into the lower slopes of Mount Eagle which here fall steeply towards the Ocean.

The headlands are rich in archaeological features such as the famous stone 'beehive' oratories and other even earlier artefacts, ancient ogham stones, promontory and ring forts, pillar stones, in all the greatest concentration of such remains in Ireland. A mile offshore from the mainland are the Blasket Islands, the largest of them Great Blasket rising 950ft out from the foaming Atlantic ocean. It actually consists of the steep top of the drowned Slievedonagh Mountain and is far more difficult to access than it appears, being beset on every side by cliffs and jagged rocks.

In the Autumn of 1588 four ships of the mighty Spanish Armada strayed into the treacherous waters of Blasket Sound, two of them coming to grief there. The one, "Our Lady of the Rosary" a galleon of one thousand tons, foundered with the loss of all her crew bar one, a young boy, the pilot's son.

The Blaskets supported a resident community until 1953 and the ruins of stone cabins can still be discerned from the mainland cliffs. The Great Blasket is closely associated with that great early 20th century writer Robin Flower. He visited there frequently from Cambridge over a period of twenty years from 1910, becoming an Irish speaker and being much revered by the islanders who called him "Blaheen" - Little Flower.

The perilous passage across the Sound to Great Blasket was made from the tiny exposed "harbour" of Dunquin, lying below the cliffs, in traditional Irish curragh canoes, when three or four oarsmen would row the fragile-looking craft across the swirling waters.

That day of our ride Louise and I pedalled a merciless twenty five miles in total, up and down the relentless gradients that characterise the road around the Atlantic fringes of Europe. Our last muscle-aching ascent was made in driving heavy drizzle through a featureless grey landscape on the final run back to Dingle. We deposited our two machines from whence they had been hired and

Across the Blasket Sound towards Dunmore Head.

The two most westerly cyclists in Europe!

The South Pole Inn at Anascaul on the Dingle Peninsular commemorating local explorer Tom Crean.

The "cottage" at Baltimore.

wasted no time in treating ourselves to a steaming hot Irish Coffee in a bar on Dingle's main street. Never had a drink tasted so good nor been so hard earned!

By sheer chance and good fortune our friends Rob and Patricia were also holidaying in Ireland the same week as Louise and myself. They had jointly hired a cottage with another of my childhood chums Robin Rumney, and his partner Alison, at Baltimore in the far south-west reaches of County Cork and kindly invited the two of us to stay with them as their guests for a couple of nights.

Accordingly we bade farewell to Dingle and set off straightaway after breakfast with the intention of meeting up with the four of them for a lunchtime drink. Again, the enigma of those Irish miles completely beguiled us and by one o'clock we were frantically trying to telephone Rob from Killarney to inform him our earliest time of arrival would now be tea-time. All went to plan from then on and a few hours later we were all exchanging news over a glass or two in the bar of the Baltimore Inn.

Baltimore has an air of unhurried calm which works its magic on her visitors. As we stood in the late afternoon sunlight, looking out over the harbour towards the Sound of Sherkin and Clear Islands it was difficult to associate such a peaceful spot with its turbulent past. This corner of Ireland was settled by English sea farers, pirates in all bar name, in 1607, but they themselves were overrun some twenty four years later by Algerian buccaneers who invaded the settlement with the infamous "Sack of Baltimore" in 1631, taking over one hundred men,women and children as slaves. As a result the surviving community removed themselves inland to the relative safety of Skibbereen, some seven miles distant, leaving Baltimore to resume its previous untroubled existence.

The evening of our arrival we were treated to a concert of traditional music in the local inn, part of the popular "Feast of Fiddles" festival held annually in the village. As accomplished as the performers were I am ashamed to admit that Louise fell asleep in her chair and I too was not so very far from emulating her. Our early start to the day and the long protracted journey south, overlaid with the large supper we had just partaken of, had all conspired to seduce us with the charm of Morpheus.

As we had a morning flight home booked from Cork Airport it was prudent to spend our final night at a more convenient place. Thus I came to discover what a charming jewel is the small harbour town of Kinsale, sheltering in the Bandon estuary and barely twelve miles from Cork.

It is unhappily best known for the tragic event in 1915 when the passenger liner "Lusitania" returning from the U.S.A was torpedoed by a German U-Boat within sight of the Old Head of Kinsale with a subsequent massive loss of lives. There is a memorial on the headland there commemorating this awful act of war, but sadly time was pressing for us and we were unable to drive out and pay our respects at that poignant spot.

At six o'clock the following morning we slipped out of the silent White Lady

Hotel, dropping the latch on the door as we left, and stole away through the deserted streets in the grey light of that chilly spring dawn.

A couple of hours later we were in the air, winging our way back to England and home.

THE NEW CENTURY DAWNS

In late 1999, as the old year started drawing to a close with the heralding of a new century and with it a third millenium, the entire country seemed to be girding itself up for one giant celebration of the momentous event.

Despite all the ballyhoo accompanying the New Year's Eve junkettings we chose to attend our parish church event, initially a reception in the village hall then at 11.30pm a walk up the lane the short distance to the church for a brief service. At the stroke of midnight we all paused in prayer for a few moments of silent private contemplation whilst outside the dying of the old year and welcoming of the new was being celebrated with a frenetic barrage of noisy fireworks. The contrast with the peace and solitude of the old 14th century stone church in which we were knelt in quiet thought was profoundly emotional and I was later stirred to set down in a short poem this moving experience, although mere words cannot express adequately such a poignant moment.

Midnight in Teddington
A hush descends on these ancient stones, candles gutter their timeless rhythm. Two thousand years, forty generations of man's questing has drawn us together in this tiny microcosm of worship under the Gloucestershire sky.

Must we alone be their representatives on this night of all nights?

What worthy yeomen have sat as we do now in these cold oaken rows, sharing the joys and sorrows, the smiles and tears, held fast within these same stone walls.

The distant rumble from the world outside expresses our common emotion as the earth rolls inexorably towards the New Century. Old friends, old times are cast adrift now, consigned to eternity, and we alone must carry the flame on their behalf as the new dawn breaks.

If only I could have foreseen it, the year 2000 was sadly to see Loretta's and my life turned about in the most shockingly dramatic and totally unexpected way possible. For several months I had detected that Loretta was somewhat "off-colour". She had been worrying unnecessarily about an accident we had been involved in with our second Morris Minor, back in September the previous year, which was proving difficult to resolve regarding the insurance claim and I thought she was merely working herself up disproportionately over the whole business. However, one Sunday evening in March she suddenly complained of feeling generally unwell and experiencing a bizarre sensation of numbness in her left arm and hand. I immediately arranged to take her into the Cheltenham Hospital's emergency department some nine or ten miles away and by the time we arrived she had begun to feel normal again.

Nevertheless the hospital kept her there overnight for observation and various tests and ostensibly could find nothing wrong. With hindsight, and knowing what I do now it was the terrible portent of far worse to come.

That July, the day is engraved on my soul, Monday the tenth, I had arranged to open up the Bugatti Trust at six pm for a small party of ramblers and to show them briefly around before they set off on their walk. This I did, leaving Loretta at home busy cooking our supper. I was away for barely an hour but on arriving back home there was an uncanny silence in the house. To my horror I discovered Loretta prone on the kitchen floor, conscious but extremely frightened. She was very confused, saying her glasses had fallen off and as she attempted to retrieve them she had keeled over and been unable to rise to her feet again. I could see immediately that she had suffered a massive stroke which had struck down her left side. The incident four months earlier had clearly been a transient ischemic attack or mini-stroke.

The following 24 hours have become a confused whirl in my mind. I remember blindly pursuing the ambulance to the hospital and the feeling of utter helplessness, being there merely as a bystander to the emergency procedures unfolding before me. The whole awful event was like some grotesque nightmare and I was left bewildered and confused as the enormity of the incident gradually became clear. Looking back, I too was a victim, in a far lesser way of course, but nevertheless I was left floundering that night, the hospital staff quite rightly were directing all their efforts on Loretta but there was nobody to whom I could turn for information or any sort of solace or reassurance.

I returned home to an empty house, the saucepans still warm on the stove with the only evidence of what had befallen us being the overturned chair in the kitchen and the discarded blanket I had put around Loretta whilst awating the ambulance.

Life was never to be the same again for either of us.

Loretta was moved to Tewkesbury Hospital within a few days and destined to become her home for the next eleven weeks. It was to be a long and tedious process of regaining any vestige of recovery, not only in the physical sense but mentally. Stroke is such a cruel affliction, taking not just a person's mobility from them but also conferring on them a change of personality. Feelings are sharpened, worries magnified in their minds out of all proportion and the hapless victim is left emotionally fragile with the smallest comment or recollection bringing him or her into convulsions of unrestrained sobbing. I can cope with physical problems but seeing one's loved one reduced to such a pitiful state is indescribably distressing.

Loretta was deemed able to be discharged from the Assessment and Rehabilitation Unit at the hospital on October the Third but it was destined to be a short "au revoir". The following evening she was making her way cautiously across the hall at "Applegarth", supported on her walking stick, when she became caught up on the staircase newel post and went over sideways onto the soft carpet.

It was not a particularly heavy or violent fall but after her suffering a restless and tortured night it transpired that she had unluckily broken her thigh bone. Poor Loretta had to endure a further couple of weeks back in hospital having a plate inserted to effect a repair of the fracture.

Then it was back home for a second time and in a typical display of positive thinking Loretta arranged some extra physiotherapy at a local gymnasium where the proprietor had a reputation for the treatment of stroke patients. He was a huge figure of a man and Loretta underwent a course a extremely painful exercises in his hands. To his dismay and Loretta's horror he succeeded in breaking her shoulder bone, necessitating yet another return to hospital. Alarm bells must have rung with her doctor, for a bone density scan revealed she was suffering osteoporosis which had caused her bones to become perilously brittle.

Loretta finally came back home without any further mishaps befalling her. I continued taking her to the A. and R. unit for thrice weekly sessions of physiotherapy and these she supplemented by weekly home visits from a qualified practitioner for gentle reflexology on her feet. I was fascinated by the techniques used in those hour-long sessions and to learn how many of our general sensibilities and well-being spring from the structure of the foot. The treatment certainly helped to relax Loretta and imparted new confidence in her after the unbelievably traumatic previous six months.

I started taking her to a weekly stroke-survivors' exercise group in Cheltenham where she met a well-respected physiotherapist 'Mike'. He started twice weekly private home visits to "Applegarth" for half hour treatments involving manipulation, balance control, massage and stretching techniques, some of which he briefed me to provide on a daily basis. All this was certainly no magic "quick fix" for Loretta's condition but it did instil in her a more positive mindset, helping her to face the future with a modicum of hope for a somewhat improved life.

As soon as she was reasonably mobile the Tewkesbury Hospital approached her, asking if she was willing to run the local Stroke Club, a modest group of around a dozen stroke survivors who meet once a month for talks from visiting speakers, slide shows, quizzes or merely a chat amongst themselves accompanied by coffee and cakes.

With my help Loretta has enjoyed such a fulfilling and appreciated task and as I write she is currently in her eighth year of "office" as secretary, treasurer. Chairman and general factotum all rolled into one post!

For myself the last eight years have been a pretty steep learning curve and a voyage of personal self-discovery. I realise now that one does not know how you respond to a tragic situation until confronted with it. I have found skills and levels of patience within myself I never realised I possessed. Before Loretta's illness a boiled egg was the limit of my culinary expertise, but now as her carer I do all the shopping, plan and prepare the meals, operate the washing-machine (which previously had been a black-art to me!) along with all the general housework. All this effort is in addition to the myriad of routine tasks which have fallen to me in the normal course of living such as maintaining the house and garden and our fleet of four cars. It is obvious that I am never bored, on the contrary, the weeks overlaid as they are with our pattern of daily routines simply hurtle along. A huge regret was having of necessity to resign my interesting and rewarding job at the Bugatti Trust, for the greatest thing that I miss most of all is the day-to-day interaction with other people and the opportunity to use what skills I possessed and the sense of satisfaction derived from providing a much appreciated service.

Finally I must pay tribute to Loretta's elderly mother who has been a tower of strength for us both throughout these difficult years.

She thoroughly enjoys looking after Loretta in her own home two or three days every week which gives me a priceless respite from the daily commitment of a carer's responsibility.

This freedom, albeit limited, has granted me the opportunity to don my walking boots and explore the hills and vales of my native area, a camera on my belt and with only my thoughts for company.

Perambulations -1

The ancient Saxon borough of Winchcombe straddles the Isbourne valley, the infant river it contains being allegedly the only river in Britain to flow due north, a somewhat contentious claim I imagine. To the east lies the steep western scarp slope of the Cotswold Hills down from which runs the delightful Beesmore Valley, its stream joining the Isbourne by the Sudely grounds in Winchcombe town.

It is through this landscape that I regularly set off on one of my favourite local walks, passing the much-restored Sudely Castle and following the Beesmore Brook to reach the mysterious complex of disused farm buildings at Waterhatch. Here, buried in the undergrowth, lie the remains of an old water mill, its decrepit overshot wheel mounted unusually in the centre of the wide dam containing the waters of the millpond. Nature here has reclaimed what is rightly hers, tempering the scene with her curtain of natural verdure.

It is truly an enchanting spot.

A further half an hours walk takes the intrepid explorer deep into Spoonley Wood which has concealed its secret for nearly two millenia. Down an unmarked way off the path through the trees the walker who has learnt of this secret is rewarded by the thrill of discovering the Spoonley Roman Villa, the largest of its kind ever uncovered in Britain but now sadly completely surrendered to Mother Nature. Only a miniscule portion of tessellation may be seen, roughly protected from the elements under a crude rustic shelter. This tiny portion of floor, about six feet by four feet in area, was excavated under the direction of a 19th century Lady of the Manor at Sudely, Emma Dent. Some

Waterhatch mill wheel.

Spoonley Roman pavement.

Atop the Worcestershire Beacon, the summit of the Malvern Hills 1394 feet above sea-level.

Didbrook forge: Mike Hamlett busy on his anvil. April 1975.

302

cynics have suggested that she actually had the pavement built up from new, but whether this is true or not it detracts little from the feeling of awe in treading where once the Roman invaders lived out their lives in this hidden corner of Gloucestershire.

The wooded hills overlooking the Beesmore Valley to the north have also drawn me on my forays into the countryside surrounding Winchcombe.

You ascend Salter's Hill from the Isbourne Brook, up the stony Pilgrim's path where once those faithful seekers of the Holy Relic, a phial containing the Blood of Christ, trailed on their dedicated pilgrimage to Hailes Abbey. It is now a ruin, for the Abbey was razed during the Reformation by King Henry the Eighth in 1539, but not before it became the focus of worship for those simple believers eager to pay homage at its precious icon.

Above the hamlet of Hailes is the bizarre stone structure known as Cromwell's Seat where reputedly Thomas Cromwell sat watching the destruction of the Abbey far below him.

Modern day archaeologists have now declared the edifice to be of a much later date, probably constructed as a whimsical folly, but the old romantic legend lives on in the minds of local people.

Higher again, perched atop the Cotswold scarp, warriers of a far earlier time kept their watch. This is Beckbury Camp, now bequeathed to the fields of waving corn, its earthen ramparts a testimony to that distant "Age of Iron".

Picking my way back down from those 'high wild hills' I detoured through Didbrook village with its rural smithy, now sadly disused. The last farrier working there was an acquaintance of mine, Mike Hamlett, and I took the opportunity during his final days there, of persuading him to pose for a photograph to which he obliged very bashfully in that dark saturnine workshop.

The final leg of my walk led along the trackside path to the preserved railway station at Toddington where the thriving Gloucestershire Warwickshire Railway Society have their headquarters. The place holds pleasant childhood memories of my Sunday School days with trips along the line from Bishop's Cleeve to Toddington where we would walk out as a party to the nearby woods and gather bunches of wild daffodils which then grew in profusion amongst the trees.

Now I once again boarded the little steam train which returned me to Winchcombe station and a short walk back to my waiting car.

Perambulations - 2

When I resided in Woodmancote the hills of Bushcombe and Cleeve became my regular haunts and still they possess the power to attract me back time and again. I often drive to Prescott Hill where my car can be left at my old workplace, the Bugatti Trust. It is a steep climb from there up past Pardon Farm, a name redolent of monastic absolution, the rutted track reaching an ancient sheep dip built into the hillside, the stone chamber heavily overgrown with brambles. Its adjacent feeder pond, still fed with a little tinkling rill cascading down the bank, is now a haven for wildlife and fringed every springtime with a profusion of planted daffodils. Across a couple of steep boggy fields you gain the prehistoric track way, Grinnel or Greenway Lane, sunken between its hawthorn hedgerows. It rises from the vale below towards the pre-iron age encampments on Nottingham Hill and on further to the neighbouring camps cut into the rocky flanks of Cleeve Hill. At the former place in the late 1960's a ploughman uncovered a veritable bonanza of bronze swords and other artefacts from the cultivated field in the centre of the huge circular double embankments which define the extensive earthworks of the camp.

The track way proceeds across the modern main road onto Cleeve Common where it joins the old coaching route which once linked Winchcombe and Cheltenham in days of yore. The common consists of some 1200 acres of rolling limestone upland, pocketed with long-abandoned quarries and now bisected with an expansive municipal golf course. To avoid the fairway which monopolises the sweep of grassland along the hill's summit I usually keep to the periphery of the Common, turning off the old coaching track via the Postlip valley and another sheep washing-pool. This is the "Watery Bottom" whence rises the River Isbourne, here just a trickle of crystal clear water bubbling out from the pure limestone strata deep below. Walkers with the legs and breath to spare can continue from the top of this valley and attain the westernmost heights. Hereabouts were run the earliest Cheltenham races, on a huge figure of eight course constructed in 1818 and where the first Gold Cup was won in 1819. It was to here that upwards of fifty thousand followers of the noble "Sport of Kings" would regularly swarm and hence provoke the Reverand Francis Close into publishing his famous sermon in 1827 "The Evil Consequences of Attending the Racecourse Exposed" - strong stuff indeed!

The views from this edge of Cotswold are spectacular and far-reaching, for the informed eye can detect the Severn Motorway bridge in South Gloucestershire, Gloucester Cathedral tower rising from the general murkiness of the city, and May Hill towards the Forest of Dean, crowned with its symbolic clump of trees planted for Victoria's diamond jubilee and immortalised by Poet Laureate John Masefield's "Everlasting Mercy".

A glance westwards reveals the long line of Malvern Hills and the nearer Whaleback of Houseman's Bredon.

In the immediate vicinity of this unique vantage point the observant rambler will identify the massive ramparts of another encampment, now truncated by later quarrying and immediately below, the great block of hewn stone, Huddlestone's Table, marking King Kenulf of Mercia's farewell to his "illustrious gathering of departing guests". Beyond is the remnant of Queen's Wood, named in honour of Edward's Eleanor of Castile, and the adjacent Nutter's Wood, the scene in my Mother's time of the ritual gathering of herbs and simples by local witches, who nightly went a'foraging under the darkening trees.

Watery Bottom above Isbourne's source: rounding up the flock c. 1920's.

Huddlestone's Table, Cleeve Common with a youthful self in November 1963.

"Linger and Die" farm ruins, Gotherington in 1997.

*Wyche Cutting, Malvern: A Morgan three-wheeler makes a competitive ascent in 1913
with the company's founder H.S.F. Morgan aboard.*

And so I reluctantly turn back towards whence I came, under Cleeve Cloud's rocky outcrops and along the spine of Nottingham's outlier, through the familiar path-ways of Bushcombe and Gotherington Woods to drop down past the eerily deserted ruins of the farmstead, "Linger and Die" to finally close the great circle which I had been transcribing around the Cotswold height. For here once more I gained the old demesne of Lord Ellenborough's Prescott Estate and wearily reached my destination and my car waiting to transport me home.

Perambulations-3

Occasionally my wanderings take me further afield and that distant range of "blue remembered hills", the Malverns, are one of my favourite destinations. Those familiar summits, North Hill, the Worcestershire Beacon, the Herefordshire Beacon and British Camp and Midsummer's Hill were thrust from the 'slumbering Midland plain' over six hundred million years before man walked the Earth and represent some of the earliest rocks in the British Isles.

The small residential towns which cloak the eastern flanks of the Malverns sprang from the gracious age of the Georgian spa health resort, for the waters that flow abundantly from the aquifers of those ancient stones have been considered from time immemorial to confer health restoring properties, either by means of bodily douches or imbibing regular vast quantities.

The tradition is perpetuated in the ornamental conduit supplied from a spring at the top of Great Malvern's main street where enthusiasts for the water fill their containers from the never-ending stream which gushes forth.

A steep climb up St Anne's Lane, snaking past the St Anne's Well and its Gothic spa building, now a café, leads to the summit of the hills.

Here the walker can enjoy the sheer exhileration of stepping out along the crest, buffeted by the ceaseless wind, with views westward across the Herefordshire plain into Wales and eastwards across the roofs of the town towards the familiar hump of Bredon Hill and beyond to the Cotswold escarpment.

Cut into the western contour of the Malverns is the scenic "Jubilee Drive", linking the British Camp with the famous Wyche Cutting. At this latter place, a narrow steep defile representing the original pass through a gap in the centre of the range, early hill-climb trials were held in those pioneer days of motoring before the Great War. The locally built Morgan three-wheeled sports cars regularly competed for the honours here on their 'home-ground' with great success.

Along the Jubilee Drive is the historic café "The Kettle Sings" so beloved of composer Sir Edward Elgar who drew much of his inspiration from walking these hills. When time permits I break my own walk with a refreshing brew partaken sitting in those quaint wooden premises, enjoying the panoramic vista across the countryside of Herefordshire and South Worcestershire with a relaxing few minutes of musing. Then follows the tramp back across the hill, passing the old red sandstone Abbey en route and on through the grounds of the Wintergarden Theatre to the car park and so to home.

Perambulations -4

"In Summertime on Bredon my love and I did lie" so wrote A.E.Houseman in his "Shropshire Lad" anthology. I sometimes wonder if he was referring to the same Bredon Hill that I know and enjoy, but nevertheless the sentiments are equally applicable. It is a wonderful height on which to lose oneself, physically and also in the spiritual sense. One can range freely over its network of paths and track ways, never far out of sight of distant views across the Gloucestershire and Worcestershire rural landscape and nearer, Shakespeare's Avon winding lazily through the patchwork of grassy water meadows.

The summit of Bredon is truly a mystical place, surmounted by the earthworks of its prehistoric encampment, the scene of much bloodshed in those far-off embattled times. The nearby Banbury Stone was reputedly the altar on which ritualistic sacrifices were executed and its huge elephantine form has given rise to the fanciful local legend that it metamorphoses into a living beast on the stroke of Pershore Abbey's midnight chimes when it lumbers down the hillside to drink from the River Avon!

A much later embellishment to the scene, and built on the embankment of the camp itself, is the squat stone tower of a folly standing four-square to the winds. It was erected by the 18th century Squire Parsons of Kemerton who apparently viewed its construction as a means of adding forty feet to his hill thus raising its natural height of 960ft to the all-important one thousand feet necessary to define it as a mountain!

For many years it was the home of a rather disreputable hermit who by local accounts lived off the bountiful rabbits on the hill by catching them with his bare hands!

The northern slopes of Bredon are generally uncultivated, representing scrubland, a landscape which can hardly have changed since the Dark Ages. The southern aspect is mainly agricultural farmland, worked now from a large parent farm at the hill's foot, but at one time this land supported a number of smaller farms established on the upper slopes. These have become long-abandoned and decaying ruins though still clinging tenaciously to the land they once worked. My own theory is that these farms suffered from an acute water shortage; due to the peculiar geology of the hill what springs there are all rise on a line following the present roadway. This winds around the hill's contour on the lower slopes and along which the original settlements have developed into the circular string of fifteen modern-day villages. The road linking these communities is some seventeen miles in circumference and a popular local cycle route, where one has

Parson's Folly, Bredon Hill.

The Banbury Stone on Bredon, often referred to as The Elephant Stone.

Eckington Wharf on the River Avon.

A lunchtime sojourn for 'the gang' at the Coal House Inn on the River Severn.

the pleasure of passing the village with the distinction of boasting the longest place-name in Britain which does not use the same letter twice - Bricklehampton!

Standing atop of Bredon with a pair of field-glasses it is possible to follow the progress of boats navigating their way along the picturesque Avon, working through Nafford Locks to moor downstream at Eckington's village wharf. It is an idyllic spot, with the waters of the Avon gently flowing past, under the arches of the old red sandstone road bridge and onwards with their timeless journey to swell the Severn stream at Tewkesbury.

The ancient bridge inspired Sir Arthur Quiller-Couch to pen his immortal lines of contemplative verse "From Eckington Bridge" and to stand today, as he also did, ensconced in one of its parapet niches and gaze down into the dark waters sliding past below can seduce the observer likewise into such philosophical reverie.

The wharf is a convenient place to pull in from the public road and enjoy a picnic lunch on the river bank or to merely sit and view the narrow boats and cruisers with their burdens of happy voyagers, the resident swans and ducks animating this colourful scene with their amusing splashing and cavorting.

Eckington Bridge has become one of Loretta's favourite places to visit since her illness, for this quiet unhurried and timeless rural scene engenders a therapeutic effect in relaxing her with its innocent magic.

"A Gang of Eight"

Since those early years of visiting the "Gardener's Arms" at Alderton the friendships forged with certain people met there through our regular evenings still flourish. We have come together as a small coterie of eight, meeting regularly to enjoy the mutual company of each other in various ways.

To the casual observer we may appear as a very disparate circle of individuals - myself and Loretta, Rob with his motor sport interests and tastes in traditional music accompanied by Patricia, Nigel and Irene from Red Barn Farm and David and Veronica "Ron" Cramp, the latter couple being enthusiastic and knowledgeable ornithologists and lovers of the great outdoors. Despite our apparent differences we seem to co-exist quite comfortably as a group, originally coming together when we all decided to embellish the music nights at the Gardener's Arms with an occasional booked supper. Gradually we have explored further afield over the intervening years and discovered a number of acceptable eating establishments within thirty minutes drive to partake of luncheon as a table of eight. So absorbed are we in our discourse that it is common for us to be still sat around the table at teatime with the proprietor hovering anxiously and making suggestive noises as to the lateness of the hour.

On one memorable occasion we had lingered over a summer lunch enjoyed 'al fresco' on the banks of the Severn at Chacely Stock's 'Ferry Boat Inn' when the landlord locked up the premises and disappeared off down the lane in his car, leaving us all sat at leisure to finish our drinks, his hens and ducks scratching and pecking about our feet.

The sun was sinking below Wainlodes Hill before we summoned up the strength to rise, with the ever-lengthening shadows of eventide stretching across the river bank as we finally departed.

When studying for her English Literature degree Loretta was given an insight into the world of poets and their works and as a result she came up with the notion of a home poetry evening for our group. The formula was simple, each person brings along a few of their favourite poems to read aloud and accompanied by some tasty nibbles lubricated by several bottles of acceptable wines it made for a highly entertaining night.

Any tendencies towards seriousness were leavened by Rob and his much cherished anthology of Limericks, choice examples from which he proceeded to recite with great gusto, reducing us all into helpless mirth and henceforth any pretensions towards literary decorum rapidly evaporated!

It was through the kindness of Nigel and Irene that we participated as a party in several Scottish holidays. They owned a splendid seven-bedroomed lodge standing in its own grounds of some seven hundred acres situated on Mormond Hill in Aberdeenshire, six miles inland from the fishing port of Frazerburgh.

On the occasion of our first visit we all flew from Luton Airport in Bedfordshire except Nigel who made the tiring five hundred miles road journey in his Jeep loaded with the party's luggage and other requisites for the week.

Nigel had an arduous day for that same evening he turned out again to make the eighty miles round trip to Aberdeen Airport, in convoy with an estate employee driving the Range Rover kept at Mormond Hill, in order to meet us and convey us back to our accomodation. It was an unforgettable week of sightseeing in that much neglected corner of Scotland. The coast from Inverness around the north-east shoulder of the landmass to Peterhead and Aberdeen abounds with quaint steeply-accessed fishing villages and other places of interest whilst the skies and the seas teem with bird and aquatic life.

Every day that week the group of us went out and about with Nigel and Irene playing the part of perfect hosts, guiding us around that fascinating area.

We covered the tract of country from the Spey valley in the west, visiting the family firm of Baxters where they produce their famous range of culinary wares on the banks of the river in an enormous factory alongside the immensely popular visitors centre, "Baxter's Village" complete with a busy cafeteria.

In the course of the next few days we went on to enjoy a guided tour of the

Mormond Hill Estate near Frazerborough.

Frazerborough Harbour.

Pennan Harbour and village.

Rattray Head's sand dunes.

314

Strathisla Distillery at Keith, home of the Chivas Regal Scotch Whisky, eastwards along the coast to the deep-sea fishing museum at Buckie and further on to Banff with its sea-aquarium housed in a modern circular building of local granite built on the quayside. We were held spellbound by its breathtaking collection of exotic marine life, amazingly all indigenous to the local waters. Despite the capacity of several of the enormous glass-sided tanks being many thousands of gallons of sea-water certain specimens occupying them outgrew their homes and then had to be removed by lifting them carefully from the tank by an overhead crane. The creatures were then taken by boat far out to sea for release. We were awestruck by one of these Leviathans, a giant conger eel lurking among the rocks on the aquarium floor, its girth bigger than a man's arms could encompass.

I was thrilled when we dropped down the steep lane into the tiny harbour of Pennan used as the principal setting for the acclaimed film "Local Hero". Those who have seen the production will recall the iconic red telephone box on the quayside which now enjoys listed status and attracts cinema aficionados from across the world.

Frazerburgh is the archetypal Scottish coastal town as characterised on the covers of the Dundee "People's Friend" magazine, but it has sadly suffered from the general decline in deep-sea fishing and consequently has lost much of its former prosperity. Nevertheless the harbour is the home port for several huge trawlers, each with a holding capacity of some four hundred tons of catch, taken during their long forays up to the fishing grounds of Scandinavia and beyond, sometimes even as far as Nova Scotia and Newfoundland.

These enormous vessels appear to monopolise the harbour, dwarfing all the other smaller boats which cluster about their bows. Around them all go the seals, scavenging through the oily water for discarded fish offal and quite oblivious to the human activity taking place above their heads. We took the opportunity of going around the lighthouse museum in Frazerburgh which boasts collections of huge glass Fresnel lenses and other artefacts salvaged from the increasing number of condemned historic installations around Britain's coast. The Frazerburgh lighthouse is itself constructed within the ruins of the town's castle when the latter were narrowly saved from demolition and preserved as an ancient monument through a protest movement spearheaded by no less than Sir Walter Scott himself.

A few miles out of town is the R.S.P.B reserve at Loch of Strathbeg near Rattray Head, where we all spent an hour in the hides and looking around the visitor centre. Here David was a font of knowledge, explaining how this north eastern coastline was the first landfall encountered by returning migrants and consequently attracted many interesting and more unusual species of birdlife.

Rattray Head, familiar as a name to millions of listeners to the BBC Shipping Forecasts for Inland Waters, has its shoreline buttressed by a spectacular array of sand dunes. We were glad of the extra traction provided by our four-wheel drive vehicles enabling us to gain the seclusion of the picturesque beach overlooking the Rattray lighthouse and beyond to the restless waves of the North

Sea stretching away to the far horizon.

Mormond Hill became a familiar landmark to us that week, marking out our home when returning from our daily excursions.

It rose some 768feet from the lowlands with its summit crowned with the installation of huge dishes serving the international telecommications station established there and visible for miles around. It had once been the site of an American early warning post during the days of the infamous Cold War when its antennae were trained constantly eastwards towards the ominous Soviet Communist threat.

A curious feature of Mormond Hill was the outline of a giant deer marked out on its upper slopes and visible from several miles away. It had been constructed many years previously by a former Laird of Mormond as a poignant memorial to his late son who had lost his life under tragic circumstances. The recollection of these visits to Scotland, made in such convivial company, will continue to give me pleasure for many years to come. It was part of the British Isles I had never visited and I returned home with pleasant memories of that hospitable and gentle area, of its softly spoken kindly people and the local herring fishermen returning on the flow-tide bearing their bountiful harvest of the "silver darlings".

Robust good health has been a blessing I have enjoyed throughout my life and consequently taken somewhat for granted. Therefore in 2003 I was caught entirely off my guard when it became evident my long run of fortune was at last beginning to falter. I started suffering regular indigestion attacks, especially at night whilst lying in bed, and a complete intolerance to anything sharp or slightly acidic. At dinner one evening a glass of white wine caused such a severe burning sensation in my oesophagus and upper stomach that I irrationally attributed it to an over-crisp vintage. This state of affairs continued for many months and culminated in my collapse one night at three A.M. in the bathroom after the gastronomic rigours of the Christmas period.

The following morning it became evident that I had suffered internal bleeding. Even then I stubbornly refused to admit that anything could be seriously wrong and as things appeared to have settled down it was to be a further two months, when I had occasion to visit my doctor on an unrelated matter, that I casually mentioned my previous problem. He straightway arranged a blood test which indicated anaemia.

So it came about that I reported to Cheltenham General Hospital endoscopy department a few weeks later for an internal oesophigal examination. As I had been concerned with the design and development of simple endoscopes nearly forty years earlier I was intrigued by the latest modern technology confronting me as I lay on the couch. The equipment at the hospital was manufactured by a company by the name of 'Key-Med' who had been producing primitive instruments all those years ago, basic rigid optical devices around a foot in length and horrendously expensive, several hundred pounds each at 1960's prices. At that time flexible fibre optic piping presented huge difficulties in manufacture, to draw out the long lengths of exquisite fine hair-like fibres into coherent orientation and robust enough to resist internal breakage.

I forbade regaling the doctor operating the device with the tragic story concerning an unfortunate 'Key-Med' salesman who had been demonstrating one of the early endoscopes on a sick dolphin at an aquarium somewhere on the south coast of England, only to contract a rare strain of disease off the ailing creature, becoming seriously ill himself sadly with fatal consequences.

The inspection procedure carried out on me was the most uncomfortable twenty minutes I have ever endured in my life, exacerbated by my opting to undergo the ordeal without sedation. One disappointment was being unable to view the monitor screen which is positioned behind the patient enabling the doctor to observe the progress of the endoscope's probing lens and to point it at areas of particular interest. The 'umbilical cord' connecting its business end with the outside world contains flexible 'sinews' which not only rotate the viewing lens but can also operate miniature forceps to enable biopsies to be taken. It was a cleverly designed piece of kit and an invaluable tool in the doctor's armoury, well worth the many thousands of pounds it undoubtedly cost.

At the conclusion of my examination I was casually informed that there was no sign of any cancer, a remark which shook me emotionally as I had not even considered the possibility of there being anything seriously wrong. The doctor did pronouce however that I had been suffering from severe gastric reflux disease, inflammation of the sphincter valve which normally prevents gastric juices backing up into the oesophagus which in turn becomes inflamed. He was amazed that it had not been troubling me to a greater degree. It was to be a long healing process involving a daily course of stomach acid reducing capsules, technically classed as 'proton pump inhibitors', and only some four years later did they appear to have worked their magic and my digestive system was once more back on an even keel.

The new century continued to unleash its unhappy train of personal grief on me when in the late autumn of 2005 my brother David died. He had suffered a lifetime of health problems, principally with asthma, and some of my earliest childhood memories are of our home filled with the acrid smoke of David's "Potter's Asthma" herbal remedy which he had ignited in a saucer.

The final blow was the lung cancer which sadly was to claim his life. David was living then in West Wales, at Dinas Head near Fishguard and our small party of mourners from Gloucestershire travelled there on the day of his funeral in a hired minibus.

It was the saddest of occasions to stand in a 'foreign field' on that bitter December afternoon and bid our final farewells to our beloved brother. In the short time he and his wife had lived there they had so endeared themselves to the local community for the village church was full to overflowing. In tribute to

David the villagers all sang a rousing hymn in their mother tongue, a most touching gesture and one which made me feel so proud of him.

The Christmas of 2006 heralded a special birthday in my personal calendar for on the twenty seventh of December I marked my sixtieth year. As other Capricorns may testify, being a Christmas baby inevitably means one's annual celebration becomes swamped with the general festive fandangle. To a child it is a major disappointment in being so overlooked but as adulthood advances one is quite happy for such poignant reminders of the passing years to be ignored. However as my contempories had all celebrated their own respective 'milestones' I organised a birthday luncheon for our 'gang' of eight, plus daughter Louise at the well-recommended restaurant "Russells" in the tourist honey-pot village of Broadway. Its name derives from the world-famous arts and crafts furniture manufacturing concern of Gordon Russell which occupied the site until that business's demise a number of years ago and the restaurant is carrying on in the culinary fashion that same tradition of high-quality craftsmanship.

We were not disappointed, for whilst the final bill was somewhat higher than might be expected from a country restaurant it was worth every penny. Our happy little party enjoyed the whole experience of superb food and drink served impeccably in a discrete manner and partaken in the relaxing company of one's fellow companions. The jollification had yet to be laid to rest for a couple of weeks later Rob Dewey and I held our Annual Winter Romp in the local village hall and despite my reluctance Rob organised it around a theme of my birthday. It was a thoroughly enjoyable evening although I was somewhat abashed by the generous gifts and cards that our guests were bestowing on the 'birthday boy'.

The party was crowned by the rendering of a specially written song in my honour by all the assembled guests and musicians followed by a surprise presentation. A bespoke iced cake was borne into the hall with great pomp, ablaze with candles and its top adorned with a humorous portrayal of 'yours truly', cleverly printed in full-colour edible dyes.

The onset of my sixty first year had been well and truly launched.

LOUISE

I have thus far refrained from any great mention of my daughter as she justifies a small chapter of her own in this account of my life's experiences. For the better part of twenty years Louise characterised and influenced Loretta and my early married life and, as with the offspring of most other parents, she represents the flowering of personality conferred upon her by we, her own parents, throughout that time. No doubt a learned professor of human behaviour could reduce such an outcome into a neat clinical explanation but to us it has been a source of supreme pleasure and satisfaction to have played some part in shaping the well-balanced, talented and popular young woman she has developed into.

For my part I have always endeavoured to be a friend, companion and confidant on whom she can depend and trust as well as a mere father figure. It has not been an easy or straightforward journey to make, for along the way there have been the joys and tears of childhood and the ecstasies and agonies of teenage angst to bear, as one minor drama after another unfolds.

I can recall when Louise was as yet only a toddler, rushing her to the local hospital's accident and emergency dept in 'Dumpy' after she had fallen headlong into the door post at home, cracking her temple open and necessitating a row of stitches. So traumatised was poor Loretta that she fainted at the hospital and ended up in the recovery unit there that same evening!

In later years Dumpy again became a conveyance of mercy when I rushed Louise to the local village doctor's house after an over-zealous school chum had accidently whacked her across the back of her long-suffering head with a cricket bat and I feared she was concussed as a result.

Patience was a quality which fatherhood demanded. I would stand for hours at a time with her in the village playing field teaching her French cricket and in the process unwittingly attract other children from far and wide into the game. I taught Louise to ride a bicycle in that same field, endlessly running behind her on her first small two-wheeled cycle, holding onto the saddle and going around and around the cricket pitch until unobtrusively releasing her at an opportune moment so that she went sailing off solo across the field in blissful ignorance.

Louise went through the various phases of her growing-up in the expected fashion. She joined the Brownies despite the uniform looking totally incongruous on her. A summer camp was held for her little troop at Batsford Park near Moreton-in-Marsh and many parents, we included, drove there on a Sunday to see them all. That turned out to be a huge mistake for we left most of them howling dementedly after us as we bade farewell following our afternoon visit.

We hosted several 'mini-fetes' in the garden at Nutbridge Cottage which Louise organised on behalf of various animal charities, "Save the Seals" and the like.

We came periously close to buying her a pony after being subjected to a series of prolonged melodramatic tearful pleadings but mercifully when Louise embarked on regular weekly riding lessons at a nearby village academy that particular passion receded.

At the age of eleven she moved from our village infants school to a large private one in Cheltenham. I used to battle my way there through the evening rush hour traffic in 'Dumpy' once a week to take her for piano lessons across the other side of town. At other times Loretta and I would make evening visits to the school for the regular parents' evenings or to sit through interminable school plays and concerts. On one auspicious occasion we were summoned by no less a personage than the headmistress herself for a personal discussion regarding certain misbehaviours involving our dear offspring.

Louise was very headstrong and was usually to be found at the centre of any high-spirited mischief. One weekend at "Applegarth" she had a fellow school chum staying with us. We were awoken before dawn on the Saturday by stirrings about the house accompanied by frantic whispering and then the front door was quietly clicked shut and silence reigned once more. The two girls had left, walking out into the drizzle of that still dark morning, carrying little more than an umbrella between them. Loretta and I spent a fretful day worrying as to what possible prank the two youngsters were performing. It was with very mixed emotions that we received a long-distance telephone call that same afternoon. They were calling from Lille, a town on the Franco-Belgium border! They had started thumbing for lifts on the main road at Teddington and by sheer good fortune had secured a series of lifts which took them to that far-off destination quicker than any public transport, bar taking to the air! Little wonder that fathers of teenage daughters are not renowned for their thick mops of hair.

For the convenience of studying for her 'A' level qualifications Louise managed to organise a series of bedsits for herself in Cheltenham and on several of her subsequent moves I was volunteered to load her possessions onto my ricketty two-wheeled trailer attached to Dumpy and perform the honours. One memorable journey was made across the town through the winter rush-hour with the old car packed to the gunwhales, the trailer bouncing along behind us, whilst Louise was crouched on the floor beside me, nursing the hamster cage in her arms with the terrified little creature frantically running around in circles inside.

Louise had been forever resourceful in earning money for herself, a talent she put to good use at a very young age with babysitting around the villaage and organising a delivery round of the local paper. On leaving home she wasted no time in getting on an employment agency's books and undertaking such diverse temporary jobs as waitressing, chambermaid, order picking at a wholesale distribution depot and children's nanny.

From a very early age Louise has accompanied me on quite long walks over the hills around our homes and when I purchased a rudimentary tent and basic camping kit the two of us went off further afield in Dumpy - a couple of times to Hay-on-Wye and the Black Mountains, the Forest of Dean, and even to Charmouth near Lyme Regis on the Dorset coast where we delighted in the traditional local pursuit of fossil hunting under the cliffs. This latter activity sadly did not match the fantastic discovery made by the young local girl Mary Anning in the mid-nineteenth century when she uncovered the remains of a complete fossilised ichthyosaur, several feet in length, embedded in the rocks

Louise's very first day of infants school.

At Toddington, the HQ of the Glos./Warwick railway.

On Hay Bluff.

Louise on Spirit Quay in the London Docklands near to her home.

and thus unwittingly triggered the present-day mini-industry in such artefacts.

Lyme Regis held us under its spell, we visited the aquarium perched along the end of the stone cobb and saw the exquisite sea-mice and later took a boat out into Lyme Bay mackerel fishing where much to Louise's and everyone else's surprise she managed to hook the only fish of the afternoon.

This I later attempted to cook for our supper with a conspicuous lack of success!

To crown the magic of our weekend even the heavens conspired to treat us, for we viewed a partial eclipse of the sun as we sat at ease on the grass outside our little tent

In 1993 Louise was due to start a University degree course in Law and two days in succession I took her on introductory visits to both Brighton and Essex Universities, the latter at Colchester being her eventual preferred choice. For economy I hired a small Ford Fiesta saloon for both trips, with hindsight an error of judgement, for those several hundred miles of driving over the two long days took their toll on me, mentally and physically. However my support was not in vain for she successfully completed her course and it was with pride that Loretta and I went up to Colchester on graduation day to see her receive the hard-earned diploma from the Master of the Rolls, Lord Thomas Bingham.

This was merely the beginning of a long hard road towards attaining her full qualifications and being accepted by the Law Society as a practising lawyer. Before then she underwent several years in-house training as a para-legal in two large firms followed by a year's course at the London College of Law. But this huge outlay in time and money has been well spent and has laid the foundations of a secure future for her.

When Louise eventually made London her base, work wise and socially, I visited her on several occasions at her apartment in the new Dockland's development behind St Katherine's Dock near Tower Bridge. The whole area represents an incredible transformation from the old traditional docks, including the original riverside Pool of London adjacent to Tower Bridge. This was not the first time in its history that particular part of the City had undergone radical change for the construction of St Katherine's Dock in 1826 by Thomas Telford had alone necessitated the demolition of some 1250 ramshackle houses and the ancient hospital of St Katherine's, all crammed ragbag-fashion into the 27 acres site.

During these visits I have been unfailingly made most welcome by Louise and her charming boyfriend Giles, who is himself a fellow lawyer. They have taken me out and about, introducing me to their favourite restaurants, booking us into West End shows, visiting museums and enjoying sightseeing trips on the Thames, including a "flight" on the London Eye big wheel. This latter attraction offers a bird's eye view from several hundred feet above the London landscape and such is the popularity of its thirty minute revolution that there is a continual queue of passengers awaiting the experience.

Louise and Giles shared a love of world travel and fine wines, a most fitting combination of interests. The three of us enjoyed a day's tasting at a fair organised by Australian winemakers at the Landmark Hotel, Marylebone, where I discovered to my embarrassment why it is recommended that each tiny sip is discretely disposed of and not swallowed, good advice which I chose to ignore! The hotel was built in the late 1890's by the Great Central Railway company adjacent to their newly-constructed terminus of St Marylebone and is a fabulously opulent edifice. For a while it became the Regional Headquarters of British Railways before passing into private commercial ownership and now both the hotel and station together make marvellous period settings as regular film locations.

My last trip to London on a visit to see Louise was on a day of high summer in 2006. Loretta had not made the journey for two or three years on account of transport problems associated with her disability but we solved the difficulties by hiring a locally-based London style black cab. The driver reversed right up to the front door at "Applegarth", the wheelchair folded away into the front floor well whilst Loretta and I installed ourselves on the capacious rear seats. It was a real pleasure to be thus chauffeured, cruising across the Cotswold hills on the London road and savouring the summer countryside from our lofty vantage point. There are long stretches of dedicated lanes for buses and taxis on the motorway approaching the Capital and we felt how Royalty doubtless must feel as we bowled along past the slow moving lines of private cars with their occupants sweltering in the hot sun. We met Louise at the pre-arranged rendevous outside the hotel on Clapham Common where she 'took delivery' of Loretta and I then returned home in the taxi. The hire bill at first had seemed an extravagant indulgence, but on consideration it compared favourably with the total cost involved in a conventional journey from home by public transport, which would have involved a taxi to the station, another train trip or taxi out to Clapham Common the other end and of course a repeat of all that fandangle for myself on the return home, two hundred miles in total.

Many parents harbour unease about where their offspring are heading, particularly during the turbulent teenage years. It was an apprehension that Loretta and I did for a short while share, but our worries were unfounded and we had no cause for concern. On the contrary, Louise has been a source of huge satisfaction to us and we are both extraordinarily proud of her. She has an extremely lively, almost extrovert, personality and enjoys a wide range of interesting and enduring friendships with so many worthwhile people. She has forged a successful career in law, initially with large London practices but then in a complete contrast but totally in line with her generous giving nature, she gave up regular salaried employment and devoted herself to helping the people of impoverished countries through the work of charitable non-governmental agencies.

Her first six months of 2007 were spent based in Phnom Penh, capital city of Cambodia, and as I write in 2008 she is working in Sierra Leone, supporting the innocent victims of circumstances who are ill-equipped to defend themselves against the exploitation which is all too prevalent on a world-wide scale.

Louise has found an expression for her selfless generous character, and as she herself remarked to me, the motivation was akin to the calling experienced by a missionary, something to be worked out of her conscienceness before she finally settles down.

REFLECTIONS

This concluding chapter of my life's experiences has proved the most complex one to express, in attempting to review the past six decades covering the huge gamut of developing emotions and attitudes moulded and tempered by my deeds and reactions over those years.

Through the earliest post-war days, the formative years when I was growing towards adolescence, and being the youngest by seven years of a large family, my siblings seemed always as adults in my childish eyes.

Thus paradoxically my upbringing felt as that of an only child, this feeling of isolation exacerbated by having ageing parents by today's standards. Nevertheless, this illusion of loneliness gave me an independence of both thought and deed, conferring a dogged stubborness and cussed nature which persists to this day, albeit of more tolerant proportions. I have grown up with a possessive streak in my character, having had always to fight for and hold onto what was rightly mine in those austere days of family strictures and tight budgeting.

In retrospect I regard with a respectful awe at how my parents coped so successfully with the relentless demands of raising a large family under those harsh conditions of rationing and general shortages which prevailed when I was in my infancy.

I perforce inherited cast-off clothes from the older family members, a practice unimaginable today as evidenced by the blossoming of High Street charity shops, where worn clothing and other goods, still perfectly useable, are all jettisoned quite gratuitously to make way for new.

I recall my mother making up various items of clothing from a prized pure silk ex-R.A.F parachute which she had acquired by some mysterious agency, and patiently knitting a never-ending supply of woollen wear which on the first wash lost any semblance of shape and texture, developing a character all of their own.

However, gradually conditions throughout the land improved and by my teenage years that generation were enjoying incomparably better times than those my parents had undergone. I had money to spend from a secure well-paid job, could afford modest holidays and to socialise regularly with my own contemporaries. I owned independent transport, if only the two-wheeled variety and had leisure time at my disposal to enjoy as I would. Later, my hitherto cosy world in Gloucestershire was abruptly opened up when my career took me across the face of Britain to places undreamt of by a simple village lad. It was romance of a kind, but more than that, travel removed the insularity that had been festering in me and imbued a respect for my fellow man and their diverse ways of life which co-exist in this small island we call Great Britain. I was made to appreciate just how important our industrial and agricultural concerns are to the standard of living which we can so easily take for granted. The ease with which food and all other requisites of everyday life is available does not spring from happy chance nor through the posturings of politicians, but has as its bedrock the innovation, hard work and commercial drive of the country's massed work-force, day-in and day-out, from the efforts of the engineers and scientists, the farmer ploughing his lonely furrows, to the harassed factory manager hastening his latest export orders.

All these dedicated people contribute crucially in his or her way in helping to carry forward the nation's economy and well-being.

I have been blessed with many firm and loyal friends and, to my knowledge, few enemies. From the ranks of these friends I have drawn inspiration for the interests which have sustained me over the years, interests of tremendous diversity and ones which I have enjoyed immensely in the stimulating company of those steadfast stalwarts.

Academically I have benefited from working alongside many capable scientists, engineers and successful businessmen and like to think that much of their knowledge and acumen has in part infected my own persona.

The constant love and support I have received unfailingly from Loretta and my daughter Louise has been beyond price and I have striven my utmost to reciprocate their affection in return.

As Old Father Time advances relentlessly so the daily reminders of one's mortality gather pace, the usual expected minor aches and pains and failing eyesight accompanied by a general slowing-up and lengthening reaction times to various situations. I have also become more retrospective in my outlook - in fact this autobiography was triggered by just that 'mindset'.

In growing older I have consciously become more conservative and less venturesome; seeing imagined difficulties in new undertakings can lead to a most negative attitude towards one's everyday activities. As an example, the prospect of making a long road journey becomes fraught with potential problems in my mind, with disasters lurking around every corner, even before leaving the security of my driveway.

It takes very little nowadays to persuade me to take the easier option when faced with the question whether to go out of a night or stay at home. A dozen raindrops appearing on the lounge window invariably decides the issue!

There are effective antidotes against this perceived decline. One is the companionship of younger people who generally enjoy a refreshing self-confidence and 'joi de vivre' which I have found to be a tremendously uplifting stimulus.

Other more drastic spurs can reinvigorate a lifestyle, such as moving home and changing one's career. In both these instances I experienced a restoration of my spirits and motivation and revelled in the challenge of making new friends and generally establishing myself into the new circumstances confronting me.

Finally, it is vitally important to exercise regularly, both in body and mind. I walk out as much as possible, including the long- distance stints with my old friend Olly, and also cycle on my trusty roadster, although the latter to a lesser degree due to ever increasing fast traffic on Britain's highways and byways.

Even in the garden I stubbornly cling to my hand shears and sickle to the amusement of my gadget-minded neighbours. One concession to the mechanical age is my use of an ancient Suffolf Punch four-stroke cylinder mower which I trundle around the lawns to the comforting chugging of its little engine.

When divorced as I am now from the daily duties and concerns of regular employment it is vital to maintain a mental fitness drawn from other sources. I have kept my active interests in the local music scene and thereby keep in contact with my many friends in the area by meeting on a regular basis.

Books continue to fill the 'unforgiving hour' much of my reading matter being fairly undemanding but interspersed with more esoteric tomes of non-fiction.

My photography these days consists more as an adjunct to other activities, such as countryside walks, or perhaps merely in copying local historic pictures which I unearth from time to time and print off as additions to update my albums of archive photographs.

On a more mundane level, simply completing the daily newspaper crossword or a regular game of 'Scrabble' in an evening can help keep those 'little grey cells' alert and in Loretta's case has actually aided a measure of emotional recovery since suffering her stroke.

It is a fascinating challenge to look back over the years and review that complex condition we call 'life'. It represents a matrix of experiences and emotions laid out in time and space, as a three-dimensional molecular model may be, and from which one's thought processes can extract selective fragments. The joys and sadness, elation and melancholy, contentment and anger, all can be accessed in that mysterious underworld of our brain we call 'memory'.

As human beings we possess over all other life on earth the unique ability to pass on the cumulative sum of this knowledge and experience to each succeeding generation thus enriching their own understanding of the world about them and it is this special talent which has brought the human race to its present state, for better or worse. When I consider the profound changes wrought in our lifestyles over the period of my own short lifetime, it is with apprehension that I speculate what the future holds for mankind. There are more people alive on this planet today than have ever been born and died over the entire history of human evolution and inevitably there must be a general weakening of species 'homo sapiens' as overcrowding becomes more and more of an issue.

Modern technology can 'prop up' an ailing society by means of the latest medical advances and artificially stimulated food production. The consequences of this illusory utopia is a highly unstable society and as a result people will withdraw into the sustainable secure lifestyle enjoyed by their forefathers.

On a personal level I have endeavoured to insulate myself from the ever-increasing pace and demands of modern living and thus feel more protected from such pressures.

Nearly three hundred and fifty years ago those two ancient 17th century mystics, the Welsh Silurist Henry Vaughan and his younger contemporary, the Herefordshire country parson Thomas Traherne, prophesied with uncanny accuracy the course of Man's evolution and the inherent perils awaiting future generations. In his "Centuries of Meditations" Traherne commented upon the world of man and the world of nature, exhorting us to "leave the one that you may enjoy the other". He had astutely observed that "the world was not a mine of material riches but the mirror of the eternal to be enjoyed in wonder"....

"You never enjoy the world aright, till you so love the beauty of enjoying it, that you are covetous and earnest to persuade others to enjoy it".

THE END

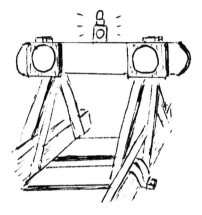

ACKNOWLEDGEMENT

I am indebted to my good friend Patricia who painstakingly transcribed over many weeks my several hundred pages of handwritten original manuscript into an orderly typescript, safely stored onto computer disc, to await final printing.

My grateful thanks for the unfailing help and interest shown by Ian, Colin and Zoe of Perfect Image UK Ltd printers, Evesham, and their contribution towards producing "Passing Time".

NOTES

NOTES

NOTES

NOTES

NOTES

NOTES

336